Complete Book
of
Athletic Taping Techniques

*The defensive offensive weapon
in the care and prevention of
athletic injuries*

J. V. CERNEY

With Illustrations by the Author

Parker Publishing Company, Inc.
West Nyack, N. Y.

Library of Congress
Catalog Card Number: 76-156762

PRINTED IN THE UNITED STATES OF AMERICA
ISBN—0-13-155572-3
BC

Dedicated to the

*National Athletic Trainers
Association*

and the

*American College of Sports
Medicine*

INTRODUCTION

This book belongs to the new breed in sports medicine. It belongs to those at professional and amateur level who have contributed untold time, effort and know-how in athletic care. It belongs to those whose names appear on the illustrations of taping techniques found in this text as well as to their brothers who have lifted their professional stature and recognition through elevated standards of education, accreditation, and service. It belongs to the relatively few men of medicine who are specialists in the care of athletic injury; those practitioners who have become a boon to athletes because athletic injury—as separate from normal civilian injury—is indeed a specialty unto itself.

This book belongs to today and tomorrow in sports, and I, as author of this book, am merely the vehicle for assembling a vast storehouse of information on adhesive tape—and the techniques for its use—which I have cut, trimmed, and polished for its trip into the future.

From coaches, trainers, and doctors every-
where have been gathered, and then culled,
those techniques which have proven themselves
consistently effective in the workshop of my
own 25 years as a sports-minded practitioner in
a couple of medicine's ancillary professions. To
the many people who have contributed to this
book go my thanks. My thanks also to the many
amateur and professional athletes with whom I
worked and the many students whom I taught
bandaging and taping techniques. My association
with their swinging tempo has helped keep me
young.

In my book the athlete comes first! As far as
I'm concerned, keeping him in condition—
through care and prevention by every means, including the art and science of taping—is para-
mount. From where I'm sitting in the press box
at this time this book is not just a complete
book on the taping of athletic injuries. It's the
wrap-up.

Jim Cerney

Contents

Complete Book
of
Athletic Taping Techniques

```
┌─────────────────┐
│     PART 1      │
└─────────────────┘
```

INTRODUCTION
TO
ATHLETIC TAPING

Contents

Tape - the
Flexible Cast
for
"Soft Tissue Fracture"

The Art and Science
of a "Tape Job"

Taping is a method of supporting tissues and limiting their function without completely immobilizing the part.

For the sake of nomenclature, *flexible cast* was the term devised to denote the procedure of taping. In athletic injuries, therefore, taping or *flexible casting* is the art and science of utilizing adhesive tape as a productive and functional tool. Taping as such is a science in the job to be done and an art in its application.

As a method of soft-tissue control a "tape job," or *flexible cast* (and we can use the names interchangeably), is a procedure whereby anatomical parts are persuaded toward normalcy and held for a short time for the purpose of healing and protection. Torn, ruptured, or otherwise violated tissues are approximated and *the flexible cast becomes a pliant but restrictive environment* that helps in the healing.

> *As such, adhesive tape is an emergency measure applied with only a temporary purpose in view. It is a diplomatic brace, a supportive crutch, and for local soft tissue compression/tension/traction it is the treatment of choice!*

The techniques of *flexible casting* and adhesive strapping are designed primarily to immobilize anatomical areas of stress. Tape, by such a method, acts as an artificial muscle, fascia, tendon or ligament. It may act as all four and thereby be classified as *an external membrane or soft tissue aid.* According to the late head trainer Allan Sawdy at Ohio's Bowling Green University—"Such an external membrane applies a desirable combined compression/traction/tension on soft tissues that have been fractured."

Like beauty, the controls of adhesive tape are little more than skin deep. Deep tissues such as tendons, muscles, and bones are never completely immobilized by tape—and a properly applied *flexible cast* is not designed to do so. Adhesive tape in athletic injury use is strictly supportive. Yet with a remarkably few pieces of adhesive tape a kind of structural human engineering is created that alleviates pain. As a defensive offensive against injury it becomes one of the best therapeutic weapons that an Athletic Department can have.

The 17 Major Assets of Tape in Athletic Injury Care

In the offensive against injuries it must be admitted that tape has a limited function and that at no time does it create total control. It controls bones only partially, cartilage only partially, and with muscles, fascia, tendons, ligaments, blood vessels and nerves, the story is the same. Because of this limited or partial control there is only a significant number of things that tape or a *flexible cast* can do. To be more specific, let's point out just exactly what tape CAN do. Let's see what a *flexible cast* can go on the offensive for.

A *flexible cast:* (1) *limits motion,* (2) *places soft tissue parts in semi-correction,* (3) *assists healing,* (4) *provides protection from pressure or contact,* (5) *provides compression,* (6) *prevents local swelling,* (7) *helps keep coapted tissues organized,* (8) *supports skin lesions,* (9) *provides an occlusive barrier against dirt,* (10) *serves as a temporary auxiliary muscle or "external ligament,"* (11) *relieves pain by stabilizing the affected part,* (12) *locks bandages in position,* (13) *maintains the position of splints or pads,* (14) *creates local traction,* (15) *helps prevent further injury to a given part,* (16) *through massagic action tape helps restore circulation to a damaged area,* and (17) *eliminates the use of plaster casts for lesser injury care.*

Because of needs such as these, easy-handling adhesive tape is a weapon of choice against injury. It becomes an efficient and adaptable tool.

Tape is admittedly not a cure-all. You can lock down a pair of loose track shoes with tape or mend a split crotch. You can wrap bat handles, patch leaking ponchos, seal a can of foot powder, batten down a thigh guard or cover the bottoms of shoes. In fact, I've even witnessed one of my more comely nurses patching a garter belt—but despite the lateral uses of adhesive tape the more important advantages in the athletic field are in the following instances:

27 Athletic Injuries Most Amenable to Flexible Casting

Here is a rough classification of sports injuries which have proven most tractable in the use of adhesive tape: (1) *strains,* (2) *sprains,* (3) *muscle rupture or tear,* (4) *myositis,* (5) *tendon pull,* (6) *torn ligaments,* (7) *tendonitis, tenosynovitis,* and *peritendonitis,* (8) *fasciitis,* (9) *joint separation,* (10) *damaged or displaced cartilage,* (11) *fracturing of small bones,* (12) *small ulcers or wounds,* (13) *compression on ganglion,* (14) *after-care of soft tissue injury or bone fracture,* (15) *prevention against new injuries,* (16) *protection for old injury areas,* (17) *emergency care of hernias,* (18) *tendon or bone displacement, subluxation or dislocation,* (19) *bursitis,* (20) *rib fracture,* (21) *fibromyositis, fibrositis or fibromyofasciitis,* (22) *general aching* (feet, elbows, wrists, knees etc.), (23) *arthritis,* (24) *contusions,* (25) *muscle "stitch,"* (26) *tension,* (27) *hemotoma compression.*

Flexible Casting as a Method of Soft Tissue Compression

ALL soft tissues under and within the immediate area of a flexible cast are involved when adhesive tape is applied. Muscles, tendons, fascia, ligaments, bursae, lymph and blood vessels, nerves, fat, and other special cellular structures are all included in the environmental *compression/traction/tension*-factor created by tape. Yet, they are not totally immobilized.

The purpose of the *flexible cast,* as an external shell, is to supply pain-relieving support to injured or weakened soft tissues. A tape job is devised to give these tissues maximum security as well as partially immobilize them. In other words—**A flexible cast is indeed a splint for soft tissues which have been fractured!**

To avoid the possibility of damaging soft tissues with adhesive tape, rather than repairing them, here are some key factors to keep in mind when applying it:

11 Star Points to Remember in Taping

1. *Apply adhesive tape smoothly* (no wrinkles or gaps).
2. *Don't fight the curves.* (Follow them. Adapt.)
3. *Equalize the application* of pressure or pull. (Avoid the abnormal tensions of speed strapping.)
4. *Develop your sense of touch or "feel"* to get an even distribution of compression/traction/tension.
5. *Avoid taping-off-the-roll* as long as you are a beginner.
6. *Always follow the line of muscle action.* (Bisecting muscle flow or expansion creates trouble for you as well as for the athlete.)
7. *Never cut off circulation* with any kind of wrap. (When blood supply stops the athlete stops.)

8. *Properly diagnose the problem* before applying tape.
9. *When in doubt DO NOT APPLY ADHESIVE TAPE.* (Check with the team physician. He will probably order X-rays.)
10. *Relax all muscle spasms before applying tape.* (If massage proves ineffectual in relieving muscle cramps or contraction, look for a possible dislocation or subluxation of bone.)
11. *Have the know-how necessary for getting the job done.* (If you don't know HOW to apply a flexible cast DON'T APPLY IT! Learn the how, when, where, why, and for whom. Then—apply it!)

Glossary
of
Terminology in Flexible Casting

In using adhesive tape for the care and prevention of athletic injuries one should know by name the segments of a *flexible cast* and identify them as such. Just as you can't know the players without a score card, you can't identify the parts of a *flexible cast* until they are defined.

So to simplify the teaching, and the learning, of bandaging techniques and *flexible casting,* I devised a glossary and illustrations. In presenting them to my students I indicated that we were dealing in human engineering, that by creating a pliant but restrictive environment with *anchors, bridges, spanners, lock straps,* etc., we were purposefully and with premeditated intent creating a mechanical device. How the various segments of a *flexible cast* are applied is indicated in the following glossary.

GLOSSARY

ANCHORS (Figure 1)

An "anchor" is that initial strap placed distal to a lesion to which all "saddles," "lockstraps," "stirrups," "obliques," or "vertical stabilizers" are fixed in creating traction or support.

Figure 1

BASELINE (Figure 2)

A "baseline" is the foundation strap from which other adhesive tape segments begin in their upward journey on the anatomy. (Not to be termed an "anchor.")

Baseline Straps

foundation for strappings

Figure 2

BISECTORS or OBLIQUES (Figure 3)

A "bisector" or "oblique" is any supplementary device or adhesive strap that angles diagonally across a vertical or horizontal strap at its midpoint. These straps are never perpendicular or horizontal to a "baseline" or "anchor" strap but are usually at a 45° angle to these planes. Their primary function is to lend added support, create additional compression, and act as "guy wires" to help stabilize and balance the structure.

Bisector or Oblique Strap

Figure 3

BRIDGE (Figure 4)

A "bridge" is any strap that runs from "anchor" to "anchor" to help maintain tractional or tension support.

Figure 4

BUTTRESS (Figure 5)

"Buttresses" are any finish-straps designed not only to cover the free ends of basic straps to keep them from curling but also to absorb some of the stress that occurs to a "tape job" at these particular points.

Figure 5

GIRDLE STRAP (Figure 6)

A "girdle strap" is any strap that has the primary purpose of tying together, or locking, the opposite ends of a strapping which partially encircles the circumference of a part.

Figure 6

HORIZONTALS or SPANNERS (Figure 7)

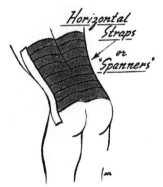

A "horizontal" strap, or "spanner," is that strip of adhesive tape which, when the athlete is standing erect, is placed horizontally with the sole intent of spanning, or locking, a given area, to stabilize it and support underlying tissue.

Figure 7

LOCK STRAPS (Figure 8)

A "lock" strap or "bridge" is that adhesive tape device used to control a given area from anchor to anchor. Lock straps may intertwine (basket-weave) or merely interlink two basic anchors.

Figure 8

PIER STRAPS (Figure 9)

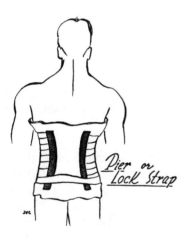

A "pier" strap, although similar to the "lock" strap, goes one step further. It not only finishes off a flexible cast like a "buttress," to cover ragged ends, but it also locks, supports, and spans a given area from any "horizontal" or "anchor" strap. "Pier" and "lock" straps are much alike. The difference is in what they support.

Figure 9

SADDLES (Figure 10)

Saddle Strap

A "saddle" is a horizontal strip of tape applied around the outer circumference of a part with the intent of fixing it to a "stirrup." (Example: — basketweave)

Figure 10

SKIN TRACTION

is that superficial immobilization in which tape, adhered to the epidermis, locks the skin only to the degree of its capacity to stretch. When stretching of the skin stops, a small amount of deep tissue-traction begins.

STABILIZERS (Figures 11-A, 11-B, 11-C)

Retention Stabilizer

(TYPE A)

Figure 11 – A

"Stabilizers" are all strappings which contain or limit the excursion of a joint. They stabilize the joint to eliminate stress.

NOTE: In positioning anatomical parts please remember that *tissues underlying the skin DO MOVE.* The *flexible cast,* as a mechanical retarder of action, exerts only partial control. To prevent over-extension, for example, a *"retention strap"* limits the amount of excursion of a given joint.

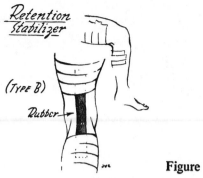

Figure 11 – B

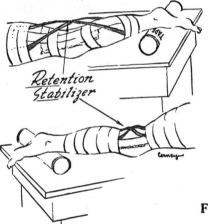

Figure 11 – C

STIRRUPS (Figure 12)

A "stirrup" strap, as in a basketweave, is any piece of adhesive tape that is literally suspended, or descending from, an "anchor" or "saddle" strap. It is looped around a body part, creates support, traction and compression, and returns to the original anchorage by ascending the opposite side.

Figure 12

STRESS FACTOR

is that physical pull, strain, torsion, or other persuasion by adhesive tape, that is brought to bear on underlying tissues to cause, or otherwise contribute to possible localized deformity, malfunction, or destruction of tissue.

STRUTS (Figure 13)

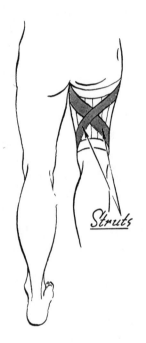

A "strut" is a supportive member of the flexible cast designed not only to take weight and pressure but also to provide a lifting type of capability in the direction of its upward progress. Like the "bisector" or "oblique," its purpose is specific in applying supportive compression and traction on the limb or body part.

Figure 13

TISSUE DRAG

is that disruptive pull on torn tissues around the periphery of an injury as the offended parts pull away from each other during activity.

TORSION

is that state of change created by pulling the tape itself (as in taping-from-the-roll), until underlying tissues are twisted by opposing torques. Such a system of unnatural forces causes rotation or twisting of human tissue, and when this happens a "tape job" adds insult to injury. In this manner a badly applied flexible cast becomes a deadly weapon and creates its own area of disaster, creating untold numbers of injuries to athletes year after year.

VERTEX (Figure 14)

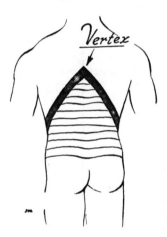

A "vertex," zenith, top or apex, is that highest point of the strapping which may or may not come to a point.

Figure 14

VERTICALS

are all straps that run perpendicular to a "horizontal," or, up and down a body part. Unlike a "horizontal" member of a steel truss, they are used to LIFT rather than support. (See Figure 3 for the "vertical" beneath the bisector straps.)

The Qualifications of
Better Athletic Tape

What you can do with adhesive tape is directly related to the job you want done. The tape you buy is of course pressured by budget, but even more important than budget are other factors that should determine your choice. The tape you buy must be judged by its grade, quality and freshness, and by your capability to use it. Your choice of tape depends on the athlete's weight, size, and the injury he has. To help you determine the tape best suited for your purpose here are some guidelines to follow:

BETTER ATHLETIC TAPE should: (1) contain **NO STARCH** in its cloth backing; (2) contain **NO SIZING**; (3) have **STRETCHABILITY**, yet (4) **NOT** be totally **ELASTIC**. (5) **The strength qualifications of tape can be determined** as follows:

GRADE	STRENGTH	Warp	Filler
Top	60 pounds per square inch or better	78	76
Middle	47 pounds per square inch or better	76	72
Economy	40 pounds per square inch or better	44	41 or less

Better athletic tape utilizes cloth backing and the strength of the cloth lies in its vertical and horizontal weaves. The vertical strands are called *warp.* The horizontal strands are termed *filler, weft,* or *woof.* The greater the amount of warp and filler per square inch the greater the strength of the cloth backing.

By using the above warp and filler guide, determine the grade of tape you need to buy. From a variety of standard cloth tapes, waterproof tapes, extra-heavy grades, elastic tapes, moleskin, hypoallergic, plastic, perforated and clear kinds make your choice.

Basic Techniques in the Application of a Flexible Cast

How to Apply a "Tape Job"

Ernie Biggs, top trainer at Ohio State University, once said: "There are as many 'tape jobs' for athletic injuries as there are trainers, coaches, and team doctors in the U.S.A."

There are indeed a lot of them. Some of the best of them are exemplified in this text because they represent taping at its best. They represent functional use—and that's exactly what every bandage should have. They represent, in turn, one common goal: —"GIVE THE ATHLETE IMMEDIATE EFFICIENT CARE!" They represent a temporary tool with no thought of permanent correction. Each flexible cast is supportive, remedial, protective and preventive, and because of this, *"taping" has to be studied as an art and as a science and applied a thousand times over before it becomes habit in its application.*

With time, knowledge, usage, observation, understanding, and often with bitter experience, the operator develops a technique of his own. He develops a *"feel"* for tape. He develops *"touch"*—and only when this occurs does he begin to comprehend how amazing, in human engineering, is the role played by a few pieces of cloth-backed tack.

It doesn't matter who invented what strapping technique, "tape job" or *flexible cast.* What DOES matter is that the application or treatment has to be right for the athlete. What DOES matter is that YOU, as the operator, develop the know-how to get the job done. To help you develop this know-how, five basic steps follow.

4

┌─────────────────────────────┐
│   BASIC STEP 1   │
└─────────────────────────────┘

Technique for Preparing
the Skin for the Application
of Adhesive Tape

How to Prepare the Skin
(See Figure 15)

1. *Cleanse the skin with soap and water.*
2. *Clip all hair in the area of injury.*
3. *Swab the area with solvent.*
4. *Apply a non-oily antiseptic to the entire area to be involved by the flexible cast.*
5. *Apply your favorite adherent. (Where an underlay such as "Pro-Wrap" is used an adherent is not necessary.)*
6. *Apply your favorite bandage and permit the flexible cast to "set." Whether you overlay the tape with cotton elastic bandage, gauze, or a coat of varnish is your prerogative.*

How to Prepare the Skin

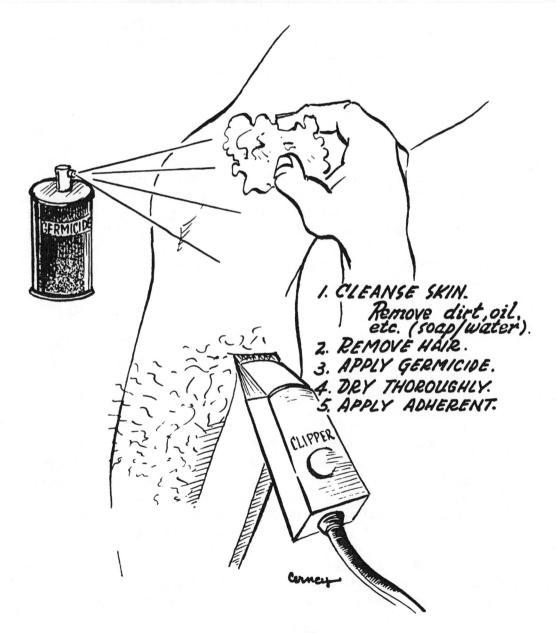

1. CLEANSE SKIN.
   Remove dirt, oil, etc. (soap/water).
2. REMOVE HAIR.
3. APPLY GERMICIDE.
4. DRY THOROUGHLY.
5. APPLY ADHERENT.

GERMICIDE

CLIPPER

Figure 15

         人 | **BASIC STEP 2** |

The Technique and Values
of "Taping-from-the-Roll"

Once you have developed the technique of "taping-from-the-roll," the procedure of *flexible casting* becomes second nature. Once you learn how to do it, the darkest locker room presents no obstacle. In applying tape from the roll here's the technique to follow:

How to Hold a Roll of Tape
(See Figure 16)

Place the core opening of the roll on the third or fourth finger of either hand. As the roll turns, the finger acts as a spindle. As the spool rotates, the thumb, index finger, and fourth and fifth fingers act as a guide. With the tack side down toward the target, place the free end of the tape at its initial anchorage and begin unrolling. Keep the index finger for the purpose of (a) *creating tension on the roll,* (b) *tearing tape,* or (c) *using it as a brake.*

Disadvantages of
Taping-from-the-Roll

In "taping-from-the-roll" there are four important factors of which to be aware, as follows:

1. *The Number One Problem Is "Hard Pull."*
   When adhesive tape "pulls hard" coming off the roll it has been either mishandled or is old. When this happens there is tension or torque brought to bear upon the skin and underlying anatomical parts to which it is attached. If the roll of tape has a flat side the flattened area pauses or drags each time around. The flat side, with its tacky side caught in the mesh of the cloth backing, stops the roll's free-wheeling. This causes the tape to pull hard on the skin and in turn subjects the skin, and the underlying tissues, to undue tension, torque, traction or twist. To prevent this "hard pull" here are some tips on what to do about tape.

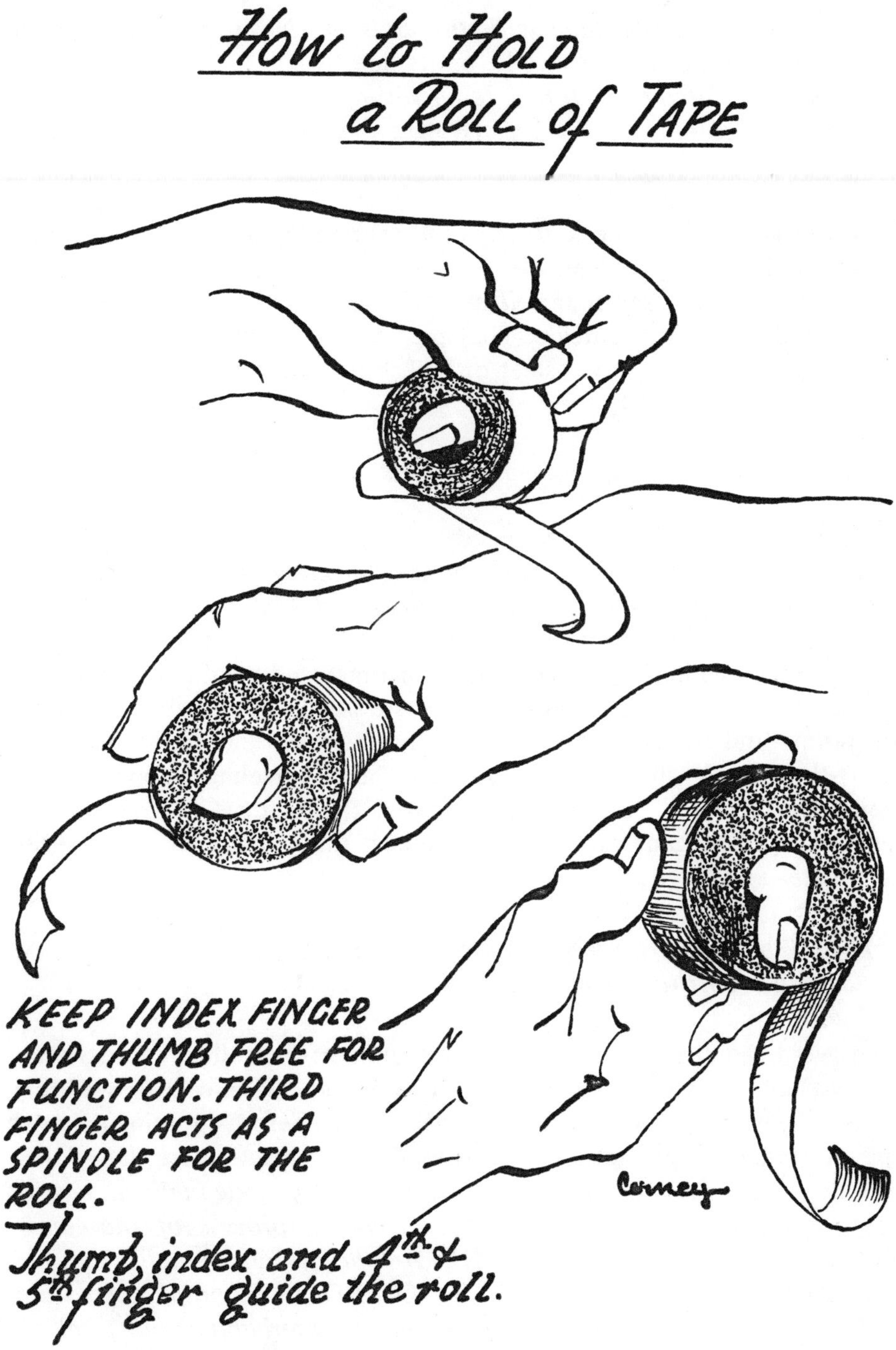
How to Hold
a Roll of Tape
KEEP INDEX FINGER AND THUMB FREE FOR FUNCTION. THIRD FINGER ACTS AS A SPINDLE FOR THE ROLL.
Thumb, index and 4th & 5th finger guide the roll.
Corney

Figure 16

To prevent "hard pull". —

(a) *Store your adhesive tape with the ends up.* Never permit a roll of tape, or its container, to lie on its side.
(b) *Provide regulated cool storage temperature.*
(c) *Buy and use only fresh tape!* (Forget that salesman who's trying to dump a "bargain" on you.)
(d) *Use a brand of tape that unwinds easily.*
(e) *Apply your tape in pre-cut strips* rather than taping-off-the-roll if you are having a problem.
(f) *Warm tape and keep it sealed* in a wide-mouthed thermos jug for fall and winter use outside. That post-season football game may have you frozen in snow, sleet or hail, but your tape will be ready to go.

2. *Speed-Applications Cause Areas of Stress*

"Taping-off-the-roll" DOES speed up tape-application. Even for the pro's, however, it has its complications. *"Speed-wrap" three squads of football men to get them out on the field and 40% of them will have tension areas, cutting edges or other points of stress contributing to new injury.* "Speed-wraps" too often become organized mayhem; if you're a newcomer to taping procedures, make haste slowly. Avoid abnormal pressure points and unjustified tensions, compressions, and traction by taping-off-the-roll. If the athlete complains about feeling uncomfortable when the "tape job" is completed, remove the bandage. Those few moments extra of diligent care may be the best thing that ever happened to the athlete—and to you.

3. *Tight Tape Cuts off Nerve and Blood Supply. Bones as well as soft tissues may be hurt.*

To avoid the stress that comes with taping-off-the-roll and constriction that cuts off nerve and blood supply, pre-pad (with cotton wadding, gauze, felt, moleskin, foam rubber etc.) the area before applying adhesive tape. Areas highly susceptible to this kind of constriction are: DANGEROUS BONY AREAS: *crest of tibia, crest of ilium, ankle malleoli, base of the fifth metatarsal, patella,* and the *olecranon process of the elbow.* SPECIFIC TENDONS TO PROTECT: *Achilles* tendon, *patellar* and *hallucis.* KEY SUPERFICIAL AREAS TO PROTECT: *nipples, scrotum, moles, eyelids, armpits, rectum, hairy areas, intercubital and popliteal spaces.* When the roll of tape is pulled on, the skin to which it is attached becomes ischemic. The local area is in a state of temporary anemia. Tissues devitalize. They weaken. They not only hurt but they also pave the way for new injury.

4. *Skin Traction is Over-Emphasized when Taping-off-the-Roll*

In applying adhesive tape, a force is automatically applied to the skin in the direction of the pull. Skin and underlying tissues "give" in the direction of traction. As a result the tissues may overlap in folds. Some of the folds may be minute. Some may occur in the underlying dermis. In turn these areas of stress convert to injury. The involved tissues may go so far as to rip or tear. Hair roots may explode into folliculitis. To conquer the disadvantages of "taping-off-the-roll," here's what former Army Trainer Rollie Bevan advised:

(a) *"Use fresh tape for free-wheeling. (b) If you're a beginner don't tape from the roll; cut tape in lengths appropriate for the part involved. (c) Use a two-handed application with one hand on each end of the cut strap so that there is an even distribution of pressure when applied to the skin."* To this he added, "Place all saddle and anchor straps in this manner as a matter of routine. *Remember that the complete purpose of the adhesive strapping, or flexible cast, is to prevent injury, or ease discomfort when injury occurs."*

How to Prevent Tape-Roll Burn on Your Finger

To avoid the cutting edge of the spool's lumen, merely dust your finger with body powder. The skin, thus lubricated, permits the spool to revolve without friction. Be certain that the powder does not get into the tape's tack. Powder kills it. Remember too that if your hands have previously been in water before you start taping they will be more tender and more susceptible to "burn" or even laceration as the core of the roll spins around. Heavy *zinc oxide powder solves the problem* but do not use graphite! It's a contaminating agent.

BASIC STEP 3

What to Do About
the Indelicate Art of
"Tearing Tape"

To "tear tape" is to save time as any trainer, coach, or team doctor will attest. When you have a large squad waiting to get out on the field you have to be fast with bandaging techniques. Every athlete comes wrapped as a rush job and there's very little time to achieve pretty bandages with scissors. The end result is that "tearing tape" by necessity becomes first choice. The trick is to learn how it's done.

How to Tear Tape

Grasp the adhesive tape with the thumb and index fingers of each hand. Hold the roll tacky side down. Adhere the tacky side to the upturned palmar side of the index finger. Now rest the thumb lightly on the superior surface, or cloth-backed side of the tape, and draw the tape fairly taut. Now with the right thumb and index finger give a sharp thrust forward and down as the left hand delivery comes up in reverse. It's that simple.

If the twist is not sufficiently sharp the cloth backing will not rip. If the fingers inexpertly roll back the edge of the cloth, the overlap of tacky edges triples the strength of the tape and tearing it becomes impossible. This is called *crimping.* Tensile strength multiplies itself so don't fight it! Find another spot to tear and finish the job. I can still remember old friend and Army Trainer Bevan saying, as we worked the A.I.U. Meet in Dayton, Ohio, "Never think about tearing tape. Just DO it!"

A fast tape-job is commendable only when you have a complete mastery of tape and its use. *Flexible casts* of adhesive tape consist of more than just the laying on of tape. It takes more than having the school janitor "wind tape" on athletes. It takes a person who *knows* tape, anatomy, injuries, and athletes, to do the job.

The fast application of tape, like taping-off-the-roll, can lead to undesirable torque and tension to underlying tissues. Through engineering delinquency a mechanical distortion of tissue takes place. The groundwork for injury is laid. For this reason it is wiser to do a "speed strapping" slowly and learn to tear tape so that wrong tensions do not occur. As Babe Ruth said the day my dad introduced me to him at Fenway Park in Cleveland, "Field 'em with both hands when you're a beginner, kid."

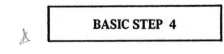

BASIC STEP 4

Tricks of the Trade
in Developing Speed Strapping

1. *Learn to tear tape* to facilitate action.
2. *Know human anatomy.*
3. *Learn to judge size and contour* of body parts.
4. *Learn the proper angle for "taking off."*
   Determine in advance where you want each strip of tape to go and where it has to stop.
5. *Adapt readily to all variations in human personality* as well as anatomy. Some athletes are rather peculiar about their likes or dislikes for tape. They are also leery of "speed strapping." They think they're getting the brush-off.
6. *Don't develop any hard and fast rules* about taping. Rules are made to be broken when something better comes along and the occasion for improvement is constant.
7. *Indoctrinate the athletes with your methods* of procedure BEFORE the season starts. Teach them to prep the skin as well as remove a bandage. It's a time saver!
8. *Organize your equipment* to make taping easier.
   Example:
   a. The height of the training table should be compatible with your own height.
   b. Locate, at your fingertips, all materials so that you don't constantly have to bend or twist. Place additional supplies within easy reach and maintain a constant inventory.
   c. Keep fresh adhesive tape on easy dispensing racks that are conveniently accessible.
   d. Lay aside tape that has been lying on its side. The "pull" zones slow you down.
9. *Acquire "speed strapping" slowly* because haste still makes waste when the chips are down.

```
BASIC STEP 5
```

Know Tape

**12 Determining Factors
That Control Selection
and Use**

One dozen major control elements should be remembered in applying tape on an athlete. The facts of life that control the selection and use of tape are: (1) *the position played by the athlete in a given sport,* (2) *the size and shape of the athlete and his injured part,* (3) *the degree of damage and type of injury,* (4) *the type and/or quality of skin upon which the adhesive tape must be applied,* (5) *the presence of swelling, tenderness or infection,* (6) *underlying tendons or bony abutments,* (7) *the length of time the flexible cast will be on,* (8) *the relative position and pathological condition of neighboring tissues,* (9) *the proximity of blood vessels or nerves,* and (10) *whether or not the tape aids and abets rather than traumatizes and interferes with muscle dynamics.*

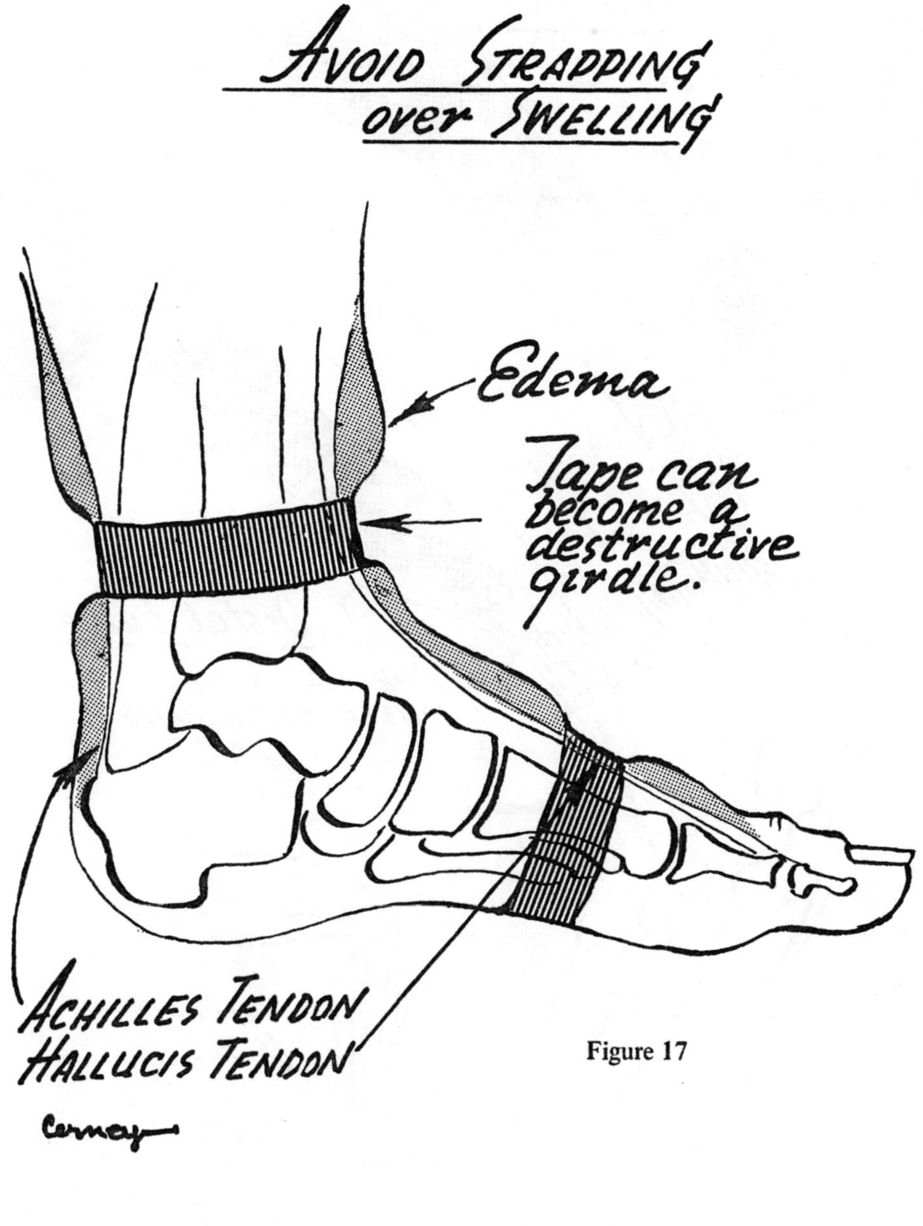
AVOID STRAPPING
over SWELLING
Edema
Tape can become a destructive girdle.
ACHILLES TENDON
HALLUCIS TENDON
Cernay

Figure 17

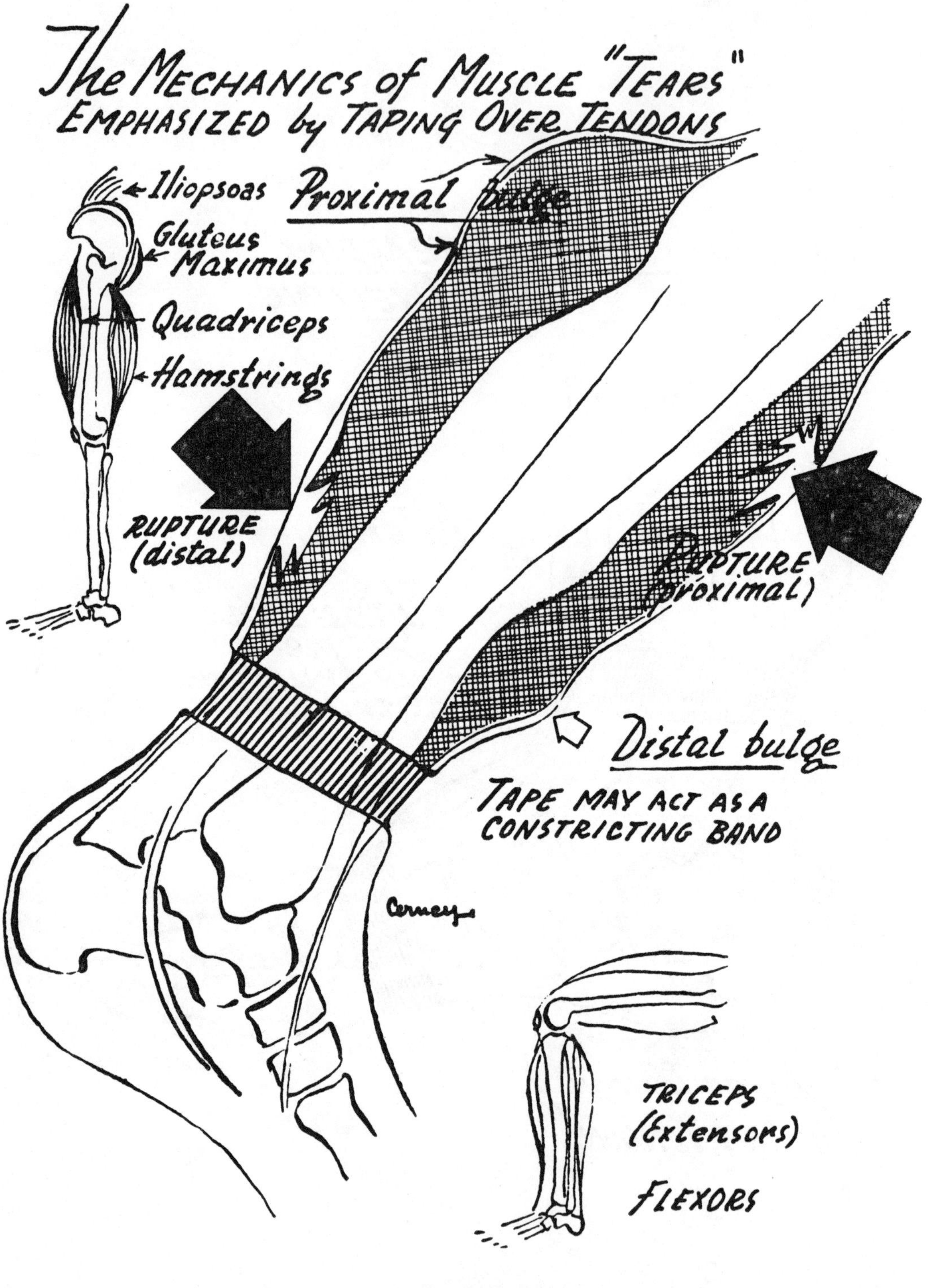
The Mechanics of Muscle "Tears"
Emphasized by Taping Over Tendons
Iliopsoas
Proximal bulge
Gluteus Maximus
Quadriceps
Hamstrings
RUPTURE (distal)
RUPTURE (proximal)
Distal bulge
TAPE MAY ACT AS A CONSTRICTING BAND
Cerney
TRICEPS (Extensors)
FLEXORS

Figure 18

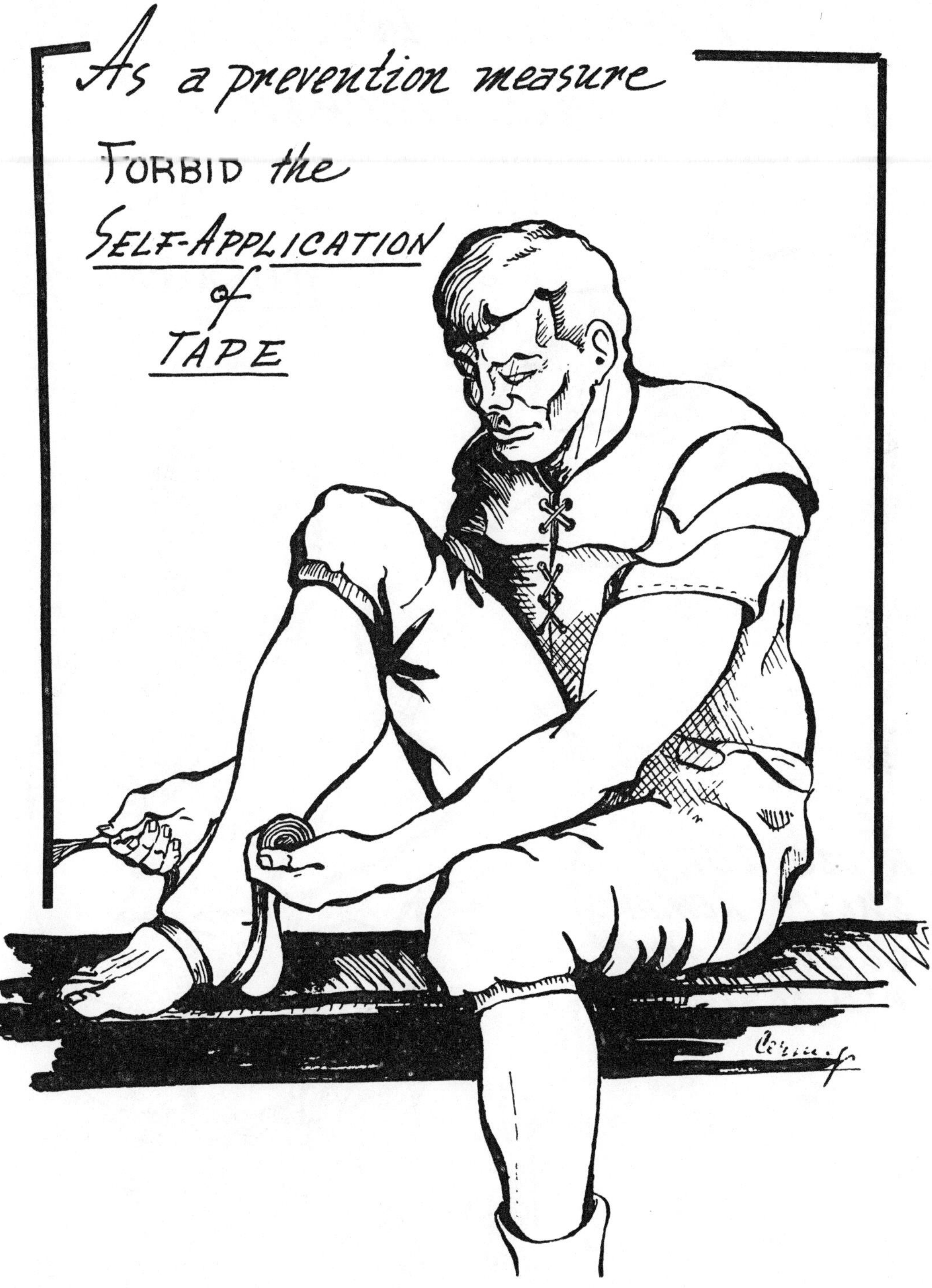

Figure 19

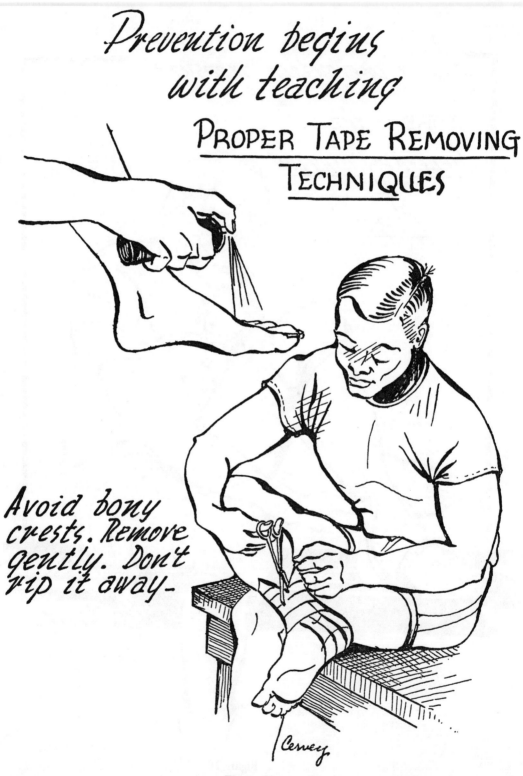

Prevention begins with teaching

PROPER TAPE REMOVING TECHNIQUES

Avoid bony crests. Remove gently. Don't rip it away—

Figure 20

Adhesive Tape
and
Its Effect on Human Skin

Adhesive tape changes the environment of the skin on contact. It does more than provide factors of compression/traction/tension. In the form of a flexible cast, and as an artificial skin or superficial integument, adhesive tape is a persuasive influence that skirts the anatomy and keeps it in a state of partial containment. However, in surrounding the contents of a human anatomical part the adhesive tape presents the disenchanting possibility of causing, or contributing to, structural or functional breakdown. How deep this goes has to be explained.

Human skin rejects all unnatural environments. In its own way it cries out against abnormality in its association with adhesive tape. It resents and reacts to the very physical make-up of the tape itself and not just to what it is doing. It reacts to bacteria that are caught between the tape and the skin. Within the warm moist confines of the *flexible cast* is a stimulating chamber that causes latent bacteria, fungi, and spores within the dermis and within the epidermis to come alive. Scar tissue from previous injury may become an obnoxious foreign body beneath an ill-fitting flexible cast.

In determining how tape acts as an environmental influence we have to be concerned about soft tissues and how they actually offer very little resistance to adhesive tape; how, when partially immobilized, these tissues react to an external force.

When a *flexible cast,* or "tape job," is properly applied to a body part there should normally be no stress, no compounding of physiological or anatomical assault. A well-applied adhesive tape wrap should create a system of balanced forces that move with the skin, and/or the underlying tissues when the athlete is in motion. Normal continuity of circulation, nerve supply and physiological action should be maintained. The part should be anatomically stable and close to functionally correct through removal of major stress.

However, if there is mechanical or chemical or other influence on the skin *underneath* the tape, the skin and its contents react.

Atypical Skin Reactions
to Be Seen Under Tape

Human skin demonstrates a characteristic pattern of change when under the influence of stress, disease, or environmental change. Under adhesive tape the pattern of this reaction is pre-determined by the structures of the skin itself. It is determined by the histology of the dermis as well as the epidermis and the forces that control them. When dermatological lesions occur under adhesive tape the change is usually the same.

Tape Reactions
and Why They Happen

Most skin reactions result from five major influences. They are: (1) *external chemical influence,* (2) *mechanical stress,* (3) *internal change in skin chemistry,* (4) *allergies,* (5) *presence of latent bacteria, virus, or spores in the skin or dermis.*

None of these changes are normal beneath adhesive tape, and none but mechanical causes can be specifically pinpointed as the exact reason for a skin reaction. But when they happen the stages of reaction go through the following evolution: *redness* (congestion) to *dryness* to *swelling* to *pimple-like structures* to *itching* to *intensified passive congestion locally* and *capillary destruction.* The tissues involved break down. They liquify to form a *bleb.* If the top of this bleb is pulled away when adhesive tape is removed the crater opens the door for *secondary infection.*

Watch for these atypical reactions. Identify them for what they are. Learn the skin specialist's terminology for what you observe. Give the lesions names, and from macule to ulceration indicate the train of change.

What begins as venous engorgement under tape becomes a local septic tank, and no matter what the cause, whether it be mechanical, chemical, allergy or otherwise, the tape is the factor that provides the environmental influence to stimulate the reaction. It's unnatural even though the excellence of compression/traction/tension is present. If improperly applied, adhesive tape creates points of noxious influence that disrupt the normal health of skin.

What Specific Factors Cause Skin Breakdown
from Mechanical Influence?

Mechanical damage to skin is caused when:

1. *Adhesive tape is left on too long.*
2. *Stress points result from "crimping" the edges of tape, causing it to wrinkle or gap, during application.*
3. *Too firm an application of the tape results in the edge cutting into a bony abutment such as the shaft of the tibia.*
4. *Foreign matter such as cinders or splinters are covered by the tape, causing them to grind into the flesh.*
5. *A "V" is clipped in the tape* (because of an error in application) so that it fails to cover the excised area.
6. *Hair is improperly removed from the skin.*
7. *Tape is strapped over edema* that has been caused by: (a) *trauma,* (b) *systemic problems,* (c) *nutritional deficiency,* (d) *post-hydrotherapy swelling,* (e) *applying tape to the skin after showering,* (f) *inordinately rough removal of tape* from the skin, permitting superimposed infection to happen.
8. *Torque or tension is caused by improper application.*

Mechanical damage may be caused by many factors, but it must be remembered that it is not just mechanical causes that contribute to the breakdown of skin.

Factors Determining Skin Response to External Influence

Individual tolerance to adhesive tape varies with all people. It varies with white skins, yellow, and black. It varies with the anatomical part involved and in the final analysis it might be indicated that the reaction of skin to tape depends on (1) *the elasticity of the athlete's skin,* (2) *the elasticity and contents of the tape itself,* (3) *the texture and age of the skin,* (4) *the basic health of the athlete and his skin,* (5) *presence or lack of subcutaneous fat,* (6) *presence of hair or foreign bodies,* (7) *allergies,* (8) *normalcy of the glands of the skin,* (9) *age of the athlete,* (10) *sex,* (11) *nutritional status,* (12) *procedures used in taping* (13) *foreign bodies in the tack of tape,* (14) *bony prominences,* (15) *applying tape counter to muscle or tendon activity,* and (16) *foreign bodies buried IN the skin or subdermal tissue* (steel, glass, cinders, wooden splinters).

As the result of a given irritation the reaction to tape begins. As the result of environmental assault the skin and its underlying structures go through the characteristic change as outlined. The end product of it is discomfort or pain.

And that's not all! There are other reasons why such changes take place and they should be given consideration. When environmental conflict takes place because of the improper application of adhesive tape, check for the following:

1. Tape applied where none was necessary.
2. An improper diagnosis of the injury.
3. Inadequate preparation of tissues that were traumatized.
4. Circulatory deficiencies or local anemia even before the constricting pressure of tape begins.
5. Any basic physiological inadequacy.
6. Basic structural inadequacies.
7. "Hidden" pathological processes that were not turned up in the pre-season physical examination.
8. Inadequate conditioning.
9. Wrapping the wrong body part when actually the pain is being referred from another source.
10. Presence of underlying adhesions from previous injuries that the athlete has forgotten or that did not get posted on the Health Card. (Just as the human knee never forgets an injury, soft tissues or other body parts that have become scarred never go back to normal and additional irritation may awaken their weaknesses.)
11. The wrong kind of wrap for the injury or the inadequate application of the right one.

These and many other factors play a role in the acceptance of adhesive tape by the human body and its extremities. As these factors predetermine the breaking down of tissues within the environment of a tape job or *flexible cast*, they must be mentioned here to develop your awareness of their existence.

Let's Wind It Up Now and Deliver the Pitch

With the foregoing in mind let's get down to the meat-and-potatoes of this book. With the basic foundation laid out, let's go to *Part 2* and build the kind of therapeutic structure that makes adhesive taping a defensive offensive in the care and prevention of athletic injuries. Let's create an environmental influence on human tissue that works! Let's make tape do the job that *can* be done within the area of its control. For athletes across the world, a big job has to be done—and they're waiting for you to do it!

PART 2

ILLUSTRATED TAPING TECHNIQUES

Contents

Section 1   LOWER EXTREMITIES

Taping Techniques for:
- FOOT
- ANKLE
- ACHILLES TENDON
- LEG
- KNEE
- THIGH
- HIP

The FOOT

> Suggested
> Tape Width 1"

Purpose: To normalize and comfort the architecture of the foot without interfering with its environment or duty.

Position: Athlete seated on training table. Foot, at ease, overhangs edge. *(Do not invert or evert the foot or maintain an abnormal 90° angle with a rein.)*

Procedure: Where necessary, the operator will manipulate foot position with each strip of adhesive tape applied to maintain the norm. **DO NOT APPLY TENSION** or correctional pull on the tape. As a productive and functional tool in athletic foot care adhesive tape is strictly a temporary supportive crutch. As a diplomatic brace for soft tissue compression/tension/traction it is a pliant and somewhat restrictive environment, but never correctional!

Adhesive Tape as an Adjunct in Athletic Foot Care

Too little attention has been given to the human foot in athletics, and the following inventory of foot conditions indicates a partial need for a working knowledge of the how, when, where, and why of conditions which warrant the use of "tape."

Foot conditions which respond to flexible casts are: *weakfoot, strainfoot, bursitis, splay foot, flabby heel, heel spurs, hard and soft "corns," calluses, tailor's bunions, metatarsalgia, traumatic arthritis, toe fractures, pronating heel, posterior transverse arch, anterior metatarsal arch, cuboid dislocation, dorsal contraction of toes, synovitis* (dorsum of foot), *hallux valgus, locked cuneiform-cuboid joint, enlarged or everted fifth metatarsal base, great toe bursitis, displaced sesamoid bone* (hallux).

What to Do About Tape on the Human Foot

Before "fixing" an athlete's feet in position for a *flexible cast* or "tape job," stop to remember the mechanics of that foot and leg. Remember the job they have to do and the restrictive environment in which they are placed.

> *Adhesive tape on feet should follow the line of muscle and tendon action or "pull." Tape should act as a temporary muscle if there is injury, until muscles, ligaments, or tendons get a chance to recuperate.*

In applying a *flexible cast* on the foot tape should be applied ONLY where required to bring comfort or relief, or to prevent injury. When applied properly, **tape should not conflict with weight bearing or function.**

Feet Are Complex and Sensitive Organs of Function

Despite its sometimes amazing size, odor, and contour, the human foot is a beautifully designed and delicate mechanism that takes tons of punishment in average civilian life and compounds that beating even more in sports. Therefore a working knowledge of the mechanics of the human foot and its function is necessary for proper care in athletics.

Weight X Force X Inept Environmental Restriction = Damage

Pull one strip of adhesive tape too tight and its *pull is multiplied by body weight times the dynamics of muscle function exploding into action.* The restrictive force of tape is magnified and the adhesive tape either snaps, aids and abets the part, or contributes to superimposed foot, ankle, or knee injury. Remember that a piece of adhesive tape is an influential guideline, an agent of control, a locking device, a method of anchoring, splinting or comforting. As such, a *flexible cast* on the foot is designed to maintain a comfortable environmental position. Because of this each strip of adhesive tape plays a key role. There is one more thing to remember about taping the human foot—if the *flexible cast* is properly applied the foot size will be one to two sizes smaller than under normal weight bearing. Because of this a track man, for example, will report that his track shoes are suddenly too big. Solve this by strapping a "ride" pad (see illustration) to the arch of the foot to compensate. DO NOT CHANGE THE SIZE OF THE SHOE!

The TOES

The average athlete has dorsally contracted toes. Some athletes have *over-* or *under-riding toes.* Almost ALL have some chronic structural deviations, and no amount of adhesive tape is going to improve the condition.

On the other hand, it is necessary to *avoid strapping those under- and over-riding toes because those key pieces of tape also lead to damage.*

Why? *When a strip of adhesive tape extends from one toe to its neighbor that toe becomes a fulcrum during violence. The weight of the athlete multiplied by the urgency of his action, and the position in which the foot is placed as he drives forward, backward, or to the side, multiplies the pressure on the strap underlying the overlapping toe. This pressure, exerted sharply, may contribute to fracturing of the toe.* This is especially true when the foot goes into violent eversion or inversion while football cleats or track spikes are anchored in turf.

Fractured lesser toes may be splinted to each other only if there is no athletic action. *Lateral splinting* (splinting toes to each other) is approved for all but the hallux. The big toe, if fractured, needs its own personal splint, which may be of metal or wood. *Dislocations* of all toes, after they have been re-set, should be bridged to the metatarsals as well as the neighboring toe. Lock straps and struts should extend backward or proximally to an anchor placed transversely across the metatarsals.

Golfer's Big Toe

Golfer's Big Toe is an acute inflamation of the big toe joint as the result of faulty stance while driving the ball and pivoting. Fatigue and foot imbalance lead to a chronically painful, rigid, and arthritic big toe joint. Wearing a postural balance pad in the shoe and putting a *retention strap* on the big toe tends to alleviate the distress.

The HEEL

"Locking the Heel" for Athletic Purposes in Arch Weakness

A great deal of stress has been laid by foot doctors, physicians, and trainers on locking some part of the foot with adhesive tape to achieve one purpose or another. Much of this has been based on happen-chance hand-me-down information that has neither physiological nor scientific support.

For example, it has been maintained for years that a *corrective heel cup appliance* or *corrective strapping* ("heel lock") will (a) correct the foot and/or (b) provide a temporary crutch as it strengthens that part of the anatomy. Some coaches and trainers today believe that "gripping" some part of the foot and ankle will re-align the arch of the foot. However, if that arch improves at all it has resulted not from the "heel lock" but from the other modalities (notably physical therapy) which have been used concurrently, and from the recuperative ability of the healthy young athlete.

The ARCH

Arch weakness is never "cured" by any "correction of the heel." Nor will any kind of adhesive strapping achieve this. A flexible cast on the foot has but one objective: *It must accommodate that foot to the environment and stress in which it finds itself!* In the human foot there is no such thing as an *arch.* The bones of the foot simply maintain their position in direct proportion to the strength of the muscles and ligaments that maintain them. The objective then, in foot or arch care, is to (a) *strengthen the leg muscles that control the foot,* and (b) *assure that foot of as much weight-bearing surface as possible* in a given environment.

The old saw about the human foot having "three weight-bearing surfaces" may be discarded. *Only a malformed foot utilizes three such weight-bearing points,* and forcing this on an athlete is a violation of the care and prevention of athletic injuries.

Today, approximately 85 percent of all athletes show some foot or leg problems. Structurally and functionally feet are never quite adequate, despite their beautiful architecture. Their design tends to contribute to injury, and it's interesting to note that *although an athlete's body is 100 percent efficient, and his head is clear, if his feet are only 50 percent efficient he is worth just half his value to the team.*

FOOT and LEG

KELLER Strap

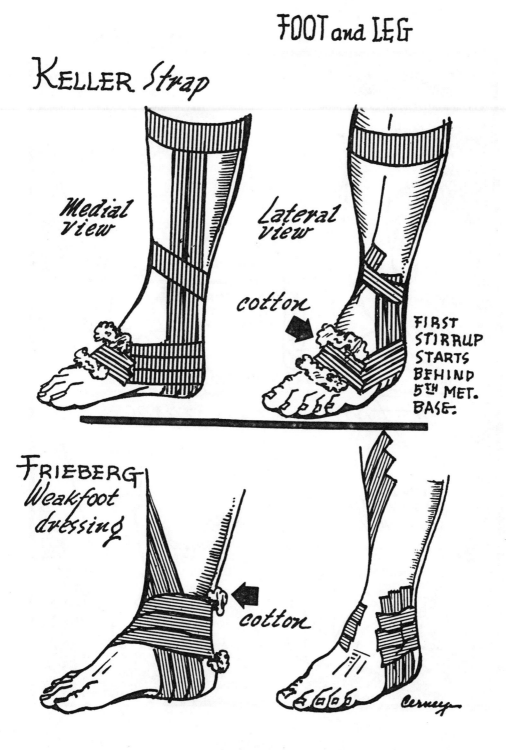

Medial view

Lateral view

cotton

FIRST
STIRRUP
STARTS
BEHIND
5TH MET.
BASE.

FRIEBERG
Weakfoot
dressing

cotton

Cerney

Figure 21

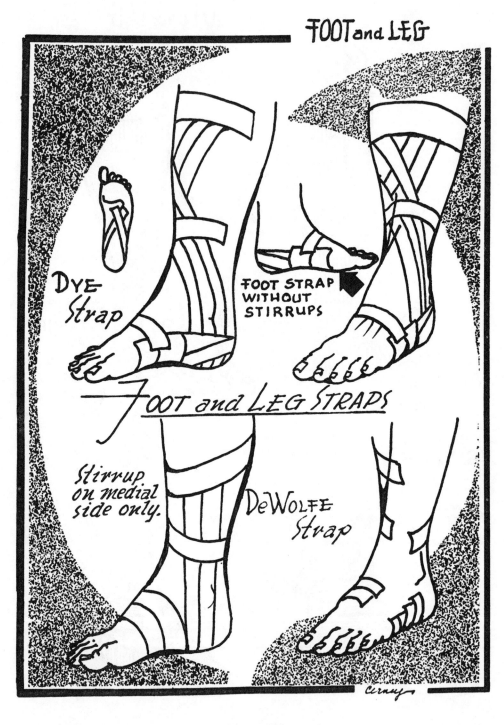

Figure 22

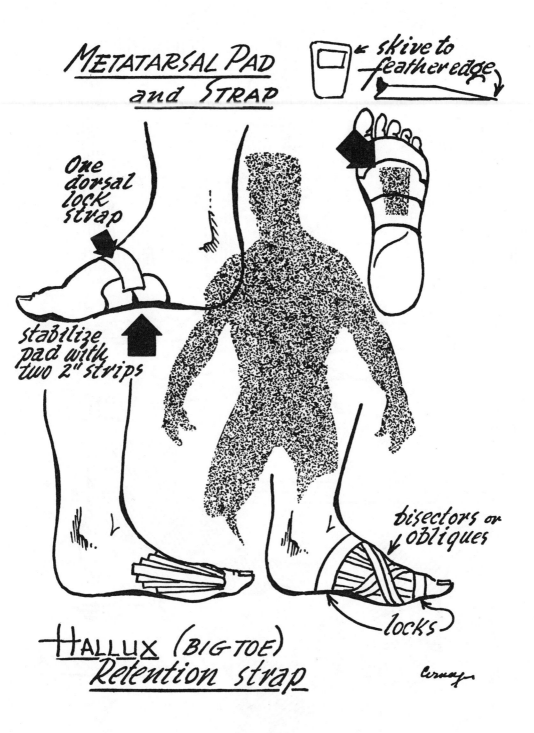

METATARSAL PAD and STRAP

skive to feather edge

One dorsal lock strap

stabilize pad with two 2" strips

bisectors or obliques

locks

HALLUX (BIG TOE) Retention strap

Figure 23

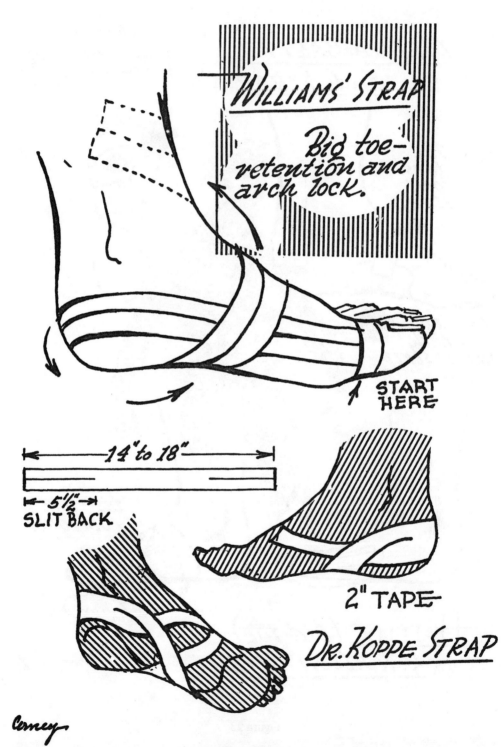

WILLIAMS' STRAP

Big toe-retention and arch lock.

START HERE

14" to 18"

5½" SLIT BACK

2" TAPE

DR. KOPPE STRAP

Figure 24

Do's and Don'ts in Taping Heels

DO TAPE HEELS THIS WAY

DON'T TAPE HEELS THIS WAY

Figure 25

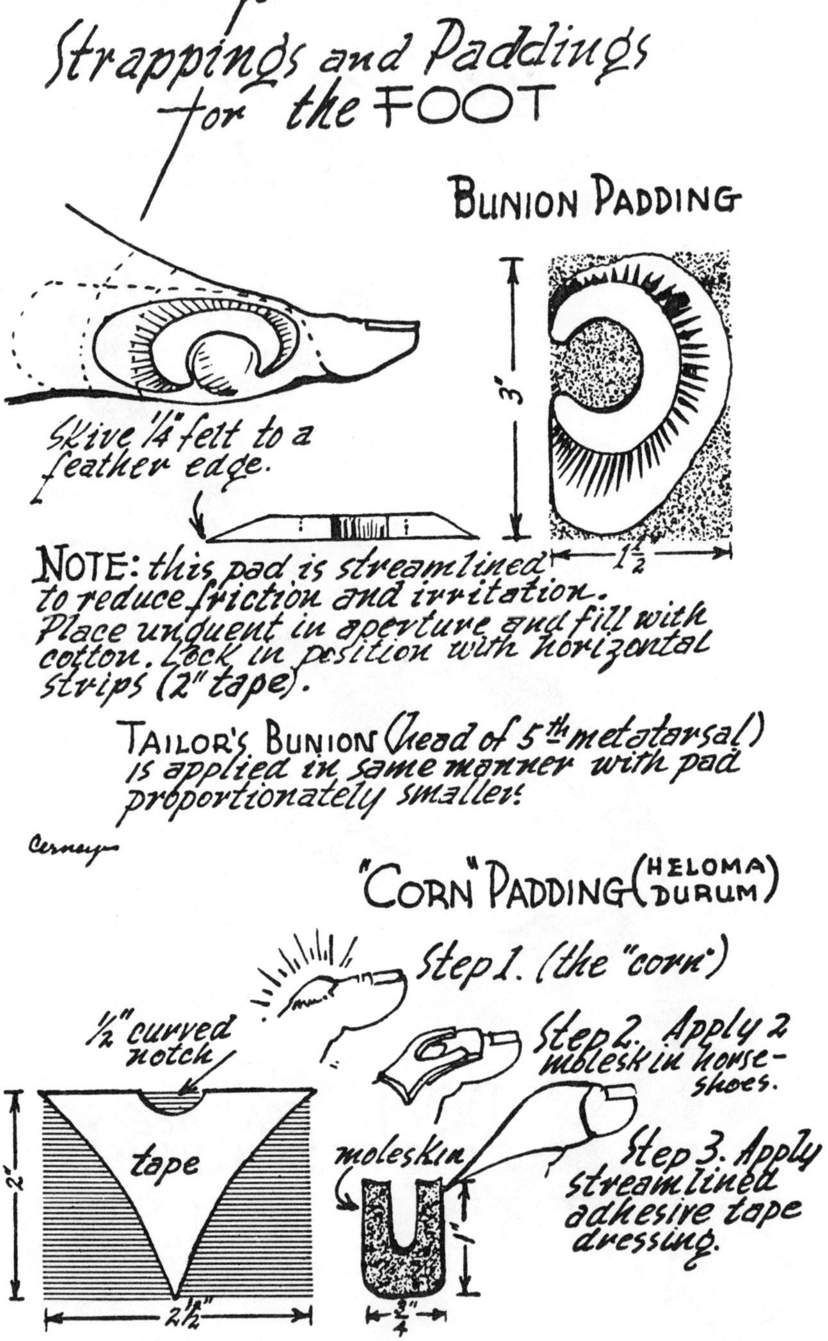

Strappings and Paddings for the FOOT

BUNION PADDING

Skive 1/4" felt to a feather edge.

3"

1 1/2"

NOTE: this pad is streamlined to reduce friction and irritation. Place unguent in aperture and fill with cotton. Lock in position with horizontal strips (2" tape).

TAILOR'S BUNION (head of 5th metatarsal) is applied in same manner with pad proportionately smaller.

Cerney

"CORN" PADDING (HELOMA DURUM)

Step 1. (the "corn")

1/2" curved notch

tape

2"

2 1/2"

Step 2. Apply 2 moleskin horseshoes.

moleskin

3/4"

Step 3. Apply streamlined adhesive tape dressing.

Figure 26

FOOT PADDING

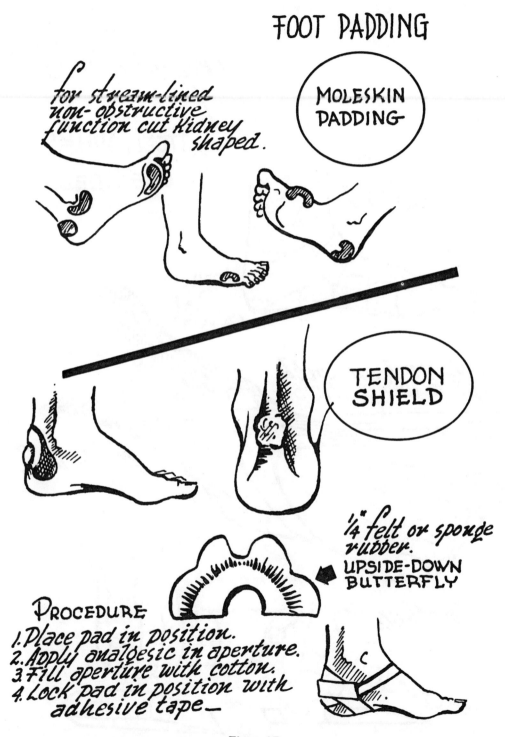

for stream-lined non-obstructive function cut kidney shaped.

MOLESKIN PADDING

TENDON SHIELD

¼" felt or sponge rubber.
UPSIDE-DOWN BUTTERFLY

PROCEDURE
1. Place pad in position.
2. Apply analgesic in aperture.
3. Fill aperture with cotton.
4. Lock pad in position with adhesive tape —

Figure 27

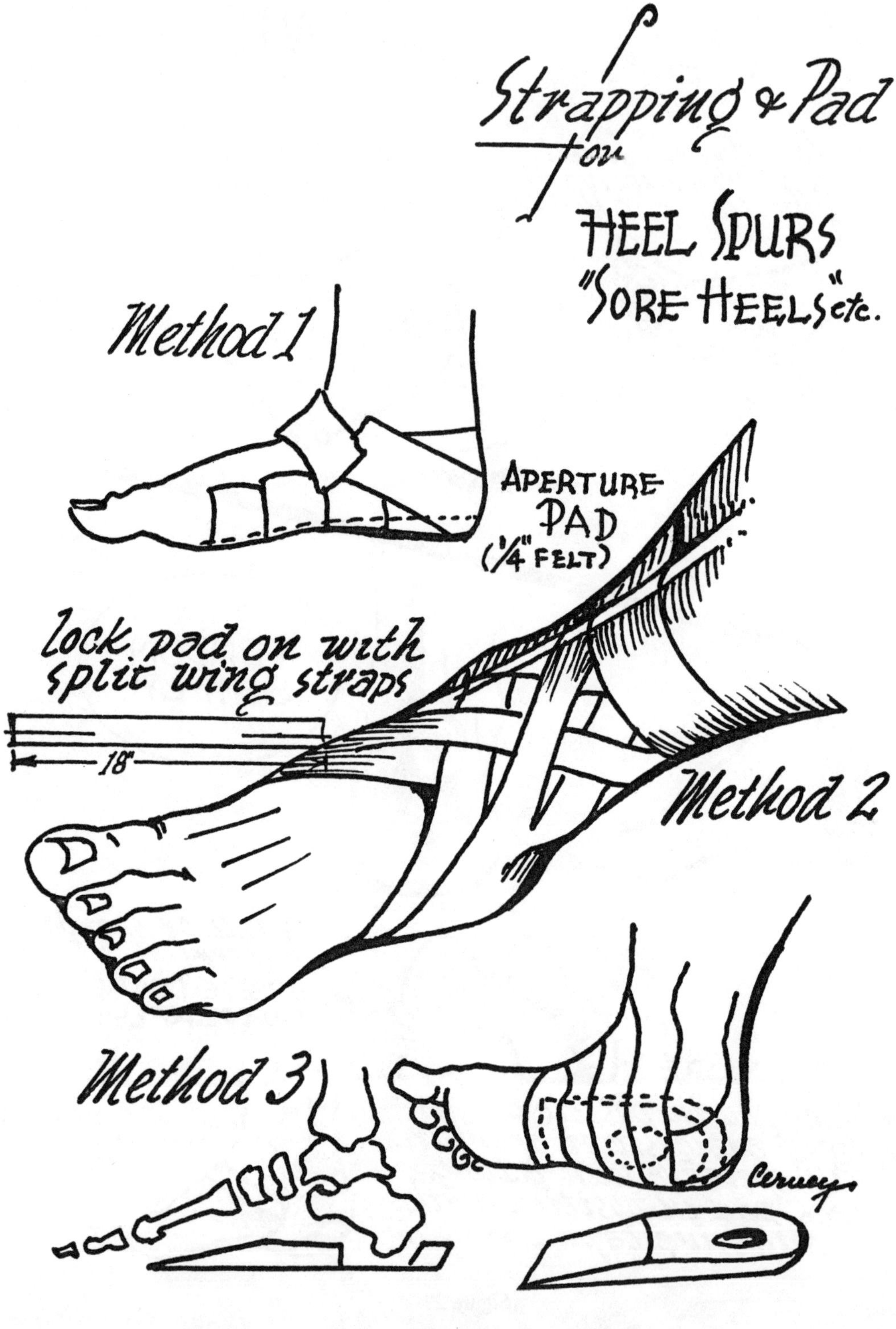

Strapping & Pad
for
HEEL SPURS
"SORE HEELS" etc.

Method 1

APERTURE
PAD
(¼" FELT)

lock pad on with
split wing straps

18"

Method 2

Method 3

Figure 28

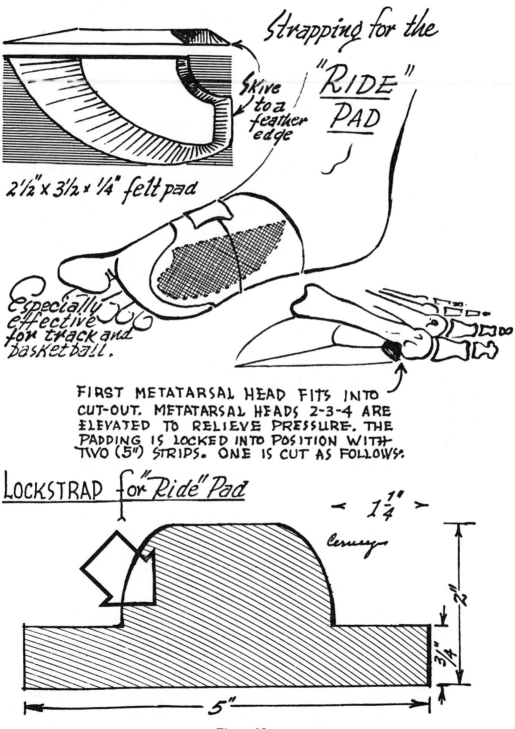

Strapping for the

"RIDE" PAD

Skive to a feather edge

2½" x 3½" x ¼" felt pad

Especially effective for track and basketball.

FIRST METATARSAL HEAD FITS INTO CUT-OUT. METATARSAL HEADS 2-3-4 ARE ELEVATED TO RELIEVE PRESSURE. THE PADDING IS LOCKED INTO POSITION WITH TWO (5") STRIPS. ONE IS CUT AS FOLLOWS:

LOCKSTRAP for "Ride" Pad

1¼"

Corners

2"

¾"

5"

Figure 29

The ANKLE

Flexible cast techniques for:

      Ankle Wrap Protection (Ariail)
      External-Lateral Collateral Ligament Wrap
      Ankle Straps (five methods)
      Ankle Strap-Split Wing Style
      Ankle Strap (Dr. Doller)
      External Ankle Strain (Millard Kelly)
      Figure 8 Ankle Wrap
      Ankle Sprain
      Ankle injury (Al Sawdy)
      Ankle Injury in Football
      Foot and Ankle Strap (Forrest Allen)
      Louisiana Wrap
      Basketweave
      Ankle Strain Strap

Taping the ANKLE

> Suggested   1"
> Tape Width 1½"

Purpose: (a) To provide support, (b) to maintain joint continuity, (c) to promote absorption of swelling.

Position: Athlete is seated on training table, foot overhangs the edge at ease. **DO NOT INVERT OR EVERT** the foot "to the side of the injury," or maintain the foot at right angles to the leg. *(Apply tape to maintain normality—not for correction!)*

Procedure: Massage leg muscles until relaxed. Prep skin for your favorite or desirable taping technique. Bandage an ankle *immediately* after an injury. Until such time as the team doctor rules out complications wrap the joint with 2" cotton elastic roller bandage and apply ice packs. Have athlete move his toes constantly to provide a muscle assist in keeping down edema or until the squad physician sees the problem. *When an ankle injury is sustained, consider it fractured until ruled otherwise by the physician and diagnostic X-rays.* Simply maintain full security and joint balance and do not worry about "strapping to the side of the weakness." When ankle "tape jobs" are used on football backfield men, punters, or basketball players keep the *Achilles tendon* and *anterior tibial* tendon free. Provide for easier plantar or dorsi-flexion. If your favorite ankle bandage overrides the *Achilles tendon* pad it. All ankle straps may be reinforced with figure-8 adhesive straps or cotton elastic roller bandage. An ankle once injured never fully recovers. It is susceptible to the same injury over and over even though it heals faster with each successive problem.

The ANKLE

Ankle strains and sprains occur from the uncontrolled inversion or eversion of the foot. Trauma is direct and fast. Ligaments rupture or stretch in direct ratio to the impact of the blow or twist. Ruptured ankle ligaments may or may not be accompanied by bone fragmentation to the distal tips of the tibia and fibula, the talus or cuboid bones. In violent twists of the foot the base of the fifth metatarsal may rupture away. *Sprain-fractures* of this type automatically preclude activity. And because bone-chipping, or fragmentation, is always a possibility in "sprains" *no sprain can be considered without fracture until the physician's X-ray verification proves it otherwise.* Sprains should be differentiated from strains for the sake of the treatment as well as for the records. To aid in this differentiation memorize the following: —

ANKLE SPRAINS

Ankle "sprains" are those changes in the ankle joint in which ligaments are extended beyond their normal limitations, and rupturing of the ligaments and fracturing of local bone structure remain a possibility.

ANKLE STRAINS

Ankle "strains" are minor injuries involving the stretching of soft tissues without leaving any of them torn. Bone tissue remains uninvolved by fracture but periostitis may be a possibility.

To Send—or Not to Send— Athletes out with an Ankle Wrap

Whether or not all athletes should go out on the field with ankle wraps has long been an element of controversy with coaches, trainers and team doctors. Trainer Ken Rawlinson and former head football coach Bud Wilkinson at the University of Oklahoma felt that their team's *lack* of ankle and knee injuries was due primarily to the fact that "Everyone who goes out on the field goes out with an ankle strap."

The late trainer Jay Colville and football coach Johnny Pont, when I interviewed them years ago at Miami University (Ohio), however, had a different opinion. "We do not believe in strapping everyone," said Colville emphatically. "When they need it they get it. That's it!"

Former Cardinal trainer and foot specialist Joe Doller put *a flexible cast on everybody on the squad,* but from where I'm sitting at this time it appears that the necessity for an ankle wrap depends on four important factors: — (1) *physical condition,* (2) *history of old injuries,* (3) *postural-structural inadequacies,* (4) *psychological conditioning and methods of prevention used.*

Actually there is only one efficient protection for the ankle. That protection is a normally healthy ankle and well-conditioned tissues that control it. To get the most uninjured efficiency out of this mortise-type joint, the ligaments and tendons that control it must be strong. Special conditioning exercises should be given the athlete for this purpose. When the athlete is in condition he is not subject to this injury.

Rawlinson and Doller are of course practicing prevention, and prevention is the first duty of any good trainer. Out on the field there is no control over mud, bad turf, ice, or having 250 pounds come down on an extended leg. There's no control over a suddenly excited ball carrier forgetting to remain relaxed and keeping his knees bent or his ankles rigid when hit.

To me ALL athletes are key men and I feel that prevention, through ankle wraps, is a matter of necessity. Whether this is done with adhesive tape, cotton elastic bandages, Webdril or combinations of gauze and adhesive, in the long run, *in the care and prevention of athletic injuries, it is wiser to wrap the ankles of ALL athletes before ALL practices and games.* In the long run it's less expensive, less ulcer-making, to spend a little time bandaging than it is to spend the rest of the season worrying about something that should have been prevented in the first place.

Tips on Taping
Ankle Injuries

1. *Ankle injuries,* and their side-effects, lead to future "Charley horses," "shin splints," knee involvements and problems of the foot.
2. *An ankle injury* is never local. It is never temporary and it demands constant prevention as well as care. When an ankle is injured ALL hard and soft tissues are involved directly or indirectly. The memory of every injury is engraved in scar tissue.
3. *Before applying tape* know the history of that ankle! Remember that *first sprains take longer to heal* than do those which follow. They are also mute reminders to tape that ankle, or ankles, *BEFORE* each practice or game.
4. *Never send an ankle "sprain" promptly back into the game* with a shot of novocaine or enzymes until approved by the team physician. Call it a fracture until an X-ray film proves it otherwise. Sadly enough too many athletes have been lost due to inadequacies just like this. And this certainly is not prevention!

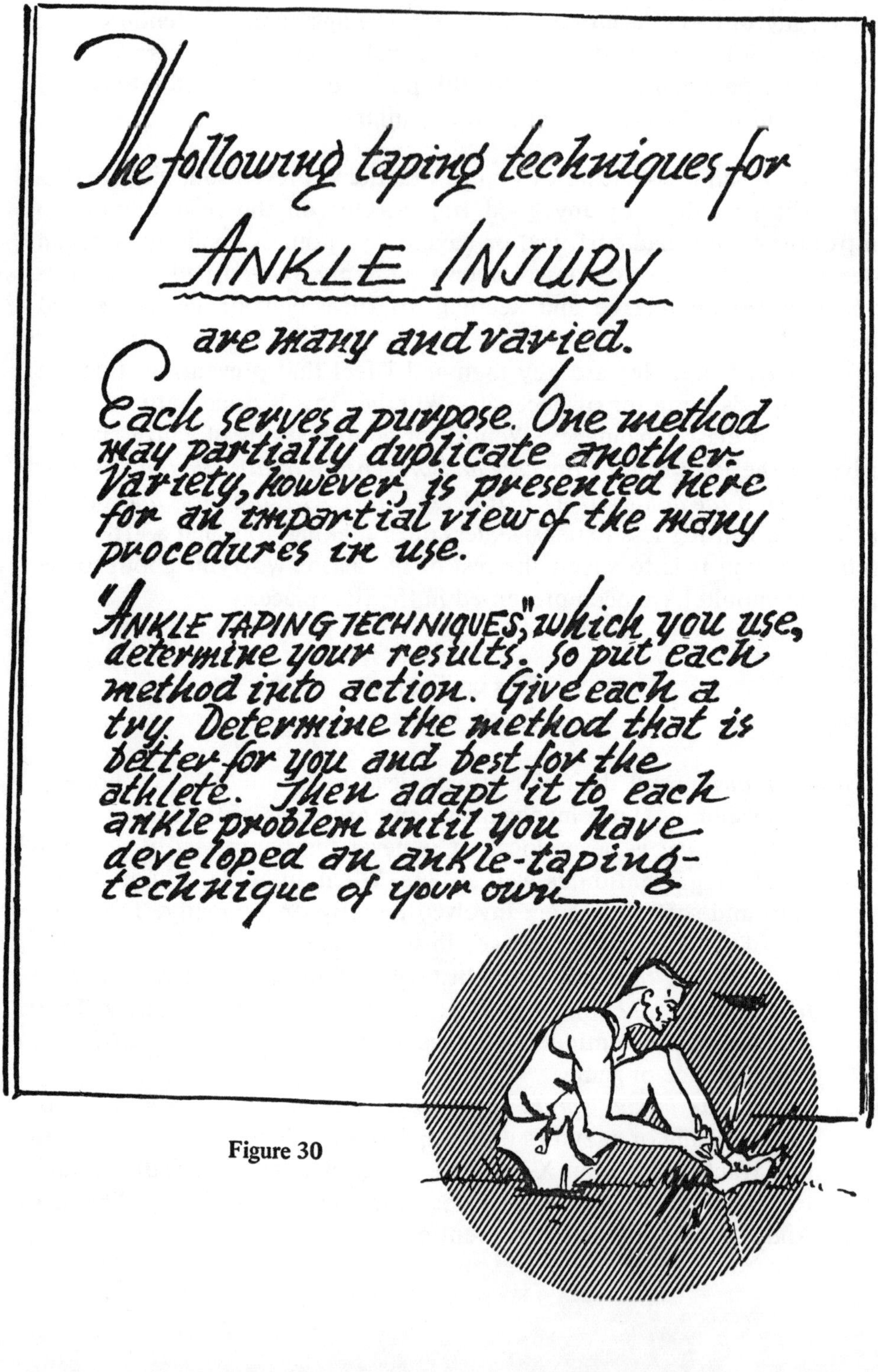

The following taping techniques for

ANKLE INJURY

are many and varied.

Each serves a purpose. One method may partially duplicate another. Variety, however, is presented here for an impartial view of the many procedures in use.

"Ankle taping techniques," which you use, determine your results. So put each method into action. Give each a try. Determine the method that is better for you and best for the athlete. Then adapt it to each ankle problem until you have developed an ankle-taping-technique of your own.

Figure 30

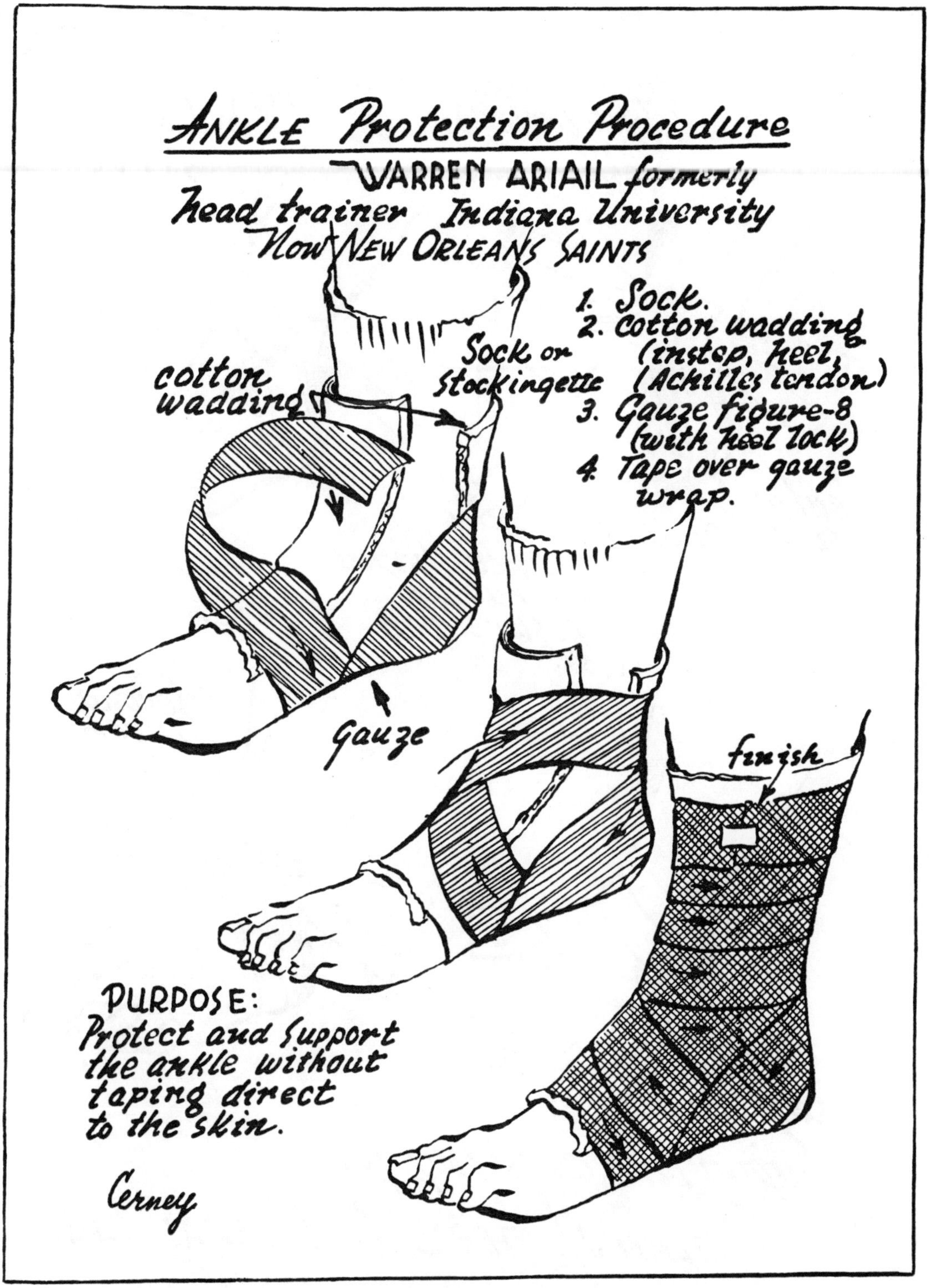

ANKLE Protection Procedure

WARREN ARIAIL formerly head trainer Indiana University Now NEW ORLEANS SAINTS

1. Sock.
2. Cotton wadding (instop, heel, (Achilles tendon)
3. Gauze figure-8 (with heel lock)
4. Tape over gauze wrap.

cotton wadding

Sock or Stockingette

Gauze

finish

PURPOSE: Protect and support the ankle without taping direct to the skin.

Cerney

Figure 31

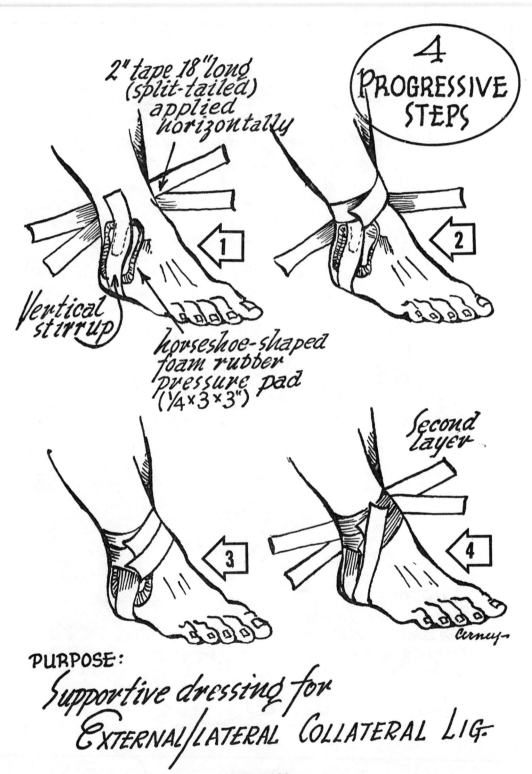

2" tape 18" long
(split-tailed)
applied
horizontally

4 PROGRESSIVE STEPS

Vertical
stirrup

horseshoe-shaped
foam rubber
pressure pad
(¼×3×3")

1

2

Second
layer

3

4

PURPOSE:

Supportive dressing for
External/lateral Collateral Lig.

Figure 32

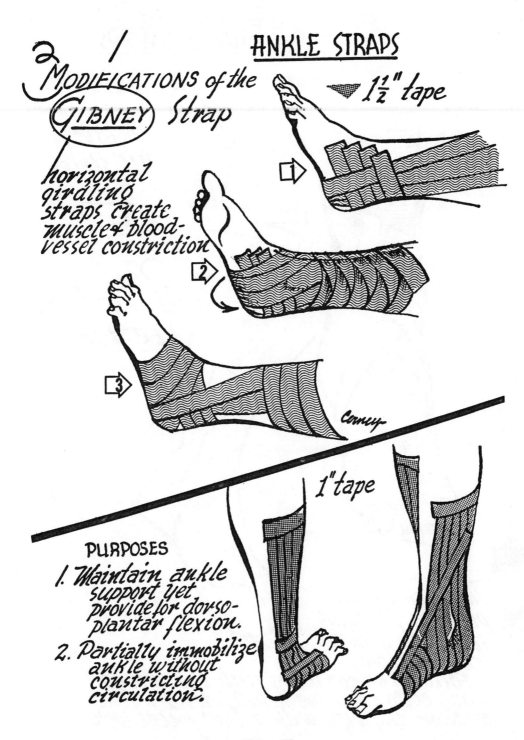

ANKLE STRAPS

2 / MODIFICATIONS of the (GIBNEY) Strap

horizontal girdling straps create muscle & blood-vessel constriction

1½" tape

1"tape

PURPOSES
1. Maintain ankle support yet provide for dorso-plantar flexion.
2. Partially immobilize ankle without constricting circulation.

Figure 33

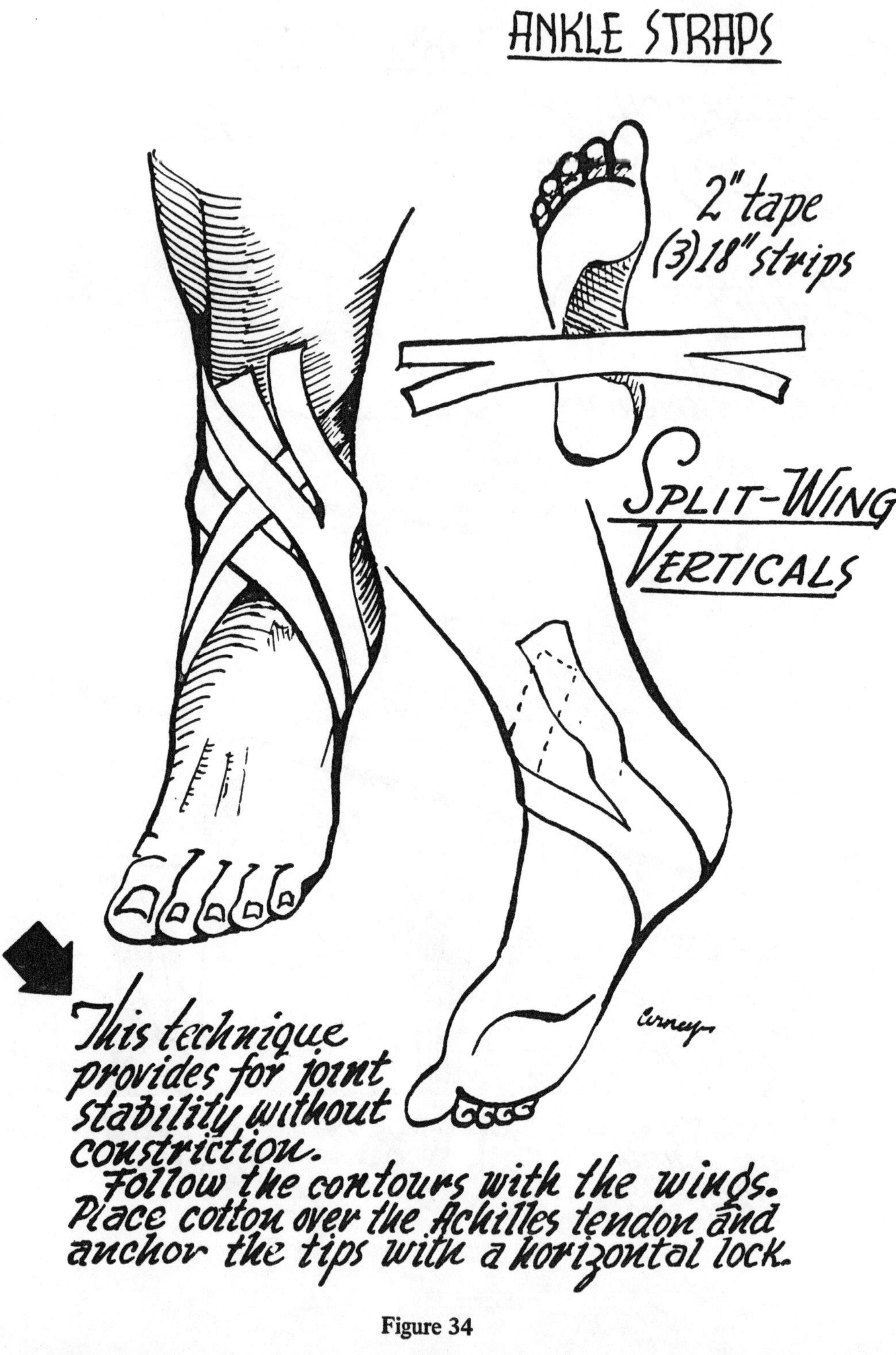

ANKLE STRAPS

2" tape
(3) 18" strips

SPLIT-WING VERTICALS

This technique
provides for joint
stability without
constriction.
Follow the contours with the wings.
Place cotton over the Achilles tendon and
anchor the tips with a horizontal lock.

Figure 34

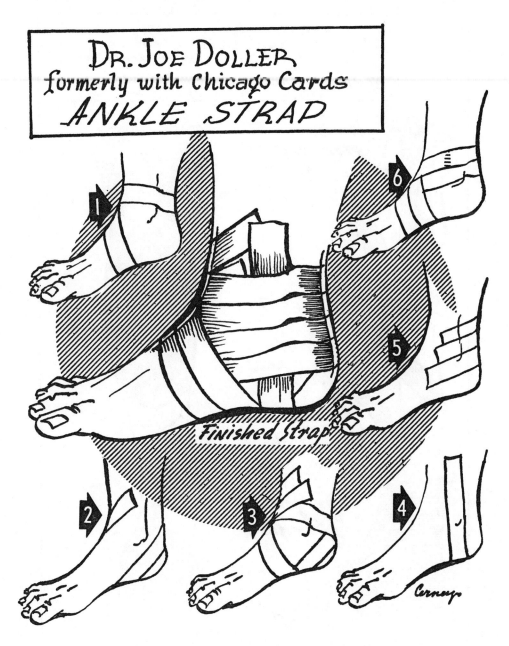

Figure 35

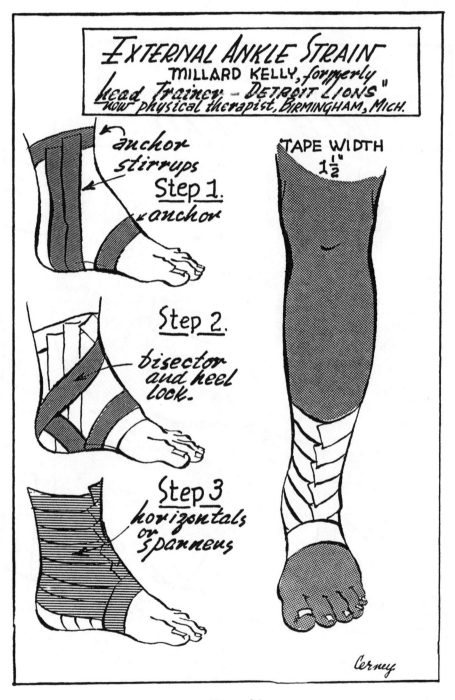

Figure 36

ANKLE STRAPS

Figure Eight with Vertical Stirrup

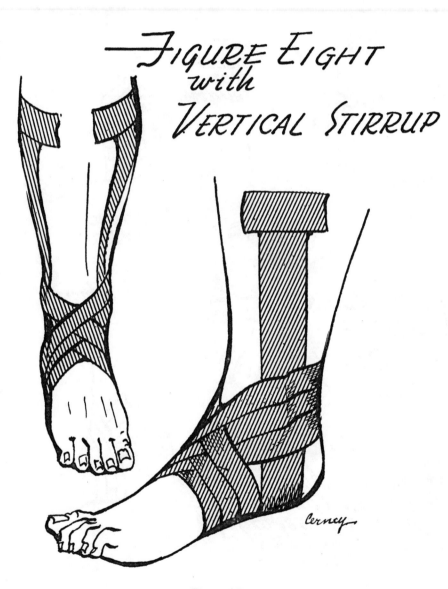

Figure 37

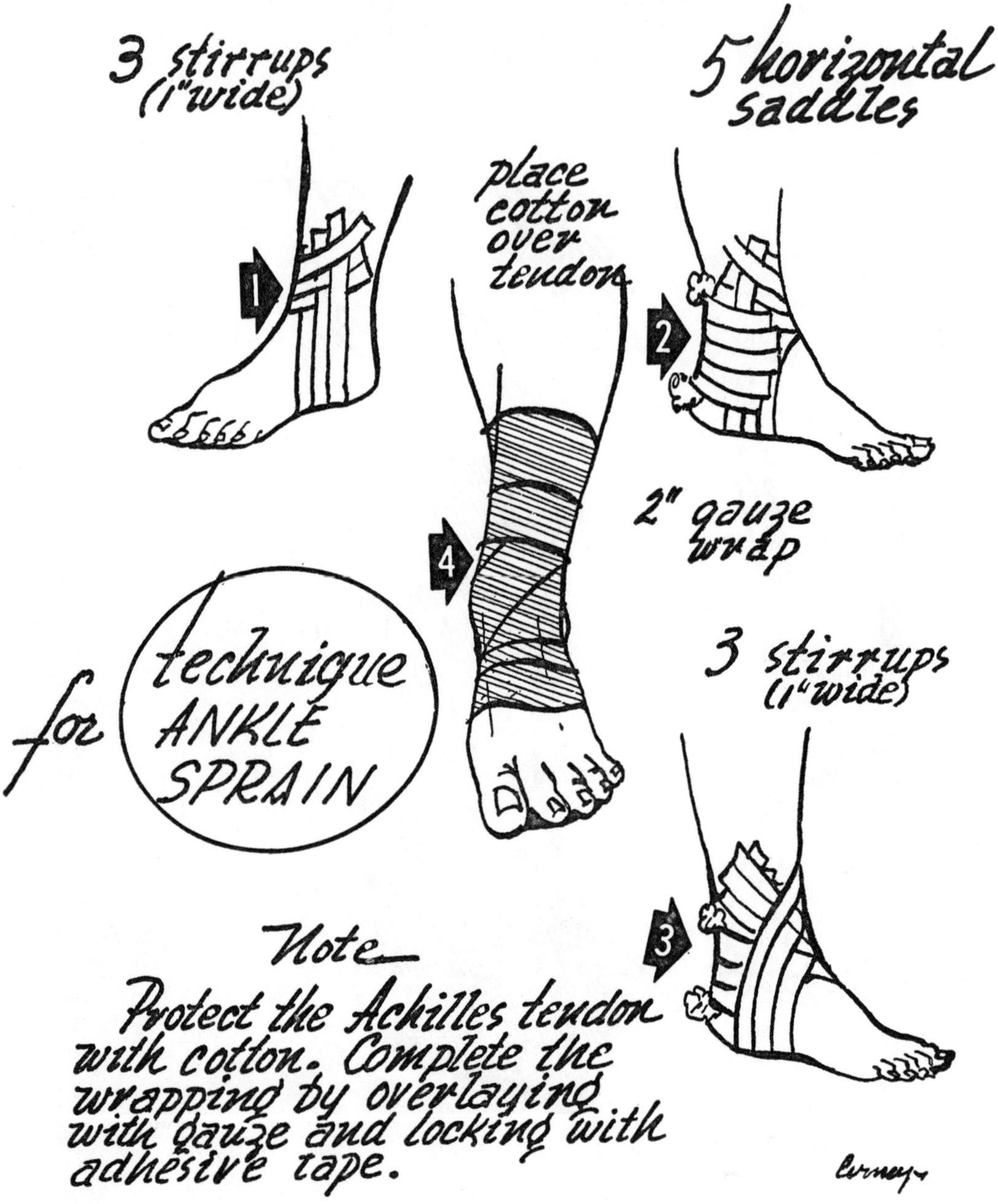

3 stirrups
(1"wide)

5 horizontal
saddles

place cotton over tendon

2" gauze wrap

3 stirrups
(1"wide)

for technique ANKLE SPRAIN

Note—
Protect the Achilles tendon with cotton. Complete the wrapping by overlaying with gauze and locking with adhesive tape.

Figure 38

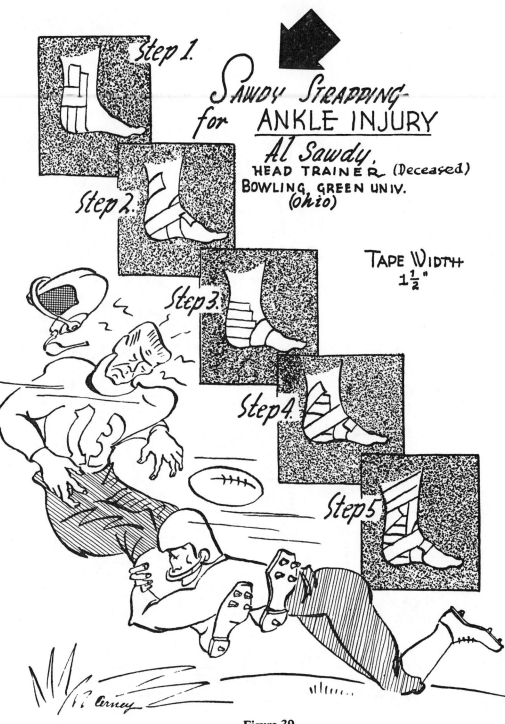

Figure 39

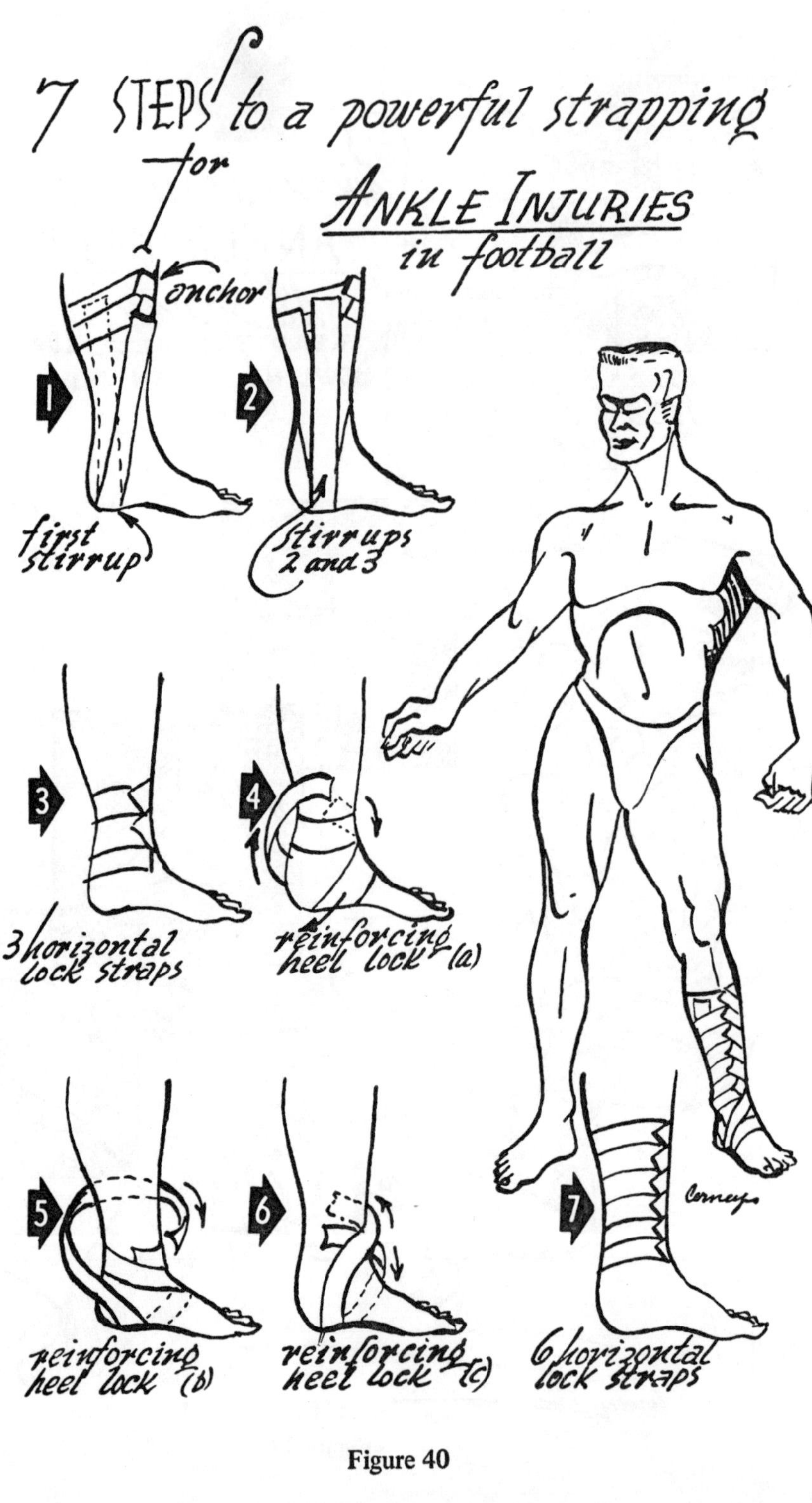

7 STEPS to a powerful strapping for

ANKLE INJURIES
in football

1 — first stirrup

2 — stirrups 2 and 3

3 — 3 horizontal lock straps

4 — reinforcing heel lock (a)

5 — reinforcing heel lock (b)

6 — reinforcing heel lock (c)

7 — 6 horizontal lock straps

anchor

Figure 40

Forrest Allen (Retired)
Foot and Ankle Strapping

Figure 41

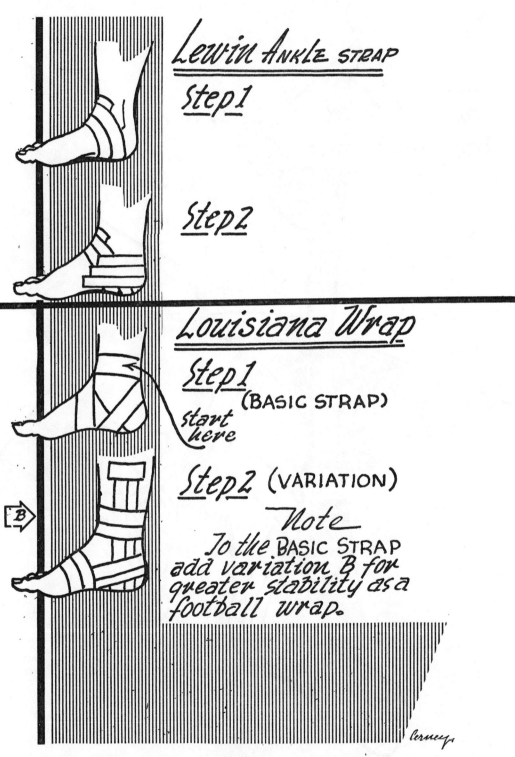

Lewin Ankle Strap

Step 1

Step 2

Louisiana Wrap

Step 1 (BASIC STRAP)

start here

Step 2 (VARIATION)

Note

To the BASIC STRAP add variation B for greater stability as a football wrap.

Figure 42

Ankle Strappings

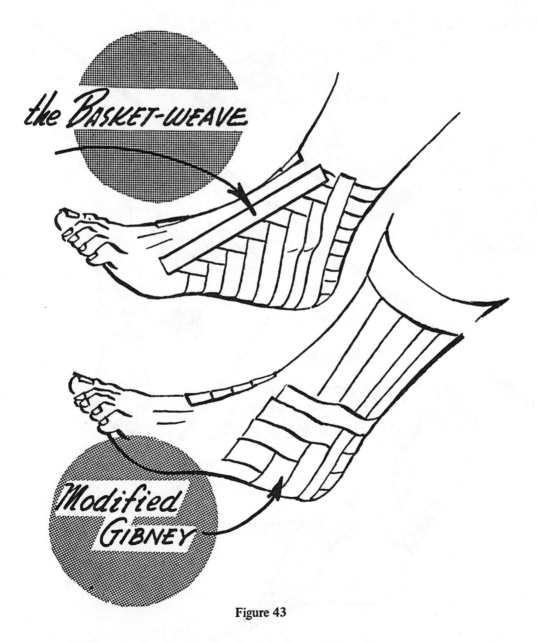

the BASKET-WEAVE

Modified GIBNEY

Figure 43

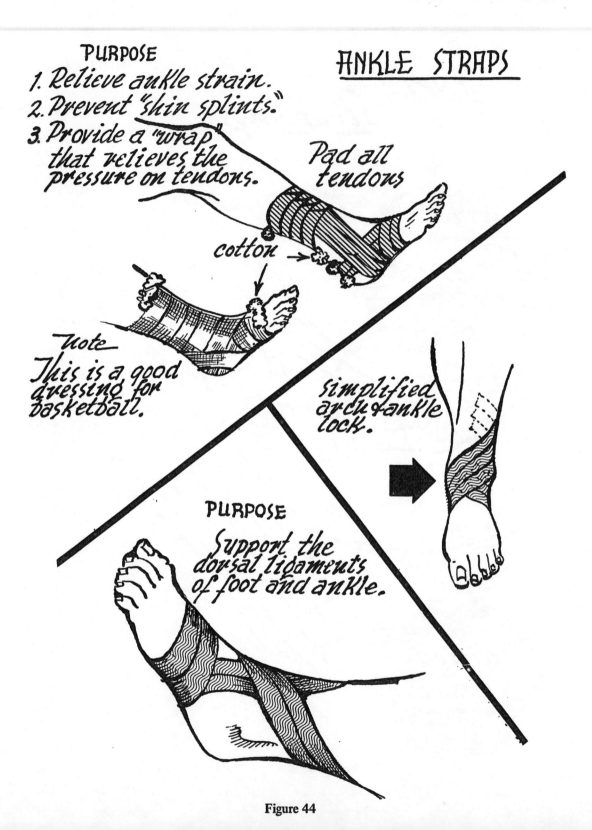

ANKLE STRAPS

PURPOSE
1. Relieve ankle strain.
2. Prevent "shin splints."
3. Provide a "wrap" that relieves the pressure on tendons.

Pad all tendons

cotton →

Note
This is a good dressing for basketball.

simplified arch & ankle lock.

PURPOSE

Support the dorsal ligaments of foot and ankle.

Figure 44

The ACHILLES TENDON

Flexible Cast Techniques for:
>Achilles Tendon Strap (Lloyd Williams)
>Achilles Tendon Strain with Heel Lift
>Achilles Tendon Ankle Wrap

The ACHILLES TENDON

> Suggested
> Tape Width: 1"

Purpose: Remove stress from soft or hard tissue attachments.

Position: Athlete prone. Feet extended at ease over end of training table.

Procedure: Massage calf muscles mildly for relaxation. After the skin work-up apply an *anchor* strap across the triceps and one plantarly behind the metatarsal heads. Run all *bridges, obliques,* etc. from the foot *anchor* up the leg. Heel padding may be placed in footgear or strapped to the foot.

Achilles Tendon Conditions
Observed in Sports

In athletics, the term *ruptured tendon* is a misnomer in its common usage. Only massive and sharp violence ruptures a tendon per se, and not once in 25 years or more with athletes have I observed this in basketball, football, track, baseball, boxing, or wrestling. On the ski slopes and in ice hockey it's another problem. The tough tendon may be cut or ripped *away* from its origin or insertion, and therein lies the misconception. *In almost all sports injuries the tendon itself DOES NOT RUPTURE!* It remains intact!

Soft tissues associated with this tendon, however, provide another story. For example: *Tendo-Achilles strain* is marked by inflammation in the triceps to which the tendon is attached. There may be inflammation at the periosteal attachment in the heel bone (calcaneum). When this occurs the tendon sheath also becomes involved. As a result of all associated tissues being involved, the functional power of the foot and leg is lost.

In *Tendo-Achilles tenosynovitis,* inflammation involves the tendon and its sheath by traumatic or infective processes. In both "wet" and "dry" tenosynovitis, adhesive tape may be used in therapy. When there is extensive swelling DO NOT USE TAPE! Wrap the area with cotton elastic roller bandage for compression and apply ice.

Where a true rupture or tearing of the Achilles tendon has occurred adhesive tape is of little or no value. The problem remains primarily in the province of the surgeon.

Achilles Tendon Strain

PROCEDURE: After skin work-up apply *anchor* straps on the triceps and plantarly behind the metatarsal heads. Now extend an 8" strip of *elastic tape* (2" width) from plantar *anchor* up over the heel to the triceps *anchor* above. Pad the Achilles tendon with cotton wadding and apply five staggered or graduated *stirrup* straps upwardly. Place a ½" thick felt pad under the heel and lock with tape. Overlay this dressing with an elastic wrap.

GIBNEY or BASKETWEAVE: After muscles are relaxed, and the skin work-up completed, pad the Achilles tendon. Start *the first 1" adhesive strip* behind the fifth metatarsal head, backward along the lateral border of the foot, around the heel to the medial arch and big toe joint. The *second strip* starts five inches above the level of the ankle bone. It runs downward parallel to the Achilles tendon, in the hollow, around the heel and up the other side. All subsequent strips overlap the initial horizontal and vertical *saddles* and *stirrups* in graduated formation. The ankle is secured with a basketweave and left open anteriorly to prevent pressure on the *anterior tibial* tendon as well as on the *digitorum longus.*

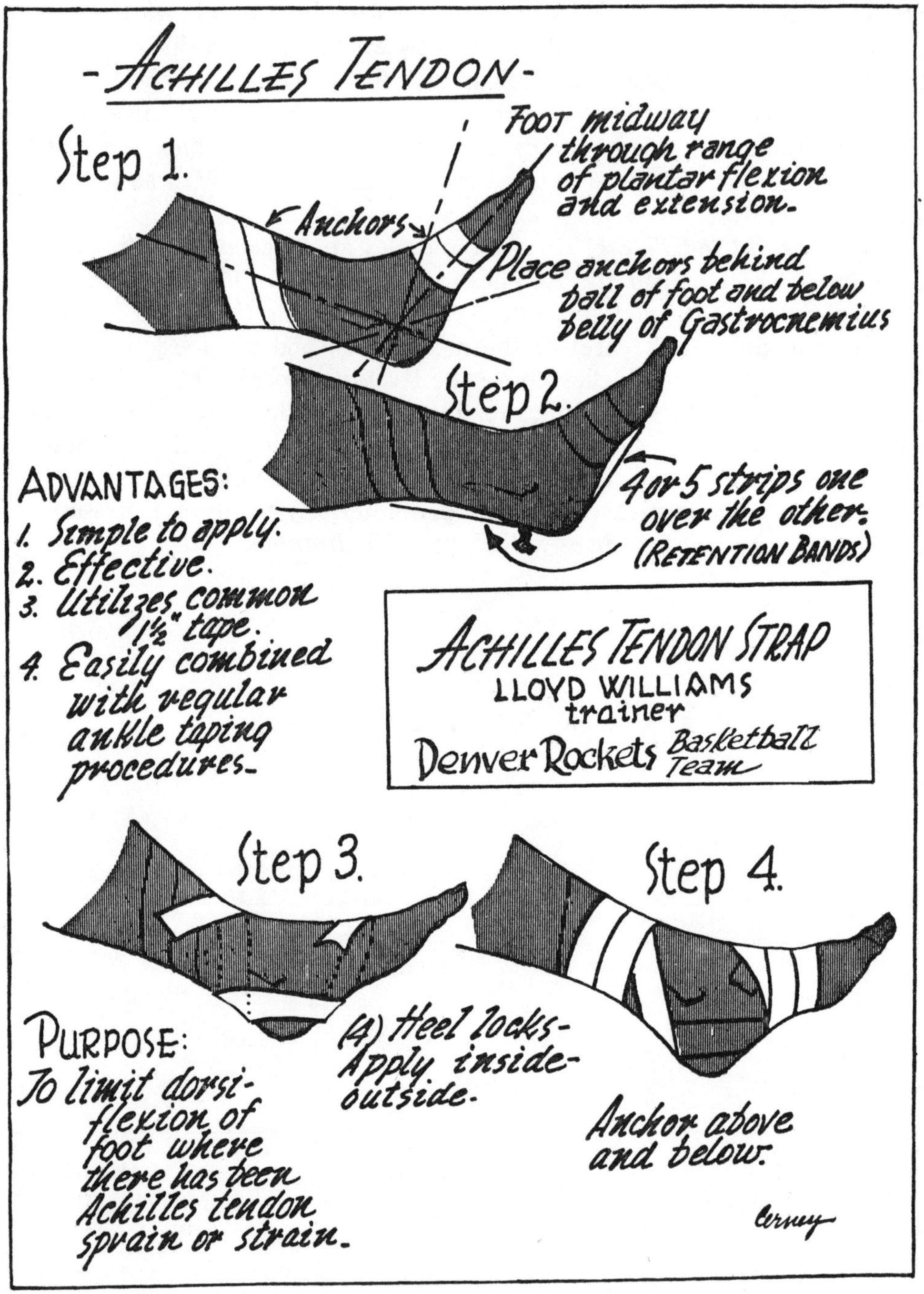

-ACHILLES TENDON-

Step 1.

← Anchors →

Foot midway through range of plantar flexion and extension.

Place anchors behind ball of foot and below belly of Gastrocnemius

Step 2.

4 or 5 strips one over the other. (RETENTION BANDS)

ADVANTAGES:
1. Simple to apply.
2. Effective.
3. Utilizes common 1½" tape.
4. Easily combined with regular ankle taping procedures.

ACHILLES TENDON STRAP
LLOYD WILLIAMS
trainer
Denver Rockets Basketball Team

Step 3.

Step 4.

PURPOSE:
To limit dorsi-flexion of foot where there has been Achilles tendon sprain or strain.

(4) Heel locks-
Apply inside-outside.

Anchor above and below.

Cerney

Figure 45

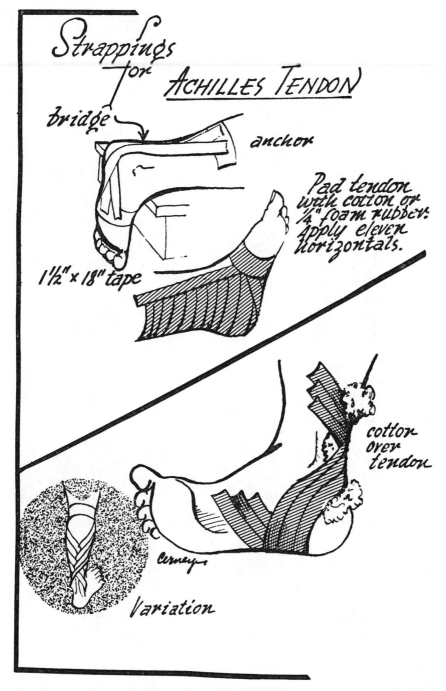

Strappings
for **ACHILLES TENDON**

bridge

anchor

Pad tendon with cotton or ¼" foam rubber. Apply eleven horizontals.

1½" x 18" tape

cotton over tendon

Cerney.

Variation

Figure 46

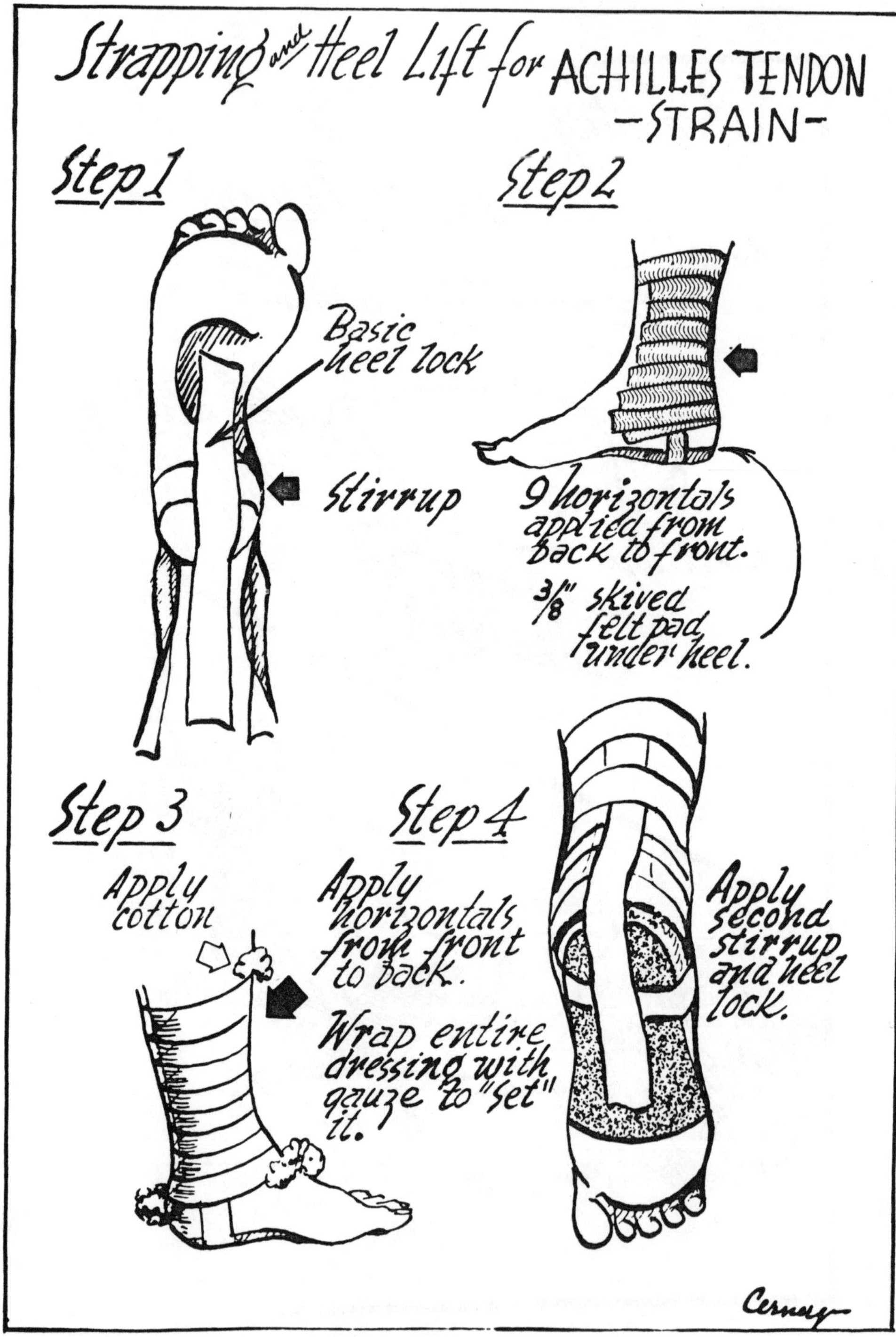

Strapping *and* **Heel Lift for ACHILLES TENDON**
-STRAIN-

Step 1

Basic heel lock

Stirrup

Step 2

9 horizontals applied from back to front.

3/8" skived felt pad under heel.

Step 3

Apply cotton

Step 4

Apply horizontals from front to back.

Wrap entire dressing with gauze to "set" it.

Apply second stirrup and heel lock.

Cerney

Figure 47

Achilles-tendon
ANKLE Strapping

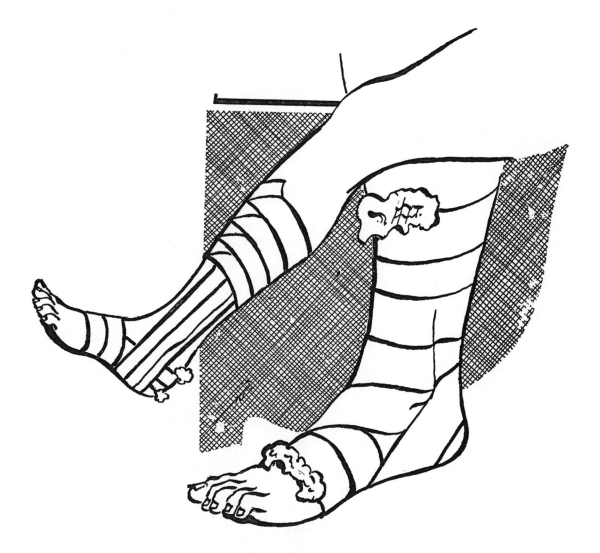

Figure 48

The LEG

Flexible Cast Techniques for:
        Peroneal slipped tendon
        Peroneal contusion
        Shin splints (Hamel)
        Contused shins
        "Tennis Leg" (Sawdy & Campbell)
        Calf herniation

PERONEAL TENDON

Slipping Peroneal Tendon

The *slipped peroneal tendon* is a condition in which either the *longus* or *brevis* tendons, or both, erupt from their normal groove behind the head of the fibula and override the talus. Such slippage may be caused by weak ankles and legs, old or new injuries, or by an ankle or foot bandage ineptly applied.

Peroneal Contusion

The wrap of preference for the *peroneal contusion* is the 4" cotton elastic roller bandage. Elastic adhesive tape may be used. Before applying it, skive and contourize a 4" x 10" x ½" foam rubber pad and place it on the contused area. Wrap as directed in Figure 49.

LEG "CRAMPS"

Leg *cramps* take an athlete out of action as fast as any direct injury. He is quickly immobilized by pain. But before "slapping" adhesive tape on him know the cause of his problem. Tape, in this problem, may be exactly what not to use. To protect the athlete against the wrong therapy and the wrong flexible casting technique, make a thorough examination of him. Be sure his *pre-season physical examination* gives him a clean bill-of-health.

As an adjunctive therapy place a ¼" felt lift in the shoe. This relieves "pull" on all muscles concerned. Also erroneous, when it comes to leg cramps, is the terminology *Charley horse*.

When, Where, Why and How to Use Tape for "Charley Horse"

The words *Charley horse* cover a multitude of sins. Too often it is a general term, like "arthritis," given to a problem because of inadequate knowledge or diagnosis. Because ALL Charley horses are usually treated the same way the same bad results occur. For example, certain kinds of Charley horses in the extremities preclude adhesive tape. It's simply contraindicated. So to help clarify this matter of whether to use, or not to use, adhesive tape on a Charley horse, the following chart was devised.

| Charley Horse Classification and What to Treat With Adhesive Tape ||
Charley Horses that DO TAKE TAPE	Charley Horses NOT TAKING TAPE

Muscle strain
Muscle spasm
Hematoma
Scar tissue in
    the gastrocnemius
    and soleus
	Muscle rupture
	Tendon tear (at insertion)
	Myositis ossificans
	Periostitis
	Tenosynovitis

Strain of superficial leg muscles such as the *gastrocnemius, soleus* and *plantaris,* is the usual cause of Charley horse. That point where the two bellies of the *gastrocnemius* meet is a common site of pain. In this injury even minor tears resulting in scar tissue start the symptoms going. **It is during the inflammatory stage of muscle strains, spasm after trauma, hemotoma after trauma, and the beginnings of scar tissue, that adhesive strapping, or flexible casting, is most desirable.**

"Poops" or Herniated Calf Muscle

Muscle hernia is any extrusion of the muscle body through its outer sheath to create a defect or weakness in the body of the muscle itself.

The most significant sign of a true muscle *"poop"* is that *the hernia disappears when the muscle contracts.* Therefore, before applying adhesive tape, have the athlete contract the muscle concerned. If the "poop" disappears, go ahead and finish the "tape job." Calf muscle herniation is more common in high jumpers and in basketball and tennis players. A "dash man" is more apt to experience the problem in the flexors of his hip. When the *anterior tibial muscle* is involved in any sport look for an advanced case of weakfoot. Biceps in the arm are subject to herniation, but in either legs or arms *don't confuse herniation with varicosed veins.*

TENNIS LEG

Tennis leg is the result of tearing one or more of the posterior muscles of the calf. When the triceps are injured, local blood vessels go into spasm. This causes a local anemia which contributes to a *Charley horse.* Adhesions follow. The more adhesions there are the less capable the muscle is of responding to action. This in turn leads to new injuries and more *Charley horses.* The problem, once begun, perpetuates itself if proper therapy is not begun. But no matter what procedure is used KEEP THE ATHLETE MOVING!

SHIN SPLINTS

Shin splints are not solved by strapping shins. In most part today's concern is with the end product and symptoms rather than with the cause; this is why so many treatment procedures fail. Many coaches, trainers, and team doctors insist on using tape to squeeze together the tibia and fibula and "ease the strain on their interosseous membrane." Some state that only ankle wraps are a solution for the shin splint. Some argue about *fasciitis, tenosynovitis* and *Sharpey's fibers.* Each of these factors may be a good explanation for a given athlete, but they do not answer the question—"Why shin splints?"

In considering the general problem of shin splints and its cause, bring the feet into focus. Remember that as the foundation goes so goes the building—and *in ALL cases of shin splints a foot problem is present concurrently!* Shin splints don't just happen. Strap the feet. Provide balance. Give the feet security with arch padding and foot strappings and well-fitted footgear. Then keep the following *Trainer's Tips* in mind: (a) *Strap the feet for all practices and games.* (b) *Avoid early season distance running.* (c) *Avoid hard running surfaces.* (d) *Use tennis shoes, not football shoes, in early spring or fall football sessions.* (e) *Keep athletes under wraps when warming up.* (f) *Avoid deep knee bends,* (g) *Avoid crouch starts.*

All Lower Leg Problems

```
Suggested  1"
Tape Width: 1½"
```

Purpose: Support the foot, stabilize and rest muscle of the leg.

Position: The athlete is seated on the training table. His foot extends over the edge when applying *stirrup* straps involving the foot. He stands on the training table when straps other than stirrups are applied. His knee is flexed slightly.

Procedure: Prep the skin after relaxing the muscles of the leg. Place *anchor* straps. Then apply other straps as indicated in the drawings. At no time totally surround the leg or its tendons. Anchor all open edges with *buttress* straps. Flexible casts may be supplemented with ¼" to ½" felt pads in the shoe for additional relief.

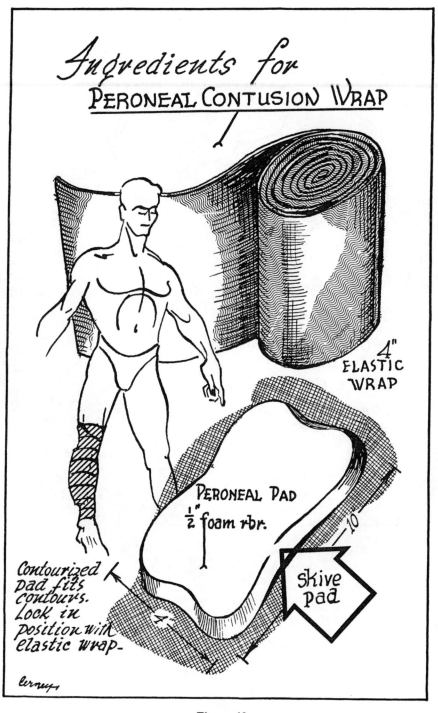

Ingredients for
PERONEAL CONTUSION WRAP

4" ELASTIC WRAP

PERONEAL PAD
½" foam rbr.

SKIVE PAD

Contourized pad fits contours. Lock in position with elastic wrap.

Figure 49

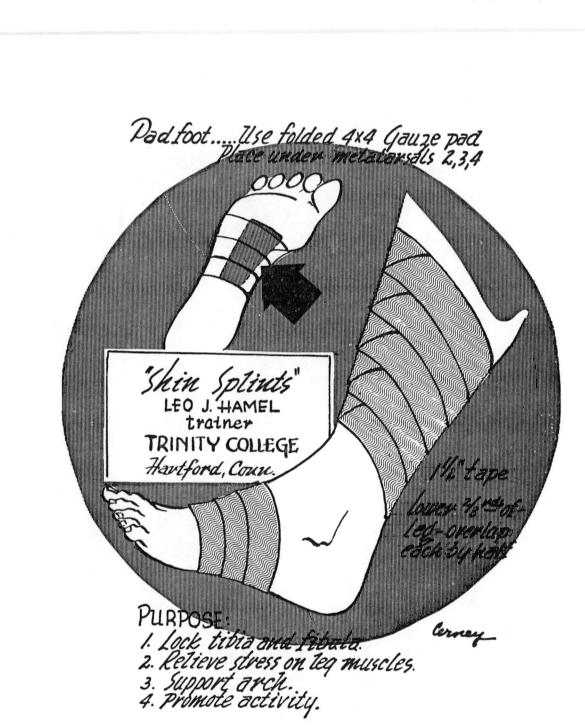

Figure 50

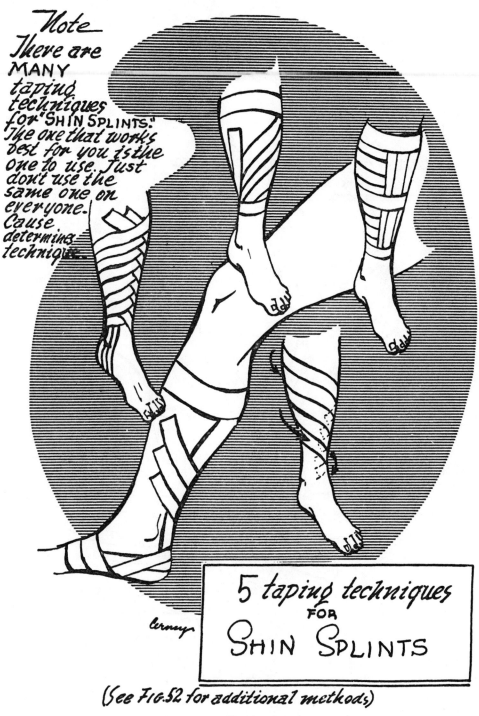

Figure 51

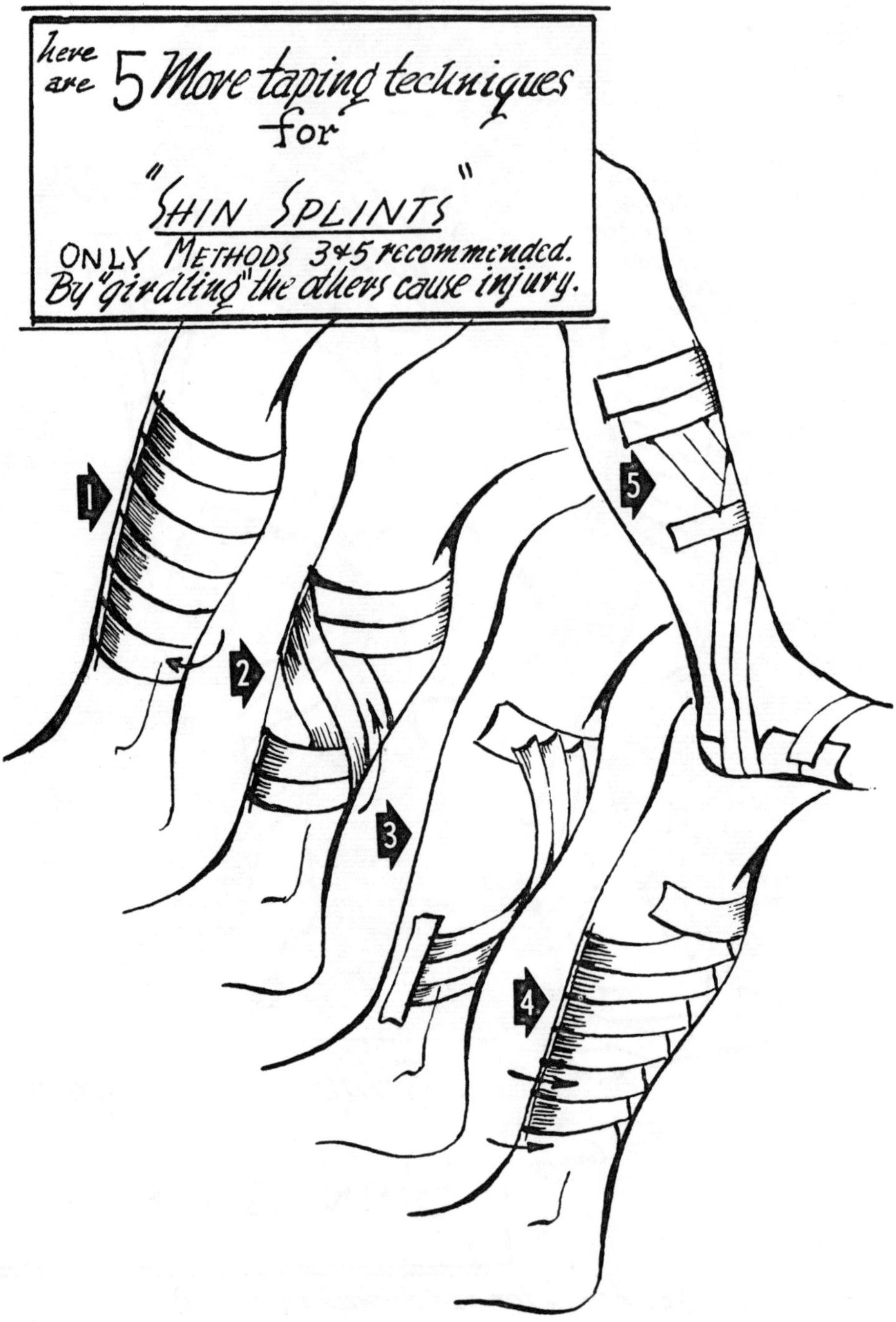
here are 5 More taping techniques for
"SHIN SPLINTS"
ONLY METHODS 3&5 recommended.
By "girdling" the others cause injury.
1
2
3
4
5

Figure 52

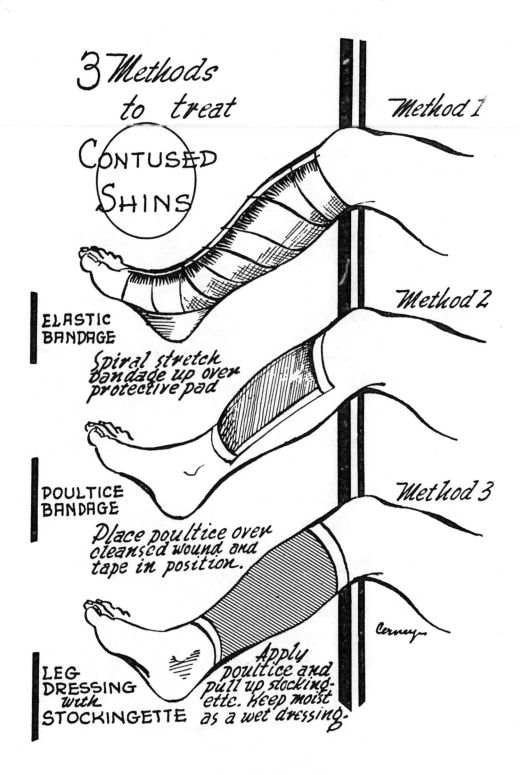

3 Methods to treat CONTUSED SHINS

Method 1

ELASTIC BANDAGE

Spiral stretch bandage up over protective pad

Method 2

POULTICE BANDAGE

Place poultice over cleansed wound and tape in position.

Method 3

LEG DRESSING with STOCKINGETTE

Apply poultice and pull up stockingette. Keep moist as a wet dressing.

Cerney

Figure 53

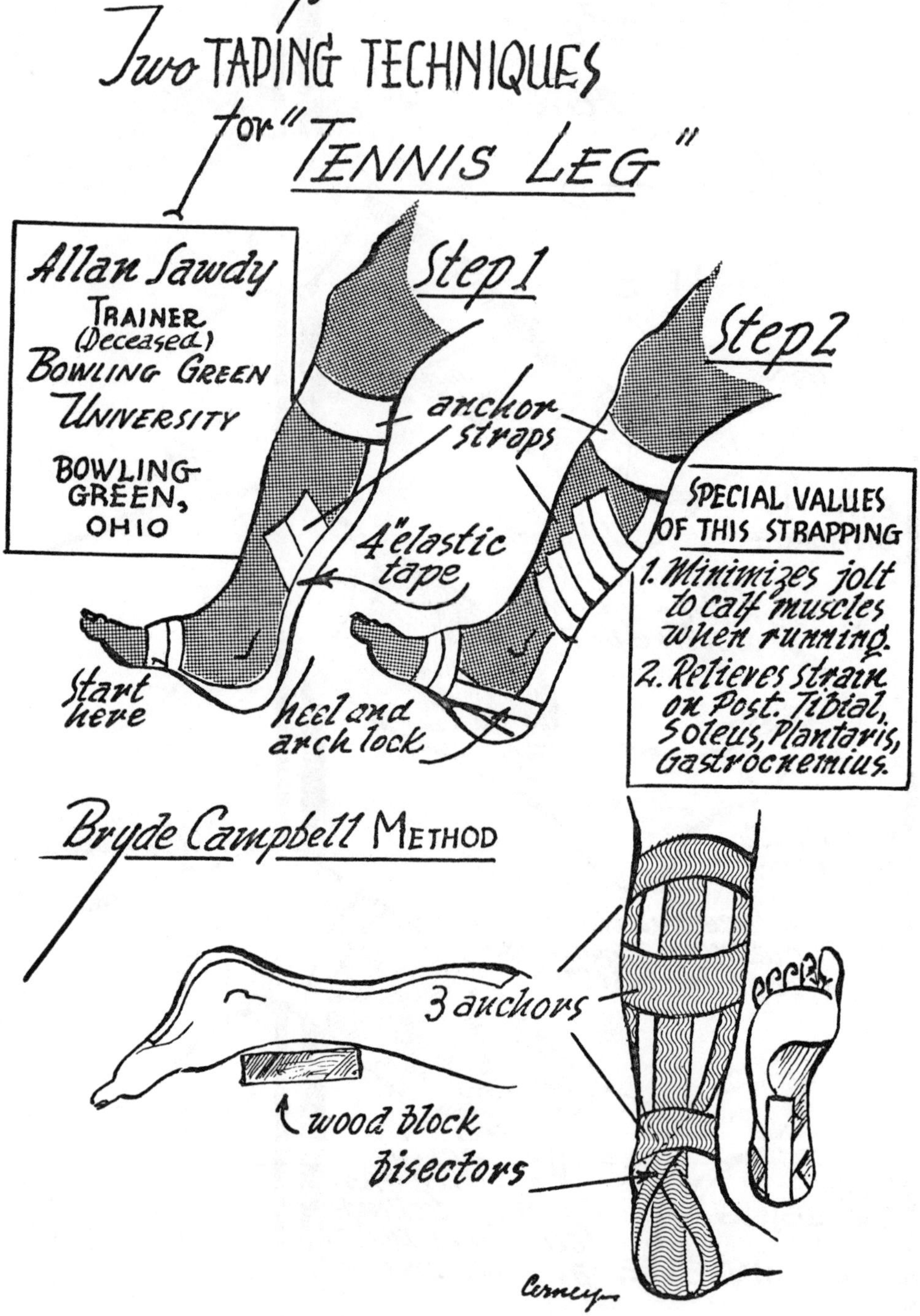
Two TAPING TECHNIQUES
for "TENNIS LEG"
Allan Sawdy
TRAINER
(Deceased)
BOWLING GREEN
UNIVERSITY
BOWLING GREEN, OHIO
Step 1
Step 2
anchor straps
4" elastic tape
Start here
heel and arch lock
SPECIAL VALUES OF THIS STRAPPING
1. Minimizes jolt to calf muscles when running.
2. Relieves strain on Post. Tibial, Soleus, Plantaris, Gastrocnemius.
Bryde Campbell METHOD
3 anchors
wood block
bisectors
Cerney

Figure 54

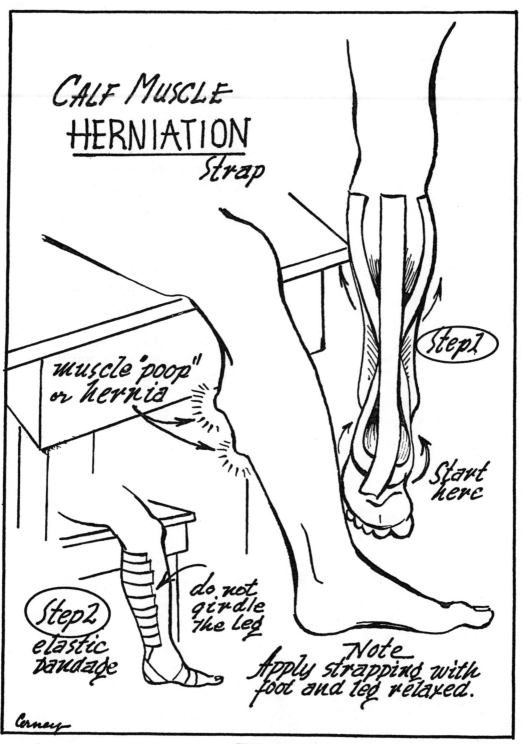

Figure 55

The KNEE

Flexible Cast Techniques for:
"False Tendon" (Wes Knight)
Posterior-Cruciate Ligament Strain
Knee Strap (Joe Romo)
Diamond Knee Lock (Brown)
Lateral Ligament strap (Sawdy)
Knee Straps (F. Allen and R. Bevan)
Knee Straps (Duke Simpson)
Knee Bursitis
Hyperextension Strap
Internal/Lateral Ligament Strap
Cruciate Ligament and Cartilage Strap
Knee Abrasions
Weak Knee Pad and Strap
Elastic Tape and Pad for Bursitis
Pre-patellar Bursitis

The KNEE

Suggested 1"
Tape Width: 2"

Purpose: Compress, protect and stabilize structures in and around the joint.

Position: Athlete to take normal standing stance. Offended knee slightly flexed. Permit no medial bend. *Where cartilage is involved* invert the foot slightly. *Where anterior cruciate ligaments are torn* the athlete sits on the training table with knee bent at 45° angle. *For hyperextended knee* the leg is flexed with the athlete standing and a 3" block or can of adhesive tape is placed under his heel.

Procedure: Prep the skin as usual and apply adherent. Apply your *anchor* straps to prevent slippage of the dressing—one anchor on the anterior and mid-one third of the thigh, the other below the tibial tubercle. All *obliques, retention stabilizers* and *bridges* will extend *from the lower anchor upward*. Do not apply adhesive tape over the patella or popliteal space. Where edema is present within or around the joint, a 6" square sponge rubber "doughnut" may be used to compress or "milk it out." Where cartilage is involved, place a ¼" x 3" skived felt pad for additional compression and security on the affected side. *Buttress* all open adhesive tape ends. When a split-tailed knee cradle is used to prevent "slipping cartilage," the athlete stands erect WITHOUT bending his knee. For this flexible cast the popliteal space should be padded with felt, gauze padding, or cotton wadding. At no time must tape impede function of tendon or muscle. When it is necessary to give added strength crimp its edges. Cotton elastic roller bandages may be used to lock your favorite flexible cast in place. Use the 3" x 5½ yard size. Start from below the tibial tubercle, and ascend in figure-8's. Use adhesive tape and not metal clips to lock it securely.

Prime Taping Techniques to
Remember in Knee Injuries

Knee injuries, common in athletics, may be superficial or deep. They may involve hard or soft tissues or both. The involvement may be *"cold"* (no inflammation or swelling) or it may be *"hot."* There may be *sprain, strain, torn ligaments, cartilage problems, bursitis, tendonitis,* or *minor subluxations*—all of which are treatable with a flexible cast if the diagnosis and supplementary treatment are right. In the care of knee injuries with adhesive tape, there are certain key factors to remember.

Trainer's Tips:

(a) *Flex the knee before taping.* (b) *Always pad the popliteal space before bandaging.* (c) *Never tape over the patella.* (d) *Avoid circular straps that constrict the thigh, knee, or lower leg.* (e) *Never tape an injured knee until X-ray film and squad physician signal the go-ahead.* (g) *Never apply tape over a grossly swollen knee.* (h) *Place firm meniscus pads over site of cartilage injury before strapping. Double the number of oblique lock straps on the side of the injury.* (i) *Utilize split-tailed adhesive tape cradles when locking protective wadding over the popliteal area.* (j) *Maintain an elastic pressure bandage and cold compresses on an injured knee for at least an hour before applying adhesive tape. Elevate the part and rule out complications with diagnostic X-ray film,* (k) *ON ALL KNEE INJURIES EMPLOY NO HEAT, MASSAGE, WEIGHT BEARING OR EXERCISES* in the early stages!

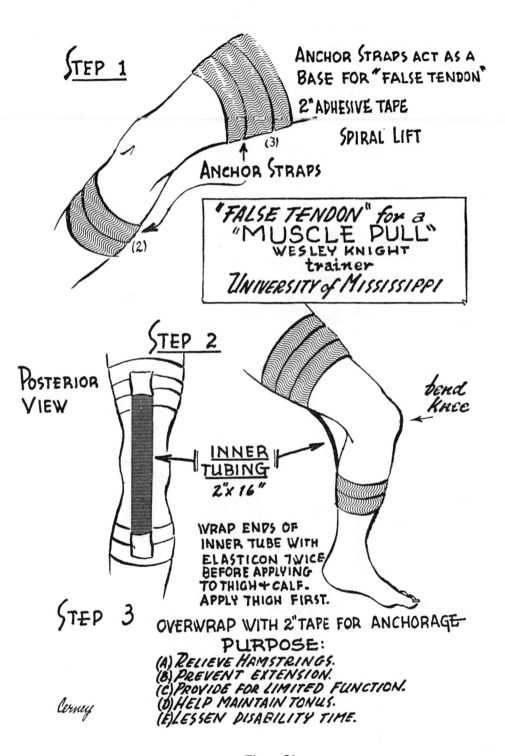

STEP 1

ANCHOR STRAPS ACT AS A BASE FOR "FALSE TENDON"

2" ADHESIVE TAPE

SPIRAL LIFT

(3)

ANCHOR STRAPS

(2)

"FALSE TENDON" for a "MUSCLE PULL"
WESLEY KNIGHT
trainer
UNIVERSITY of MISSISSIPPI

STEP 2

POSTERIOR VIEW

bend knee

INNER TUBING
2" x 16"

WRAP ENDS OF INNER TUBE WITH ELASTICON TWICE BEFORE APPLYING TO THIGH + CALF. APPLY THIGH FIRST.

STEP 3   OVERWRAP WITH 2" TAPE FOR ANCHORAGE

PURPOSE:
(A) RELIEVE HAMSTRINGS.
(B) PREVENT EXTENSION.
(C) PROVIDE FOR LIMITED FUNCTION.
(D) HELP MAINTAIN TONUS.
(E) LESSEN DISABILITY TIME.

Cerney

Figure 56

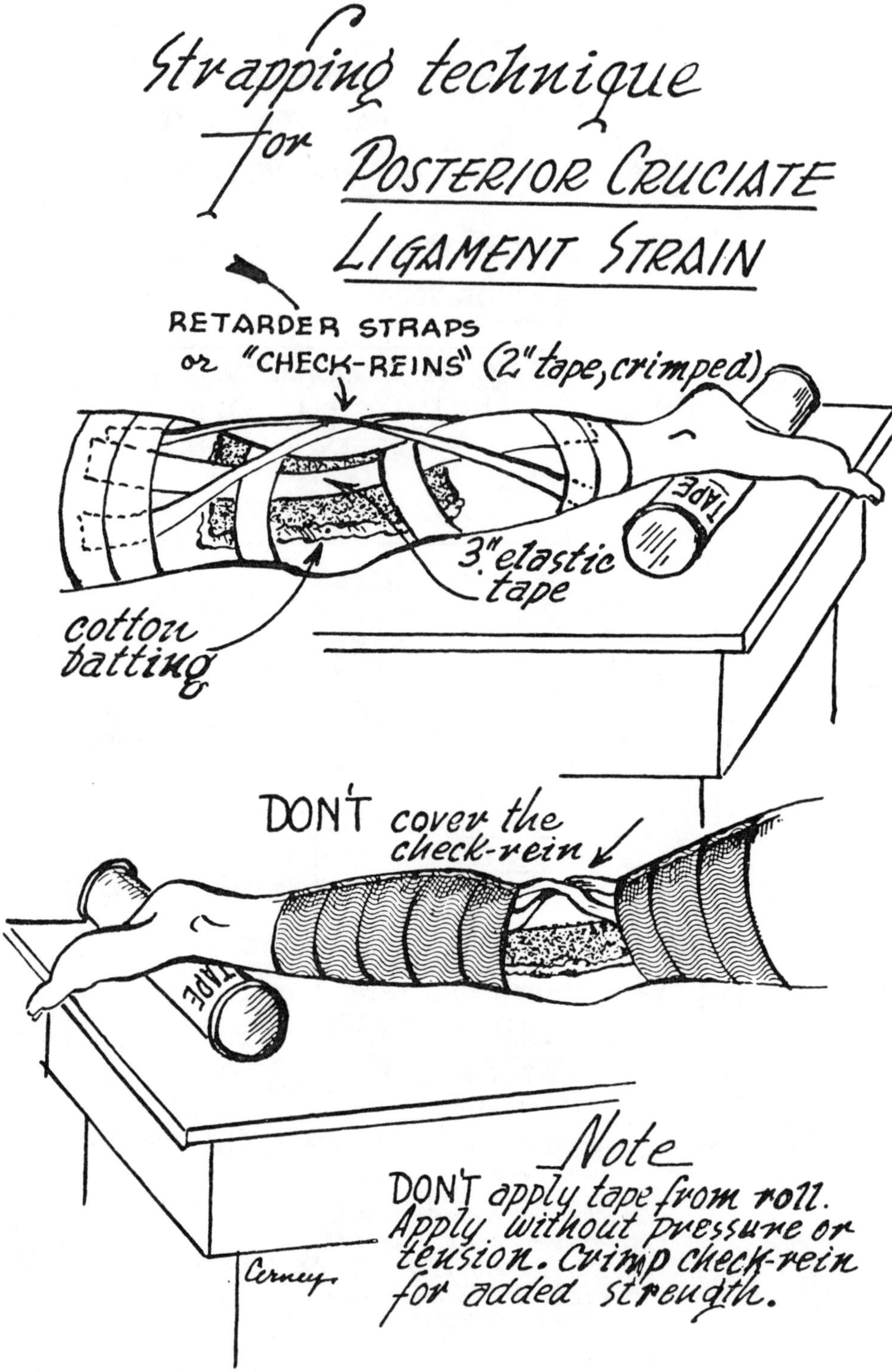

Strapping technique
for POSTERIOR CRUCIATE
LIGAMENT STRAIN

RETARDER STRAPS
or "CHECK-REINS" (2"tape, crimped)

3"elastic tape

cotton batting

DON'T cover the check-rein ✓

TAPE

Note
DON'T apply tape from roll.
Apply without pressure or
tension. Crimp check-rein
for added strength.

Cerney.

Figure 57

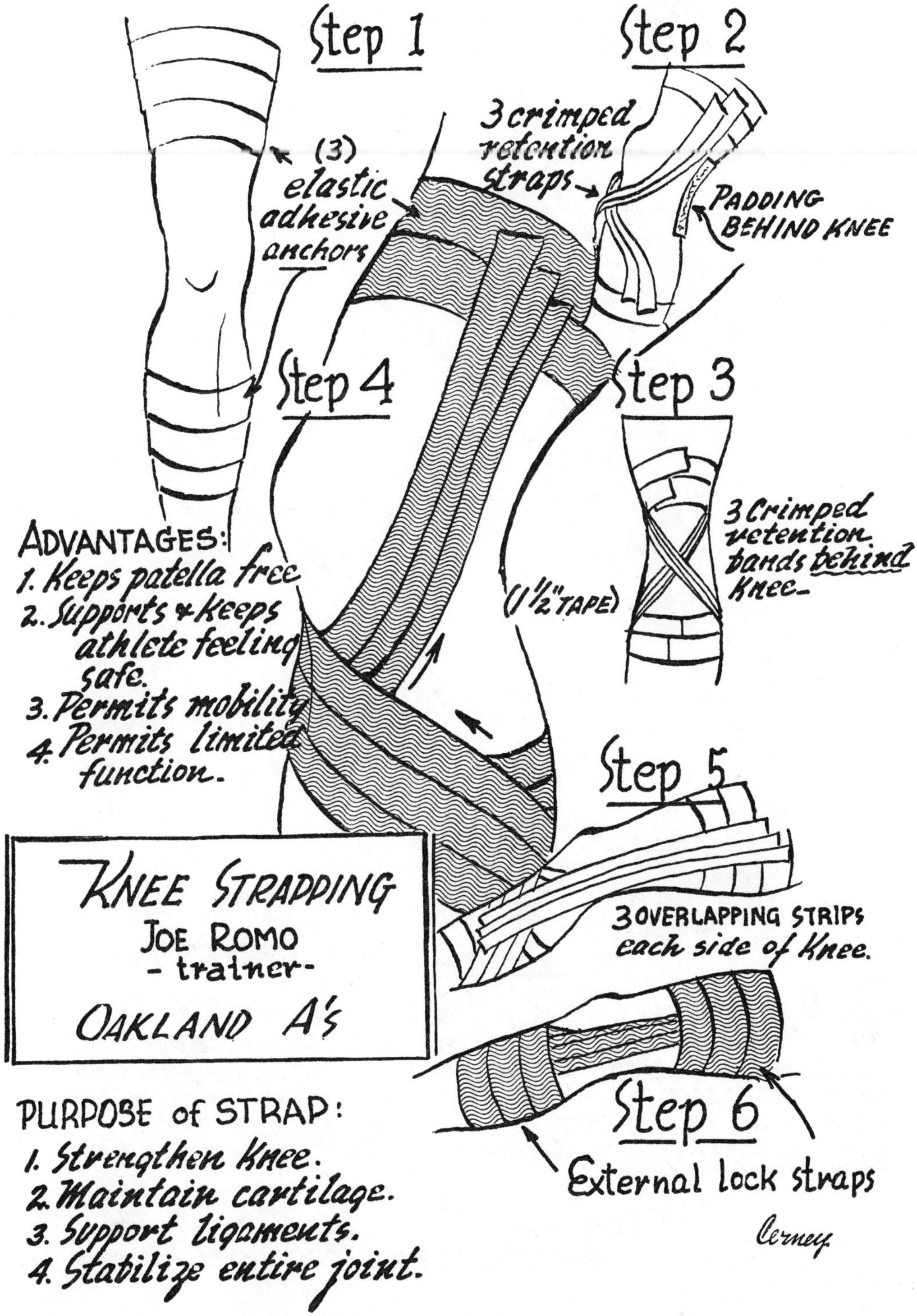

Step 1

(3) elastic adhesive anchors

3 crimped retention straps

Step 2

PADDING BEHIND KNEE

Step 4

Step 3

3 crimped retention bands behind knee.

(1½" TAPE)

ADVANTAGES:
1. Keeps patella free.
2. Supports & keeps athlete feeling safe.
3. Permits mobility.
4. Permits limited function.

Step 5

3 OVERLAPPING STRIPS each side of Knee.

KNEE STRAPPING
JOE ROMO
- trainer -

OAKLAND A's

Step 6

External lock straps

Cerney

PURPOSE of STRAP:
1. Strengthen Knee.
2. Maintain cartilage.
3. Support ligaments.
4. Stabilize entire joint.

Figure 58

· KNEE STRAPPING ·

BROWN (T.C.U.)
Strapping
for the knee

"DIAMOND KNEE-LOCK"

Technique of Application

The DIAMOND KNEE-LOCK, when pre-fabricated By the athlete on a piece of glass, saves the Trainer time. The lower strapping is anchored below the knee and pulled up to lock the joint. The lower diamond is anchored above and pulled down. The two X's are then overlayed by horizontal layers elastic tape and the knee is free to function.

NOTE: Crimp the tape above and below the patella to prevent tape from ripping.

Cernay

Figure 59

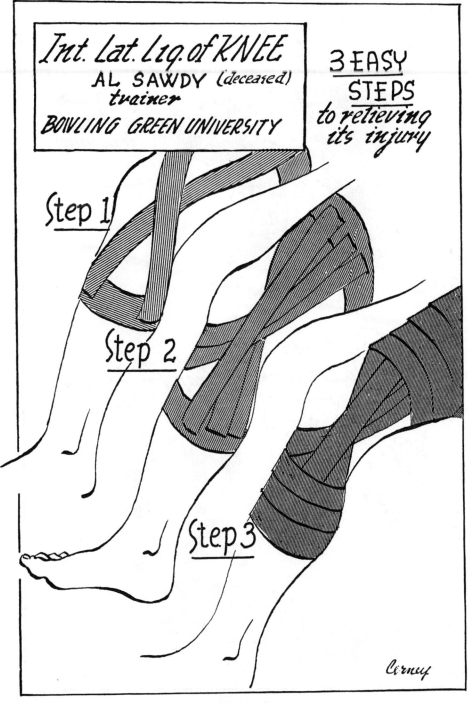

Figure 60

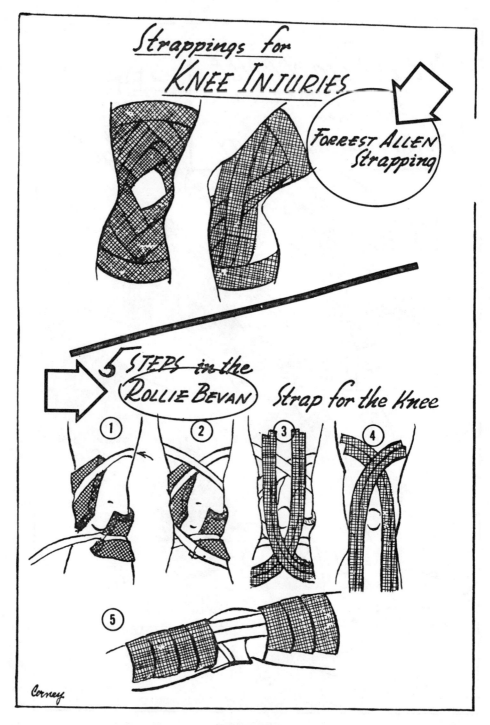

Figure 61

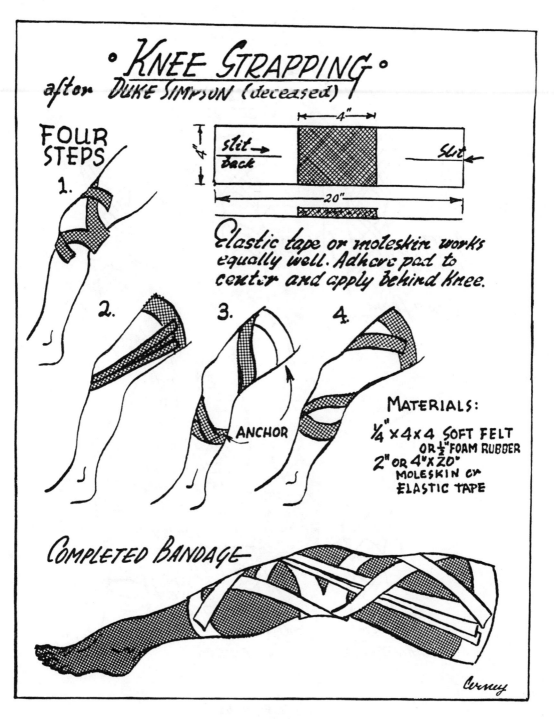

Figure 62

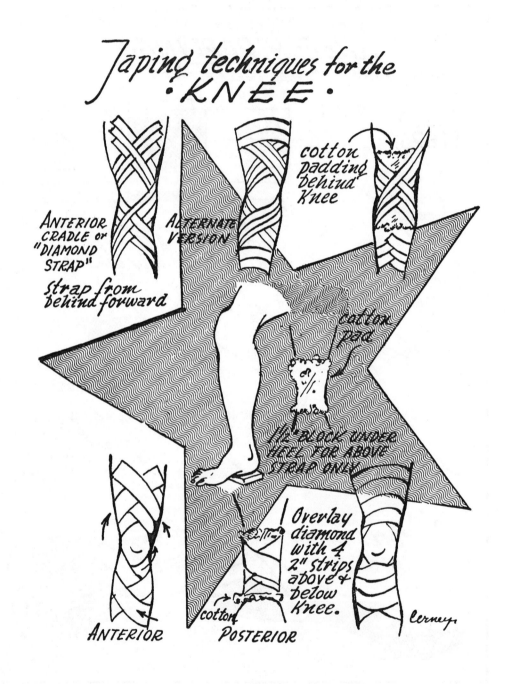

Taping techniques for the
• KNEE •

ANTERIOR CRADLE or "DIAMOND STRAP"

ALTERNATE VERSION

cotton padding behind knee

strap from behind forward

cotton pad

Use block under heel for above strap only

ANTERIOR

Overlay diamond with 4 2" strips above & below knee.

cotton

POSTERIOR

Cerney

Figure 63

PAD and STRAPPING technique for KNEE BURSITIS

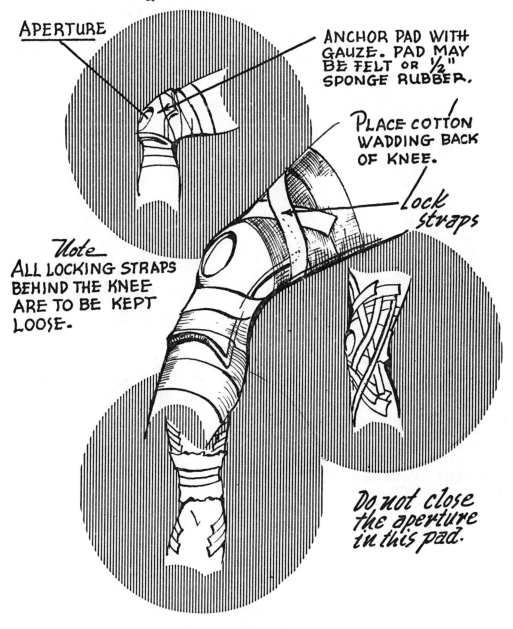

APERTURE

ANCHOR PAD WITH GAUZE. PAD MAY BE FELT OR ½" SPONGE RUBBER.

PLACE COTTON WADDING BACK OF KNEE.

Lock straps

Note
ALL LOCKING STRAPS BEHIND THE KNEE ARE TO BE KEPT LOOSE.

Do not close the aperture in this pad.

Figure 64

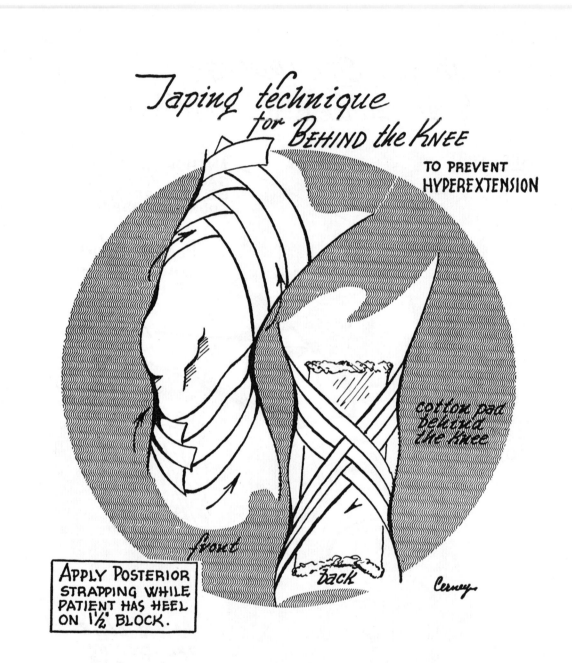

Figure 65

The KNEE CRADLE
for INTERNAL/LATERAL LIGAMENT DAMAGE

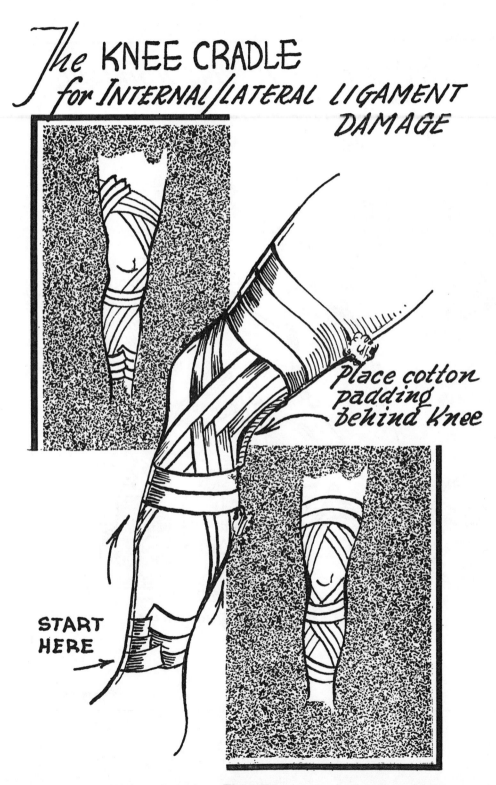

Place cotton padding behind knee

START HERE

Figure 66

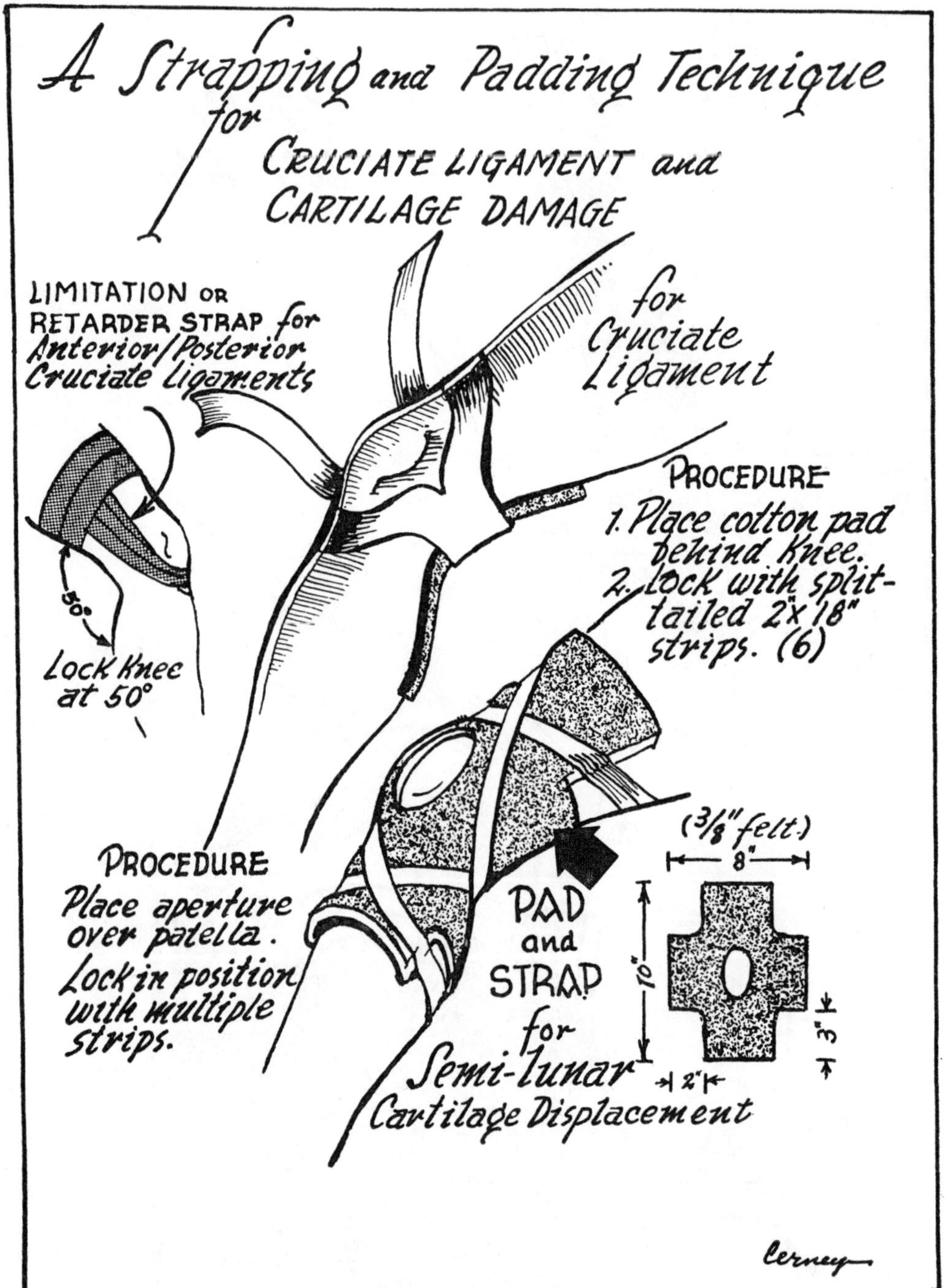
A Strapping and Padding Technique for
CRUCIATE LIGAMENT and CARTILAGE DAMAGE
LIMITATION OR RETARDER STRAP for Anterior/Posterior Cruciate Ligaments
50°
Lock Knee at 50°
for Cruciate Ligament
PROCEDURE
1. Place cotton pad behind knee.
2. Lock with split-tailed 2"x 18" strips. (6)
PROCEDURE
Place aperture over patella.
Lock in position with multiple strips.
(3/8" felt)
8"
10"
3"
2"
PAD and STRAP for Semi-lunar Cartilage Displacement
Cerney

Figure 67

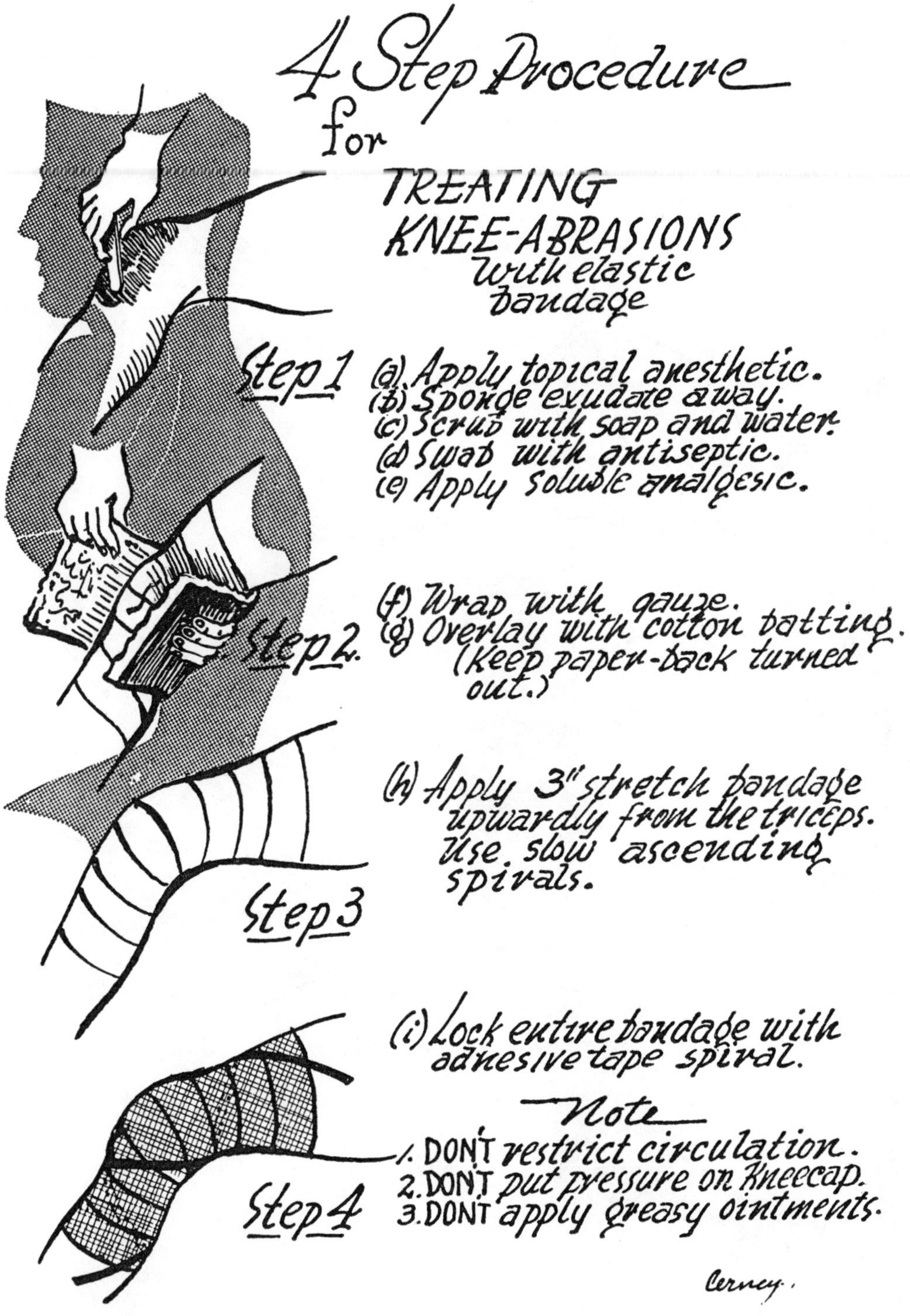

4 Step Procedure
for
TREATING KNEE-ABRASIONS
with elastic bandage

Step 1
(a) Apply topical anesthetic.
(b) Sponge exudate away.
(c) Scrub with soap and water.
(d) Swab with antiseptic.
(e) Apply soluble analgesic.

Step 2
(f) Wrap with gauze.
(g) Overlay with cotton batting. (keep paper-back turned out.)

Step 3
(h) Apply 3" stretch bandage upwardly from the triceps. Use slow ascending spirals.

Step 4
(i) Lock entire bandage with adhesive tape spiral.

Note
1. DON'T restrict circulation.
2. DON'T put pressure on kneecap.
3. DON'T apply greasy ointments.

Cerney.

Figure 68

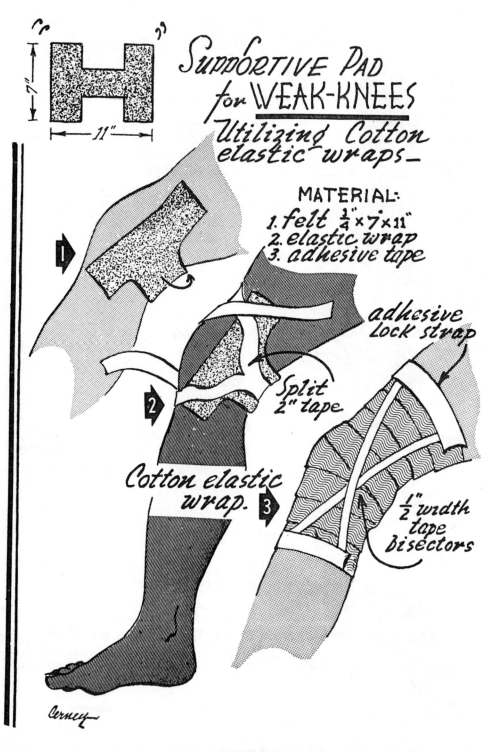

"H" 7" 11"

SUPPORTIVE PAD
for WEAK-KNEES
Utilizing Cotton
elastic wraps_

MATERIAL:
1. felt $\frac{1}{4}'' \times 7 \times 11''$
2. elastic wrap
3. adhesive tape

adhesive
Lock strap

Split
2" tape

Cotton elastic
wrap.

$\frac{1}{2}''$ width
tape
bisectors

Cerney

Figure 69

Elastic Tape & Compression-Pad for KNEE BURSITIS

MATERIAL:
1. Elastic tape - 3"
2. Foam rubber - 6x8°
3. Adhesive tape - 1"

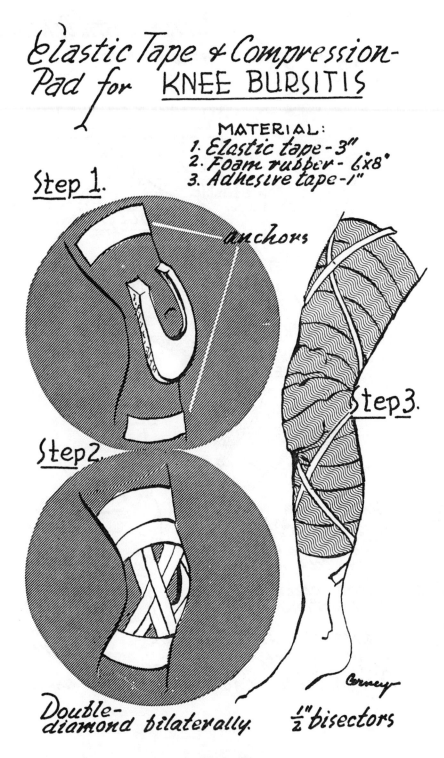

Step 1.

anchors

Step 2.

Step 3.

Double-diamond bilaterally.

$\frac{1"}{2}$ bisectors

Figure 70

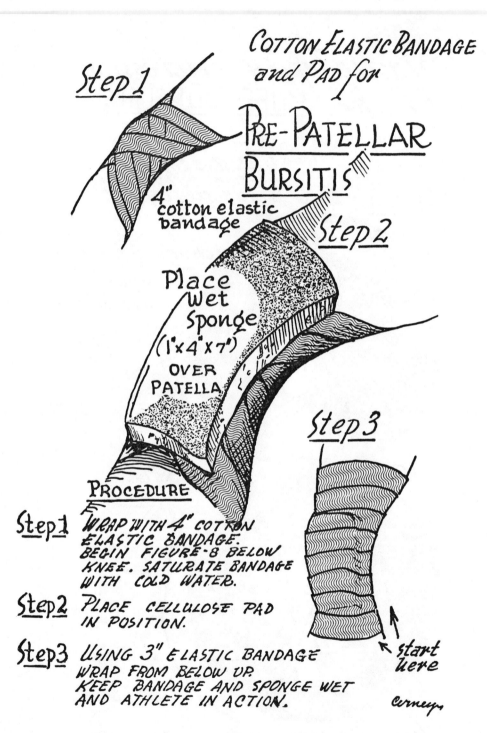

Step 1

COTTON ELASTIC BANDAGE
and PAD for

PRE-PATELLAR
BURSITIS

4"
cotton elastic
bandage

Step 2

Place
Wet
Sponge
(1"x4"x7")
OVER
PATELLA

Step 3

PROCEDURE

Step 1 WRAP WITH 4" COTTON
ELASTIC BANDAGE.
BEGIN FIGURE-8 BELOW
KNEE. SATURATE BANDAGE
WITH COLD WATER.

Step 2 PLACE CELLULOSE PAD
IN POSITION.

Step 3 USING 3" ELASTIC BANDAGE
WRAP FROM BELOW UP.
KEEP BANDAGE AND SPONGE WET
AND ATHLETE IN ACTION.

← start
here

Figure 71

The THIGH

Flexible Cast Techniques for:
        Thigh Contusion
        Quadriceps Strain
        Severe Hamstring Strain
        Mild Hamstring Strain
        Anterior "Thigh Pull"
        "Charley Horse"
        "Charley Horse" Analgesic Pack
        Thigh Compression Wrap

The THIGH

> Suggested 1½"
> Tape Width: 2"

Purpose: For strains, sprains, tears, contusions, and cramps.
Position: Athlete standing with knee flexed 20° to 30°.
Procedure: Relax both anterior and posterior thigh muscles as well as the calf of the leg before prepping the skin. Then place *anchor* straps in accordance with whether the injury is anterior or posterior. Apply all *bridges* and *obliques* from the lowermost anchor upwardly. Work up and over the injury. Use only moderate tension. *If there is an actual muscle "tear," place an anchor above and below it* for additional reinforcement. Lock down loose ends with *buttress* straps and maintain the "set" with a 3" cotton elastic roller bandage.

Thigh Conditions Most Amenable to Adhesive Tape

The heavy muscles of the thigh are constantly subject to impact and sudden stretch in all sports. How well they adapt to stretch depends on their size and conditioning, and on the weight, construction, and habits of the athlete. Conditions such as the following merit the use of flexible casts for their care.

1. *Torn Adductor Longus Muscle* is observed in acrobatics, in tumbling and in the more strenuous dance movements that utilize the "splits." The "splits" in essence may occur going over high hurdles. They may also occur to an unconditioned athlete who goes through a fast warm-up.

2. *Periostitis* occurs when the *adductor longus* pulls at its insertion. Flexible casting of the thigh is an asset in immobilizing and relieving the inflammation.

3. *Myositis* is an inflammatory process in the muscle body and may result from anything ranging from direct trauma to systemic conditions. Compression and immobilization, with other physical therapy approaches, are immediate musts.

4. *Hematomas* are the result of trauma in which blood extravasates from its tubular containers and collects between tissues in a pocket or pool. This pool is called a blood tumor or *hematoma*. The thigh needs compression when a hematoma is present, and flexible castings and foam rubber pressure pads are of value.

5. *Myositis ossificans* may occur when blood vessels are torn by direct trauma and the extravasated blood does not absorb. Instead it *calcifies*. For such a problem the compression of a flexible cast is of value only in the initial stages. Once the "hardening" sets in it is valueless.

6. *"Rider's Strain"*

7. *"Charley Horse"*

8. *"Quadriceps Tear"*

9. *Hamstring "Pull"*

Trainer's Tips:

(a) *Flex the extremity to relieve muscle tension before applying a flexible cast to the thigh.* (b) *DO place anchor straps just above and below the lesion to render added locking support.* (c) *"Set" and lock all thigh casts with cotton elastic (3") roller bandages. Lock with adhesive tape. Do not use metal clips.* (d) *Immediately after trauma apply an elastic compression wrap. Start below the knee and go up to the groin. Elevate the extremity and apply ice packs to control hemorrhage.* (e) *Get athlete to the team physician immediately.* (f) *Where contusion is simple, massage around the offended area and keep cold applications on for 48 hours.* (g) *When swelling subsides, begin whirlpool therapy at 105° F twice daily.* (h) *Use protective padding and flexible casts for all practices and games thereafter.* (i) *Remove the athlete from sports* (contact) *immediately if myositis ossificans sets in.* (j) *Where there has been extensive tearing of anterior or posterior thigh muscles, extend bridge straps from the lowermost anchor up over the buttocks, or abdomen, to the lowermost ribs. Such a flexible cast should be applied only with the patient standing. Utilize horizontal "spanners" above the crest of the ilium and below the buttock.* (k) *Place a ¼" or ½" heel lift in the shoe for added relief.*

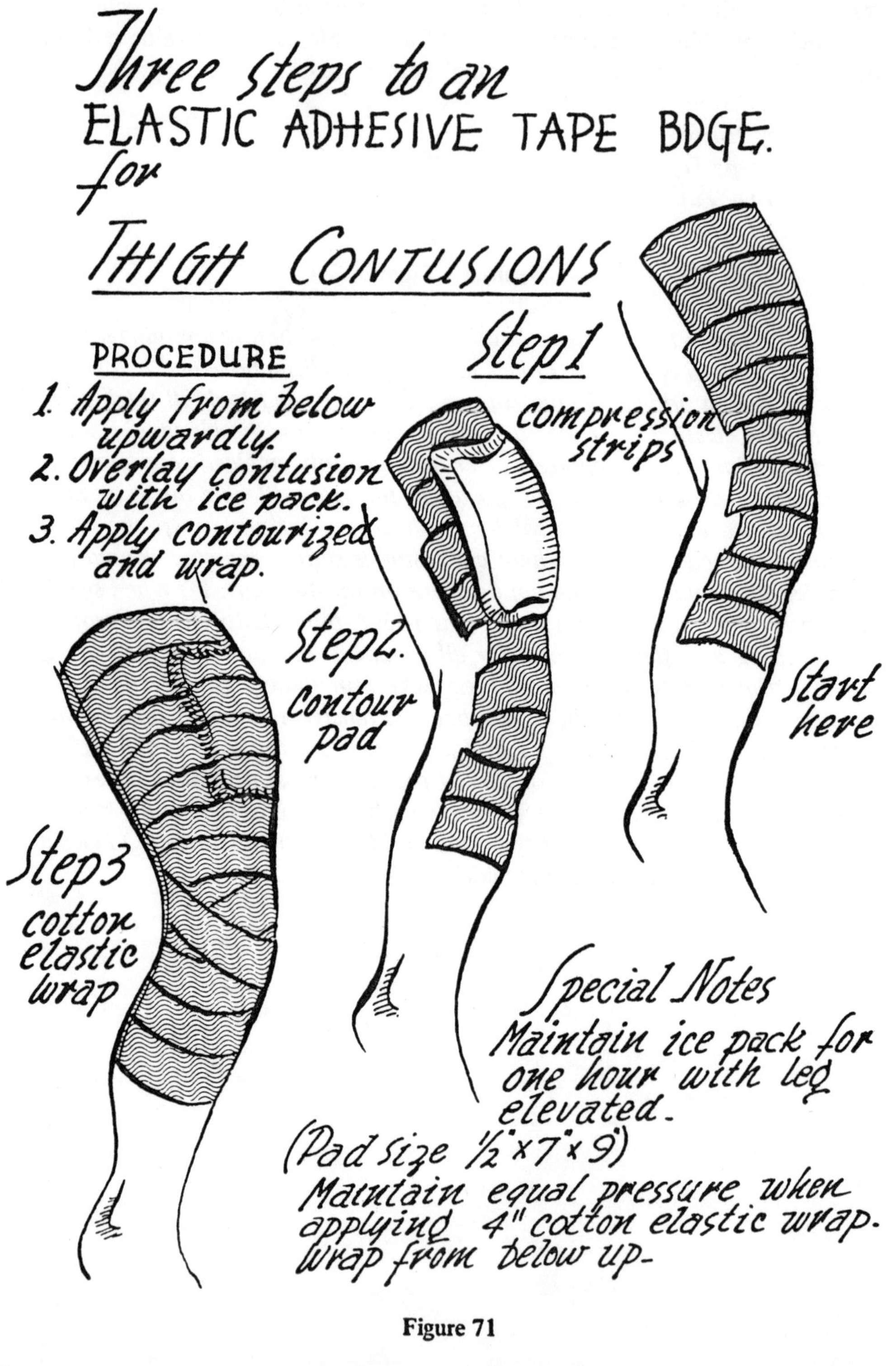

Three steps to an
ELASTIC ADHESIVE TAPE BDGE.
for
THIGH CONTUSIONS

PROCEDURE

1. Apply from below upwardly.
2. Overlay contusion with ice pack.
3. Apply contourized and wrap.

Step 1

compression strips

Start here

Step 2.

Contour pad

Step 3

cotton elastic wrap

Special Notes

Maintain ice pack for one hour with leg elevated.

(Pad size ½" × 7" × 9")

Maintain equal pressure when applying 4" cotton elastic wrap. Wrap from below up-

Figure 71

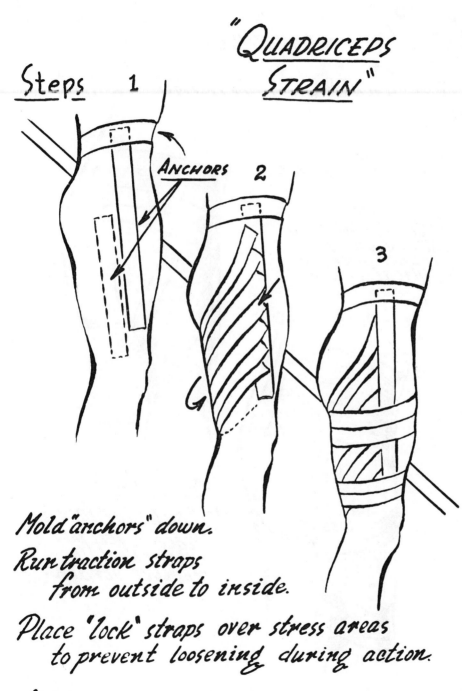

Steps 1

"QUADRICEPS STRAIN"

ANCHORS 2

3

Mold "anchors" down.

Run traction straps
from outside to inside.

Place "lock" straps over stress areas
to prevent loosening during action.

Cerney

Figure 72

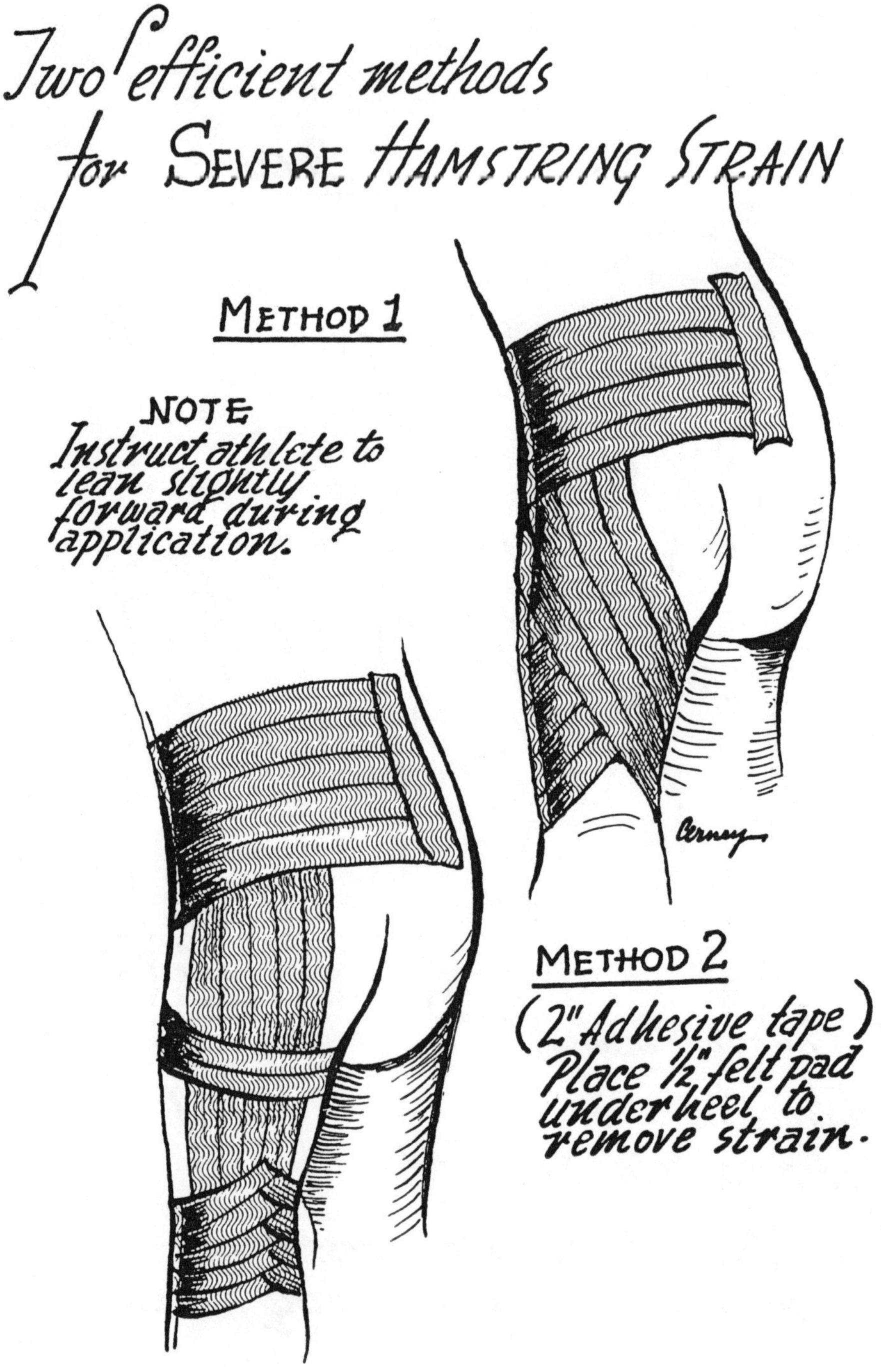
Two efficient methods for SEVERE HAMSTRING STRAIN
METHOD 1
NOTE
Instruct athlete to lean slightly forward during application.
METHOD 2
(2" Adhesive tape)
Place ½" felt pad under heel to remove strain.
Cerney

Figure 74

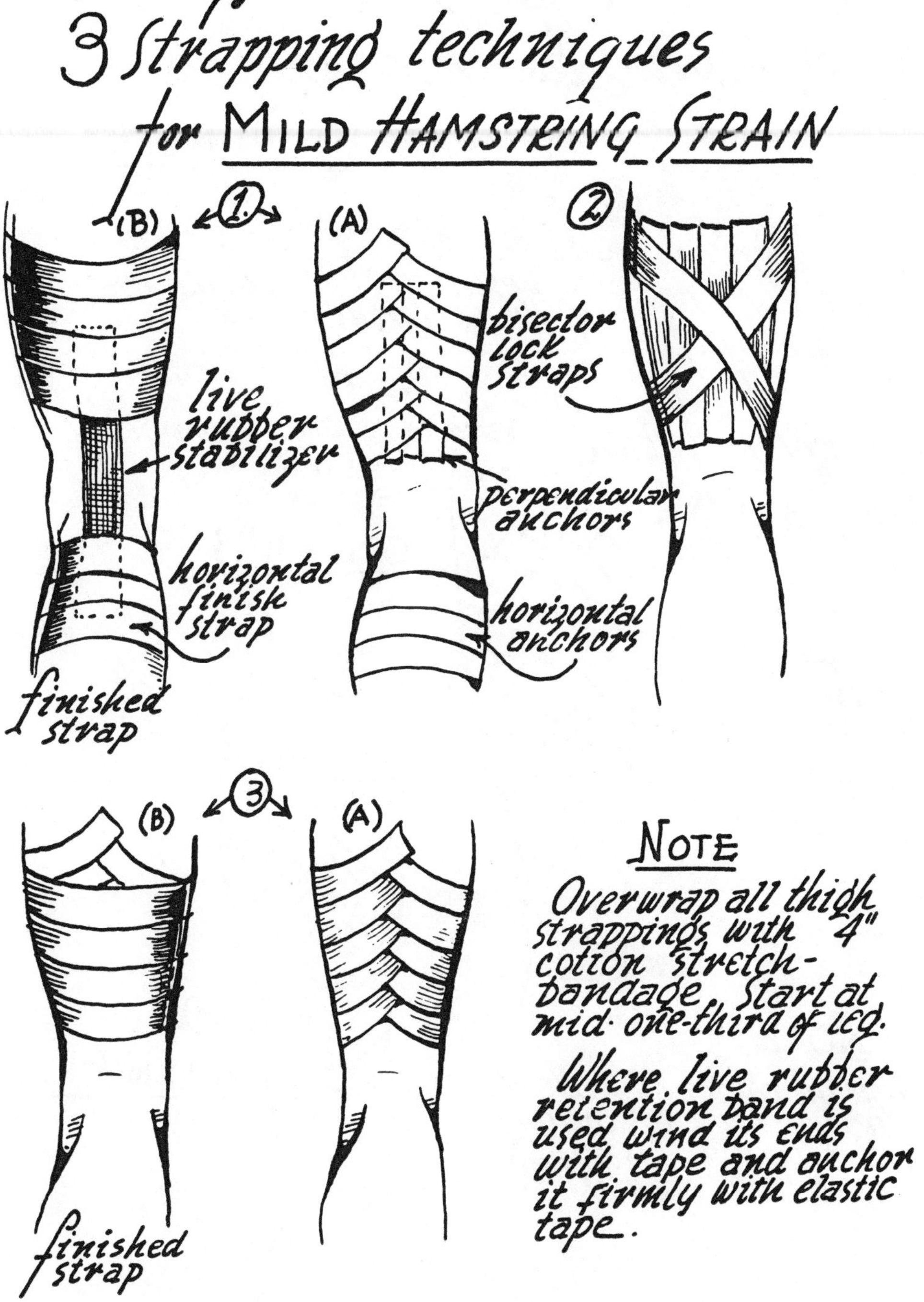

3 strapping techniques
for MILD HAMSTRING STRAIN

(B) ①→ (A) ②

live rubber stabilizer

bisector lock straps

horizontal finish strap

perpendicular anchors

finished strap

horizontal anchors

(B) ③→ (A)

finished strap

NOTE

Overwrap all thigh strappings with 4" cotton stretch-bandage. Start at mid one-third of leg.

Where live rubber retention band is used wind its ends with tape and anchor it firmly with elastic tape.

Figure 75

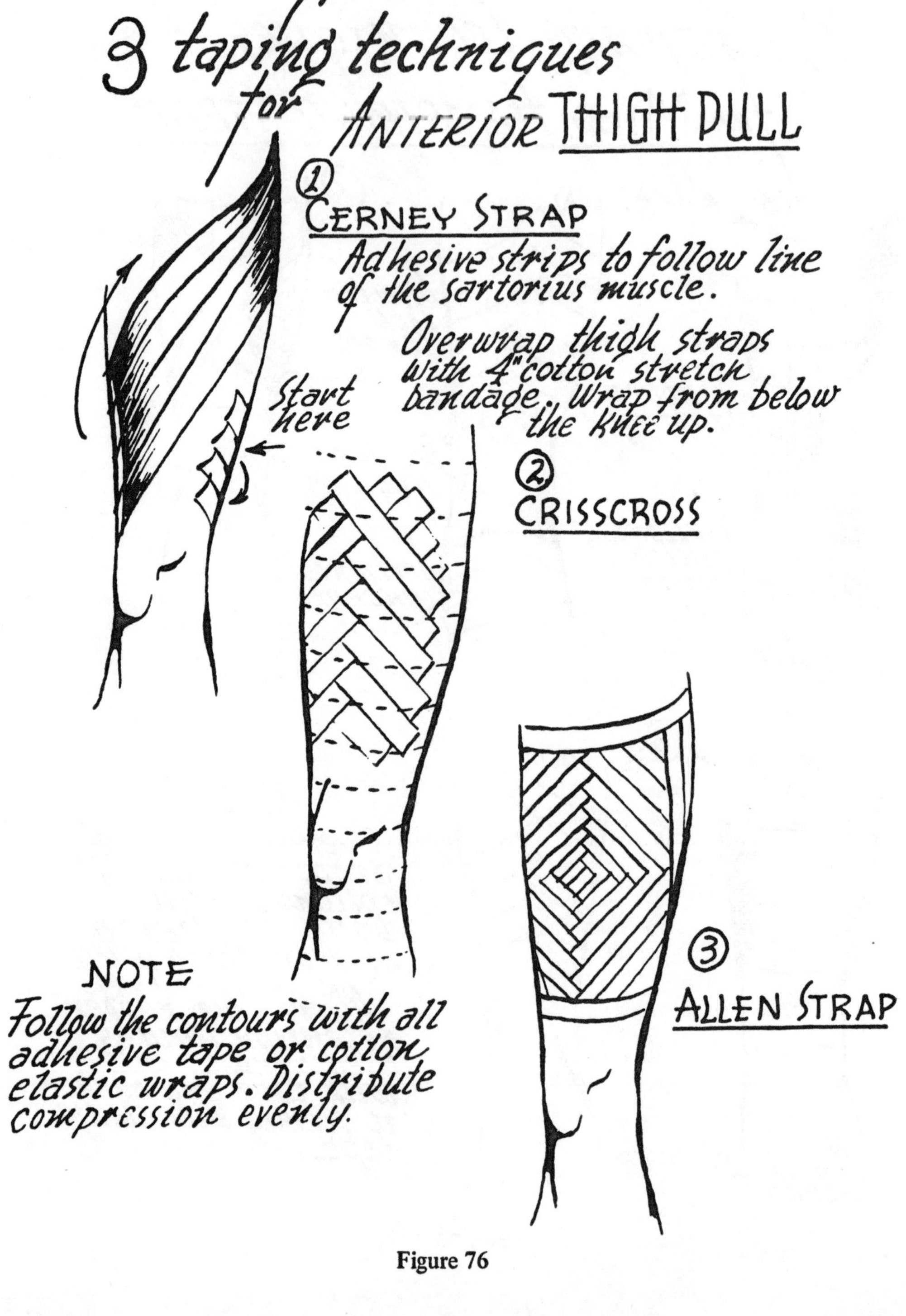

3 taping techniques for ANTERIOR THIGH PULL

① **CERNEY STRAP**

Adhesive strips to follow line of the sartorius muscle.

Overwrap thigh straps with 4" cotton stretch bandage. Wrap from below the knee up.

Start here →

② **CRISSCROSS**

NOTE

Follow the contours with all adhesive tape or cotton elastic wraps. Distribute compression evenly.

③ **ALLEN STRAP**

Figure 76

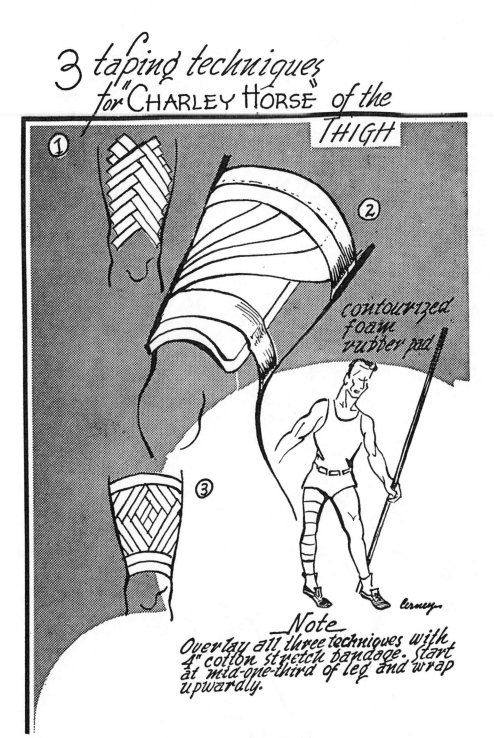

Figure 77

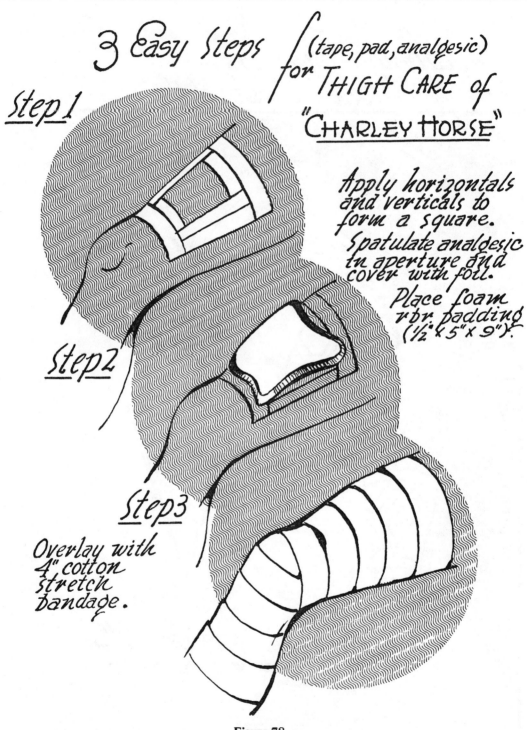

3 Easy Steps (tape, pad, analgesic) *for* THIGH CARE of "CHARLEY HORSE"

Step 1

Step 2

Step 3

Apply horizontals and verticals to form a square.

Spatulate analgesic in aperture and cover with foil.

Place foam rbr. padding (1/2" x 5" x 9").

Overlay with 4" cotton stretch bandage.

Figure 78

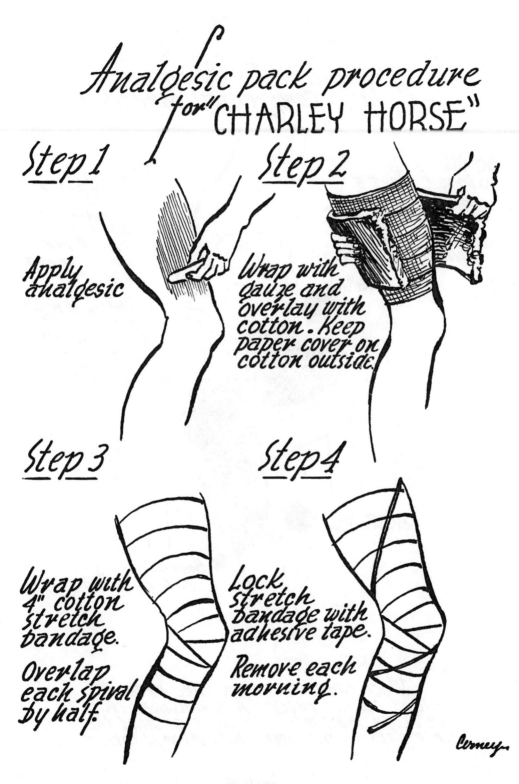

Analgesic pack procedure for "CHARLEY HORSE"

Step 1

Apply analgesic

Step 2

Wrap with gauze and overlay with cotton. Keep paper cover on cotton outside.

Step 3

Wrap with 4" cotton stretch bandage.

Overlap each spiral by half.

Step 4

Lock stretch bandage with adhesive tape.

Remove each morning.

Figure 79

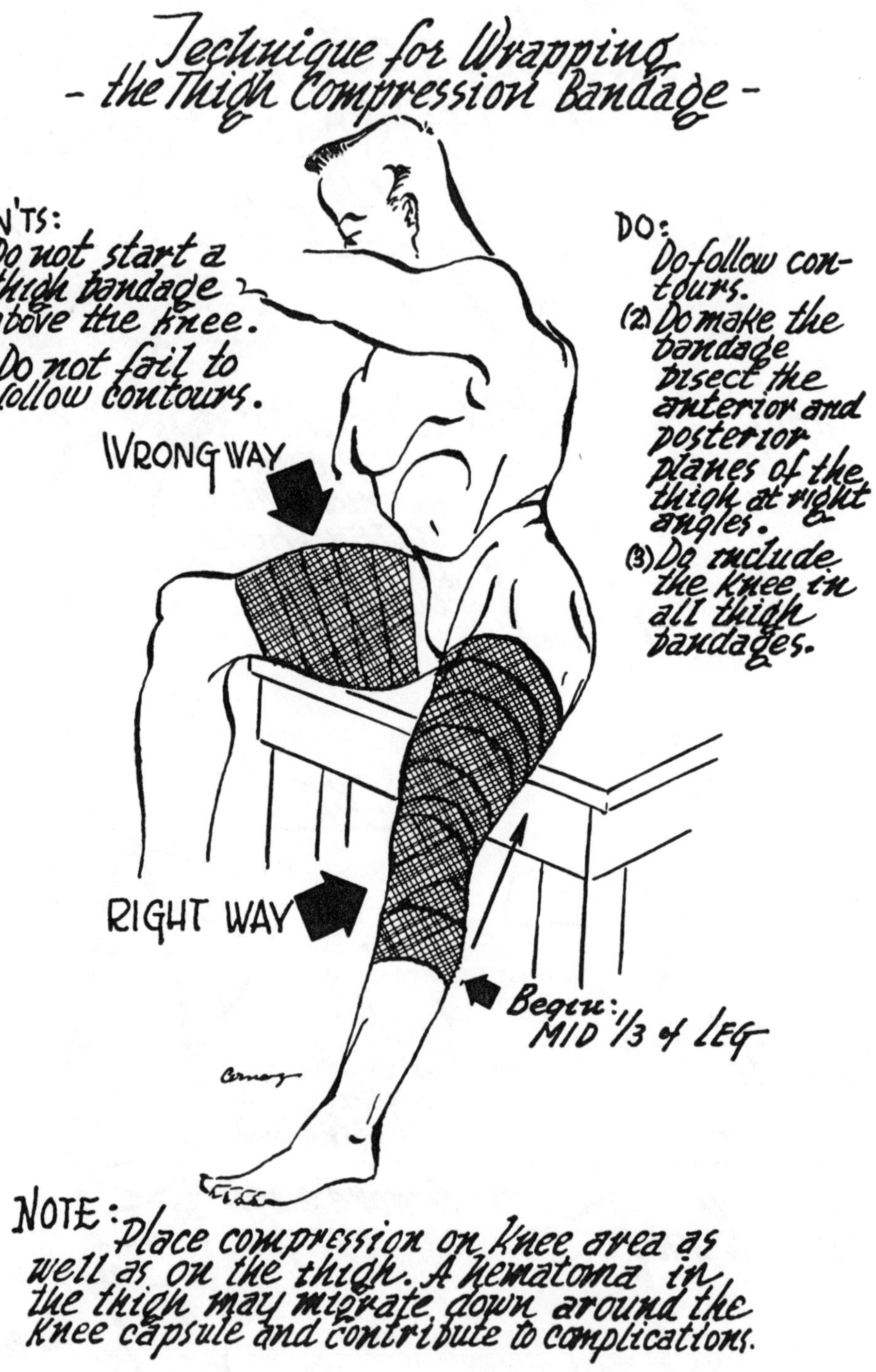

Technique for Wrapping
— the Thigh Compression Bandage —

DON'TS:
(1) Do not start a thigh bandage above the knee.
(2) Do not fail to follow contours.

WRONG WAY

RIGHT WAY

Begin:
MID 1/3 of LEG

DO:
Do follow contours.
(2) Do make the bandage bisect the anterior and posterior planes of the thigh at right angles.
(3) Do include the knee in all thigh bandages.

NOTE: Place compression on knee area as well as on the thigh. A hematoma in the thigh may migrate down around the knee capsule and contribute to complications.

Figure 80

The HIP

Flexible Cast Techniques for:
  "Hip Pointer"

"HIP POINTER"

> Suggested   2"
> Tape Width: 3"

Purpose: Immobilize the injured iliac crest.

Position: Athlete is standing. He leans slightly to the side of the injury.

Procedure: A flexible cast for the hip, unlike taping for other body parts, is designed to truly immobilize the part. In applying the adhesive tape, have the athlete bend slightly lateral on the contused side. Tape is applied with strong pressure in this particular case and must follow the line of musculature. When the athlete straightens—after getting his flexible cast put on in this position—the tape tightens even more. This pressure relieves strain on all muscles and their insertions in the area. In applying the flexible cast be certain that strands of tape brought up from the thigh and across the back or abdomen fan outwardly for greater purchase. Buttress all girdle straps or spanners. The cast should start at least 8" to 10" below the crest of the ilium but should not cover the buttocks or interfere with activity of the thigh. Overlay the adhesive tape dressing with a 3" cotton elastic wrap in figure-8 spica style to include the groin. Prep skin, after clipping hair from the thigh to the ribs, including the gluteal area, the pubic area, and lower-back.

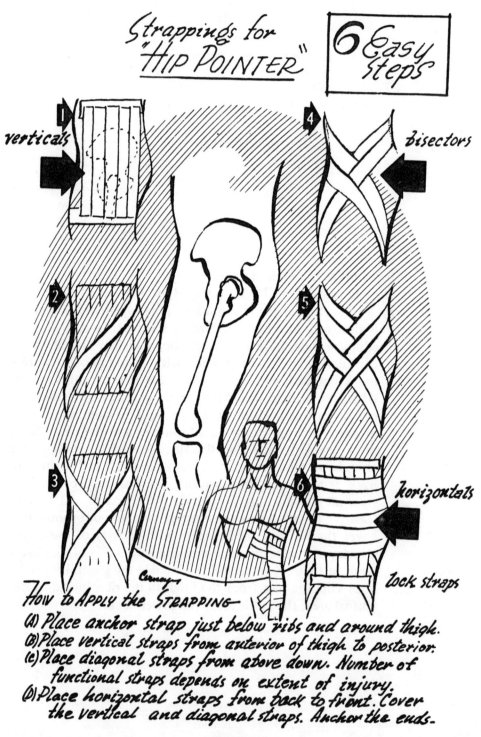

Strapping for "HIP POINTER"

6 Easy Steps

verticals — bisectors — horizontals — lock straps

How to Apply the Strapping—
(A) Place anchor strap just below ribs and around thigh.
(B) Place vertical straps from anterior of thigh to posterior.
(C) Place diagonal straps from above down. Number of
    functional straps depends on extent of injury.
(D) Place horizontal straps from back to front. Cover
    the vertical and diagonal straps. Anchor the ends.

Figure 81

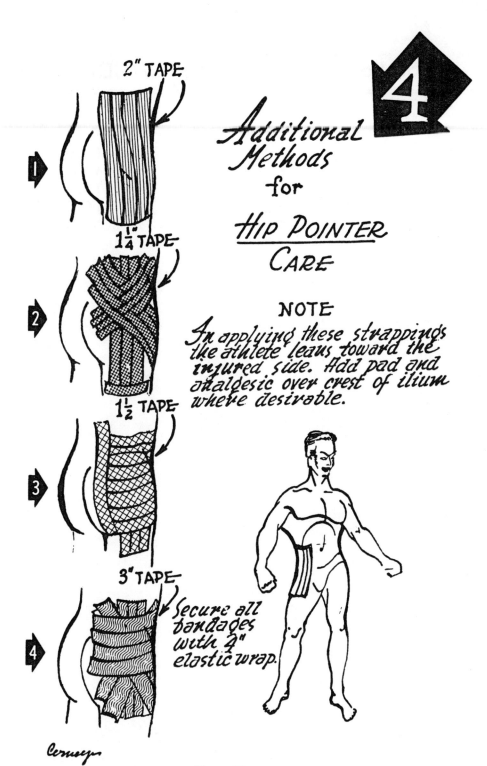

2" TAPE

1¼" TAPE

1½" TAPE

3" TAPE

Additional Methods for

HIP POINTER CARE

NOTE

In applying these strappings the athlete leans toward the injured side. Add pad and analgesic over crest of ilium where desirable.

Secure all bandages with 4" elastic wrap.

Figure 82

Section 2   UPPER EXTREMITIES

Taping Techniques for:
HAND
WRIST
ELBOW
FOREARM
SHOULDER

The HAND

Flexible Cast Techniques for:
Thumb-tether Retainer
Thumb Angle Protector
Fingertip "T" Straps
Football Hand Protector
Finger Fracture Splints
"Dropped Knuckle"
Wrist-thumb Lock
Wrist-thumb Splint

The FINGERS

| Suggested ¼" |
| Tape Width: ½" |

Purpose: Strains, sprains, dislocations, fractures.

Position: Wherever convenient.

Procedure: After skin-prep, place *anchors* on wrist, hand, or tip of offended digits. Lock anchors with *bridges* to stabilize the finger and follow with a padded splint or flexible cast of your choice. Avoid tight circular bandage straps that tend to cut off circulation. When applying hand wraps be sure that all fingers are spread wide to assure lack of hand constriction. Lock the thumb joint to the wrist when the wrist is involved.

Trainer's Tips:

(a) *All hand and wrist injuries should get immediate compression, cold application, and elevation. Apply surgical wadding, overlay with cotton elastic wrap, and apply chipped-ice pack. Continue for 24 hours.*

(b) *Apply no tape until X-ray film rules out bone damage or dislocation.*

(c) *Maintain protective support and padding thereafter.*

(d) *Where there is skin sensitivity to tape the fingers, hand and wrist may be first wrapped with gauze. Overlay with tape or cotton elastic roller bandage.*

Hand Conditions Amenable to Adhesive Tape

FINGER FRACTURES are not uncommon in athletics. As an occupational hazard they should be treated efficiently and effectively to keep the athlete functioning. Prompt care is vital to dispel the possibility of abnormal repair or deformity.

TECHNIQUE FOR IMMOBILIZATION is determined by the site of the fracture. The fracture site also determines the method of splinting or immobilizing said finger. To determine the most effective procedure to use, here's a suggested chart to follow:

Key for Immobilizing *FINGER FRACTURES*		
Proximal phalanx	Middle Phalanx	Distal Phalanx
Curved Splint	1. *Straight splint* when site of the fracture is *proximal* to the insertion of the *flexor digitorum sublimis.* 2. *Curved Splint* when site is *distal* to the insertion of the flexor tendon.	*Straight splint*

THUMB PROBLEMS amenable to adhesive tape are those of *sprain, strain,* and *dislocation.* On sprains and strains, utilize a *figure-8* wrap around the base and web of the thumb. Anchor to the wrist. Where dislocations are concerned check the thumb problem out with diagnostic X-ray. Set the bone if dislocated, immobilize with ¼" or 3/8" tape. Basketweave for strength. Overlay with gauze to stabilize or lock the bandage in position.

Thumb Tether
or RESTRAINER STRAP.

1" adhesive tape

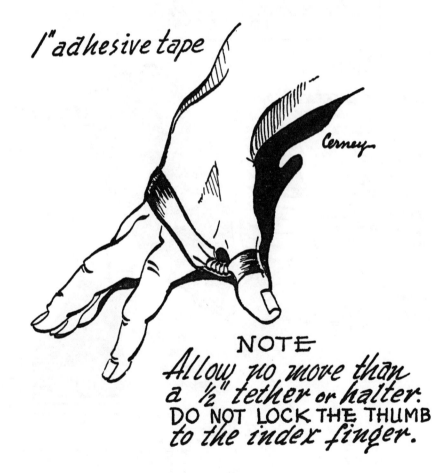

NOTE
Allow no more than
a ½" tether or halter.
DO NOT LOCK THE THUMB
to the index finger.

Figure 83

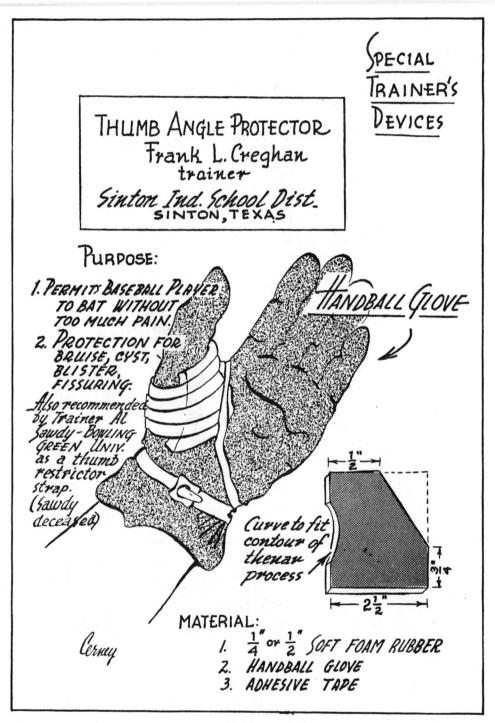

SPECIAL TRAINER'S DEVICES

THUMB ANGLE PROTECTOR
Frank L. Creghan
trainer
Sinton Ind. School Dist.
SINTON, TEXAS

PURPOSE:

1. PERMITS BASEBALL PLAYER TO BAT WITHOUT TOO MUCH PAIN.
2. PROTECTION FOR BRUISE, CYST, BLISTER, FISSURING.

Also recommended by Trainer Al Sawdy - BOWLING GREEN UNIV. as a thumb restrictor strap. (Sawdy deceased)

HANDBALL GLOVE

Curve to fit contour of thenar process

1/2"
3/4"
2 1/2"

Cerney

MATERIAL:
1. 1/4" or 1/2" SOFT FOAM RUBBER
2. HANDBALL GLOVE
3. ADHESIVE TAPE

Figure 84

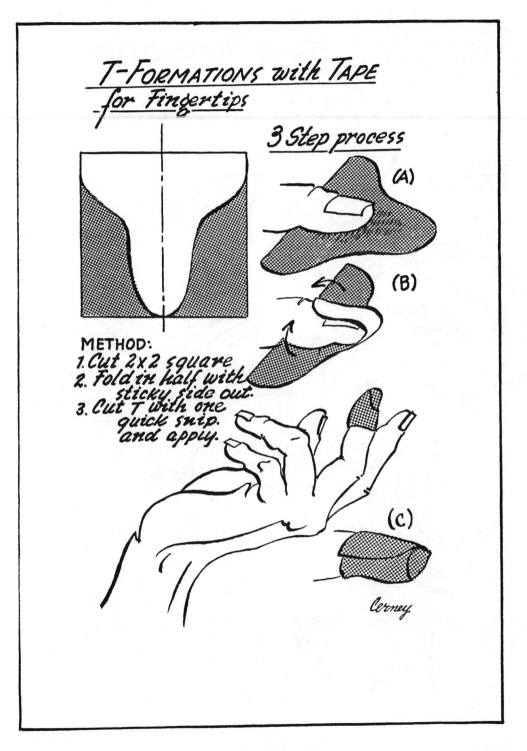

T-FORMATIONS with TAPE
for Fingertips

3 Step process

(A)

(B)

METHOD:
1. Cut 2x2 square
2. Fold in half with sticky side out.
3. Cut T with one quick snip. and apply.

(c)

Cerney

Figure 85

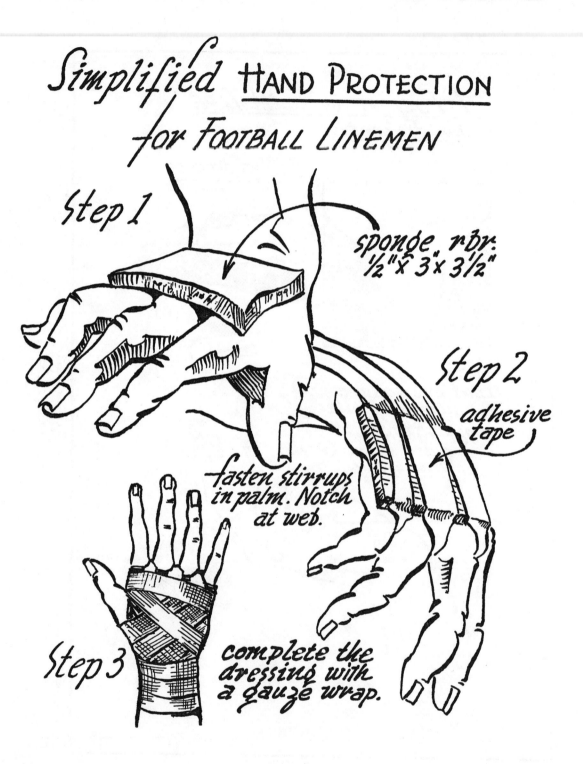

Simplified HAND PROTECTION
for FOOTBALL LINEMEN

Step 1

sponge. rbr.
½" x 3 x 3½"

Step 2

adhesive
tape

fasten stirrups
in palm. Notch
at web.

Step 3

complete the
dressing with
a gauze wrap.

Figure 86

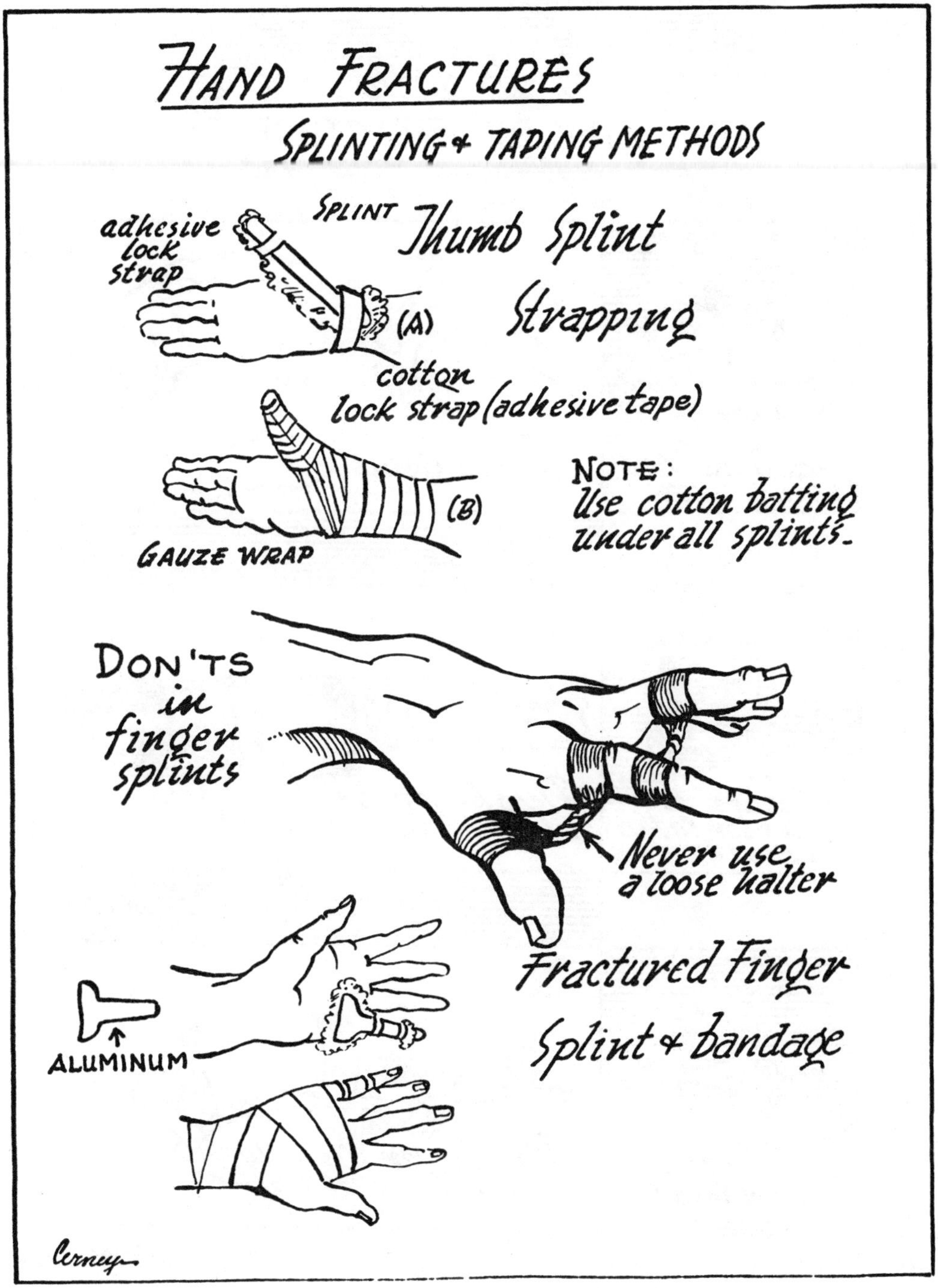
HAND FRACTURES
SPLINTING & TAPING METHODS
adhesive lock strap
SPLINT
Thumb Splint
(A)
Strapping
cotton
lock strap (adhesive tape)
(B)
GAUZE WRAP
NOTE:
Use cotton batting under all splints.
DON'TS in finger splints
Never use a loose halter
ALUMINUM
Fractured Finger
Splint & bandage
Cerney

Figure 87

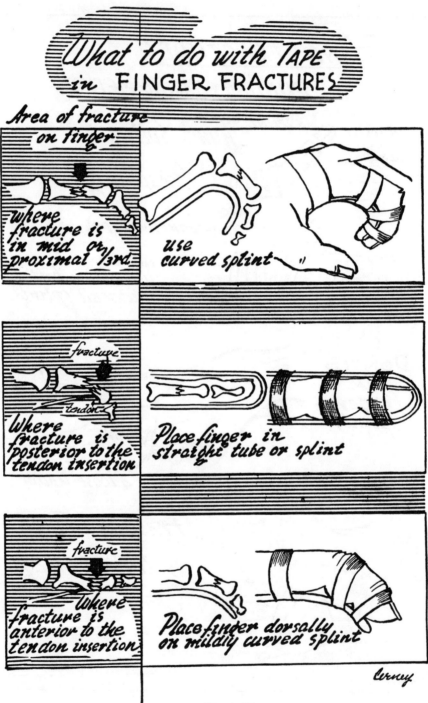

What to do with Tape in FINGER FRACTURES

Area of fracture on finger

where fracture is in mid or proximal 1/3rd. — use curved splint

Where fracture is posterior to the tendon insertion — Place finger in straight tube or splint

Where fracture is anterior to the tendon insertion — Place finger dorsally on mildly curved splint

Cerney

Figure 88

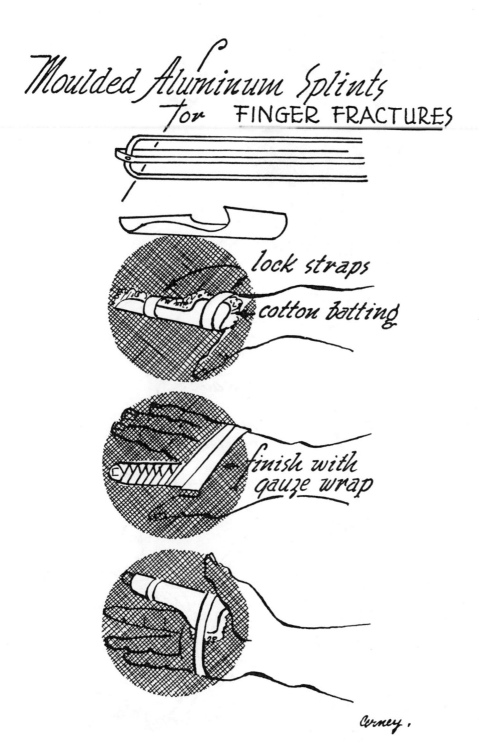

Figure 89

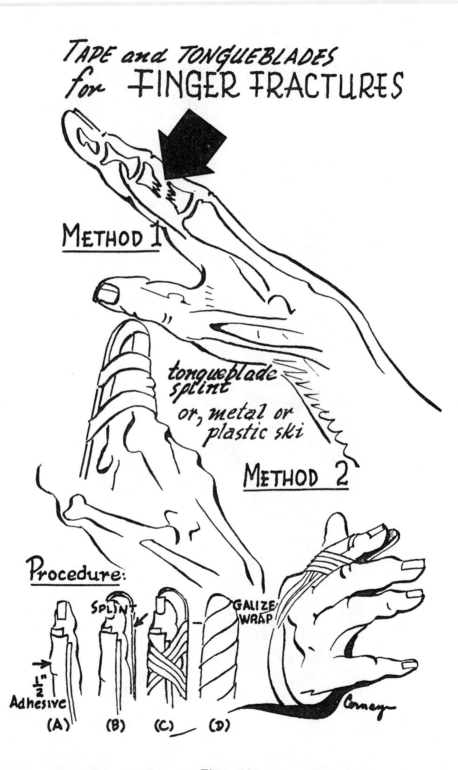

Tape and Tongueblades for FINGER FRACTURES

METHOD 1

tongueblade splint

or, metal or plastic ski

METHOD 2

Procedure:

SPLINT

GAUZE WRAP

½"

Adhesive

(A)   (B)   (C)   (D)

Figure 90

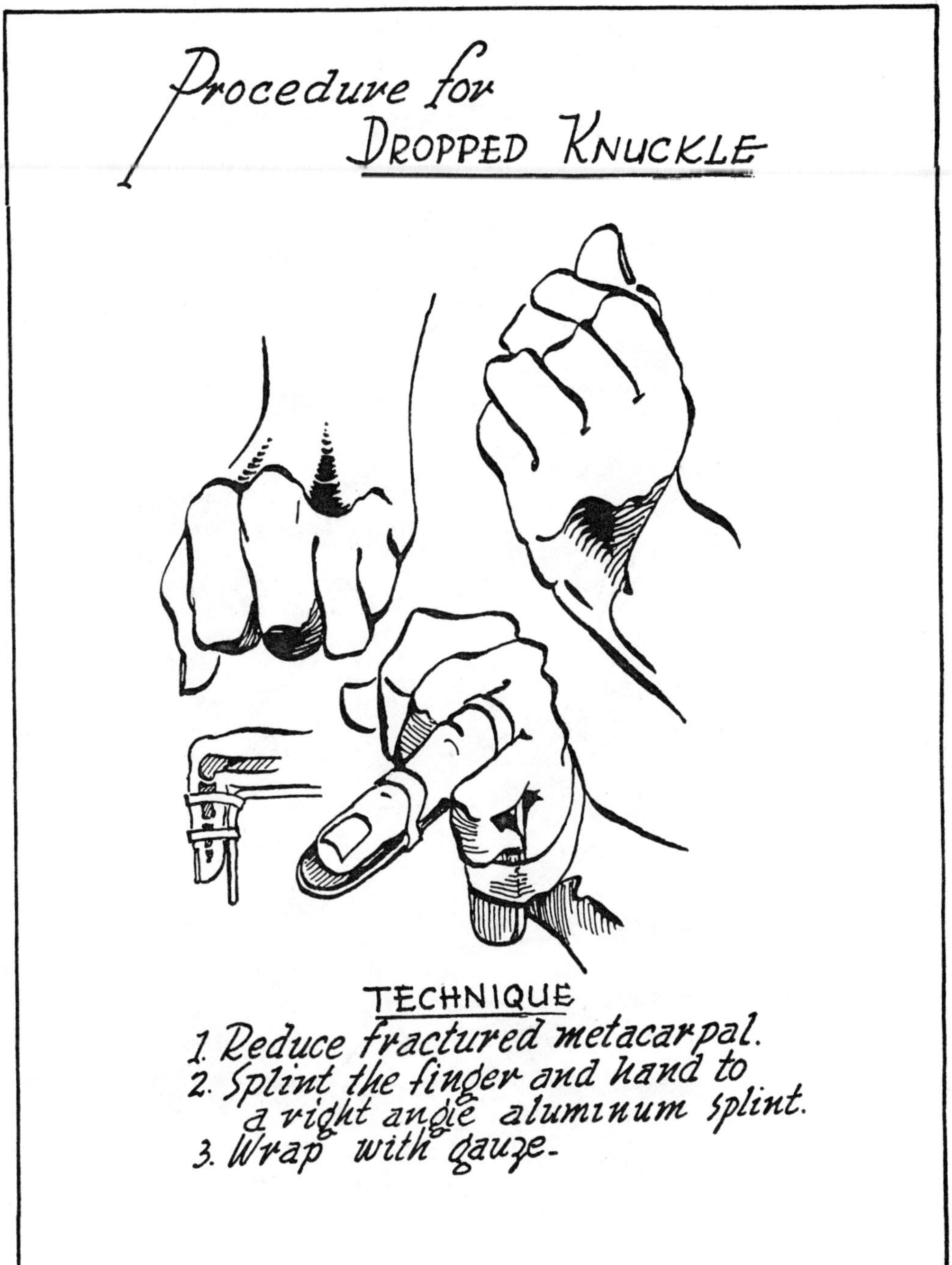

Procedure for DROPPED KNUCKLE

TECHNIQUE
1. Reduce fractured metacarpal.
2. Splint the finger and hand to a right angle aluminum splint.
3. Wrap with gauze.

Corney

Figure 91

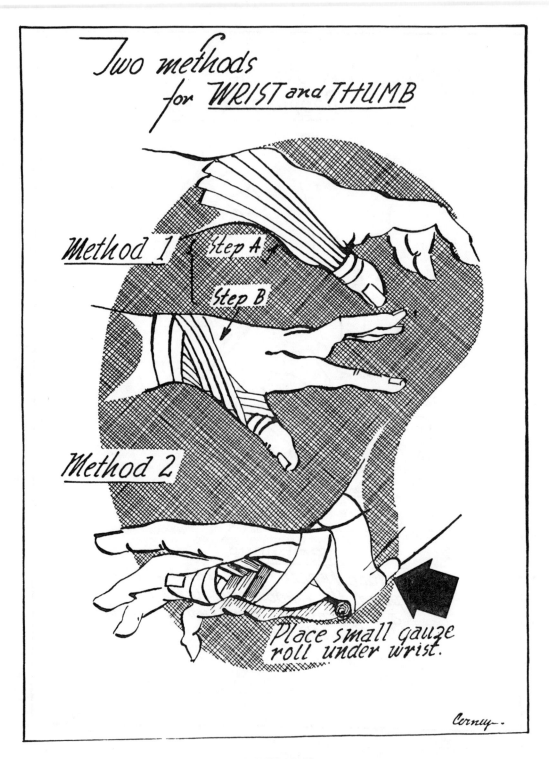

Figure 92

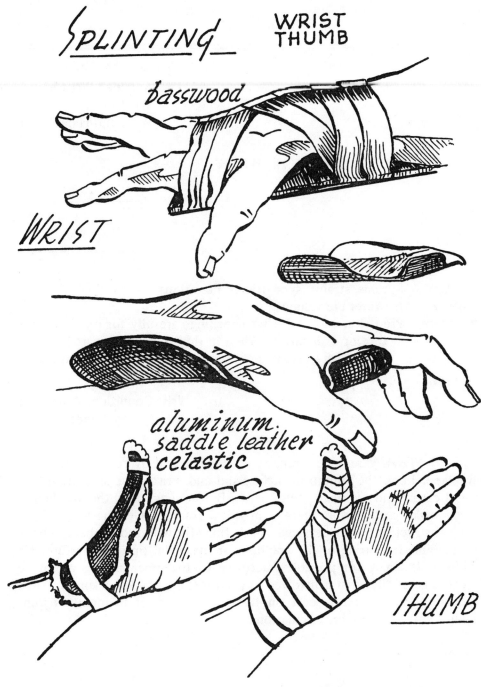

Figure 93

The WRIST

Flexible Cast Techniques for:
Sprained Wrist
Wrist Lock
Wrist and Hand Splint

The WRIST

| Suggested ¼" ½" |
| Tape Widths: 1" |

Purpose: Sprains, strains, synovitis, subluxations.
Position: However convenient.
Procedure: Prep skin as usual after checking carefully for possible fracture or dislocation. When in doubt, have the part X-rayed. Wrap with gauze if there is sensitivity to adhesive tape.

Wrist Conditions Amenable to Adhesive Tape

MILD SPRAIN may be wrapped with gauze and overlayed with adhesive tape. Lock the thumb into the hand and wrist. Give support to the dorsal carpal and radiocarpal ligaments. Before diagnosing the problem as *sprain* make certain that there is no local fracture. Get the team physician's instructions after he views X-ray film. He will also probably check for possible fracturing of the scaphoid or the distal tip of the radius. He will double check for possible fracturing of the ulnar process when the lateral side of the wrist is involved in what is thought to be a sprain. When you apply your flexible cast on the wrist, design it to maintain joint rigidity without stopping circulation.

SEVERE SPRAIN demands more yeoman splinting. After X-raying the part for possible fracture, and giving remedial physical therapy, apply gauze to the hand and wrist. Stabilize the hand and wrist with a cock-up splint and strap securely in position.

SYNOVITIS is a problem involving the extensor tendons of the wrist, and is extremely tender. Treatment of choice is adhesive tape or flexible cast immobilization. Apply after physical therapy has been used. DO NOT PAMPER THE WRIST! Instruct the athlete to use it! Do not mis-diagnose as *sprain!*

Routine
WRIST STRAP
for Sprain

May be used as a
football handwrap, and for
strains, weak wrist.

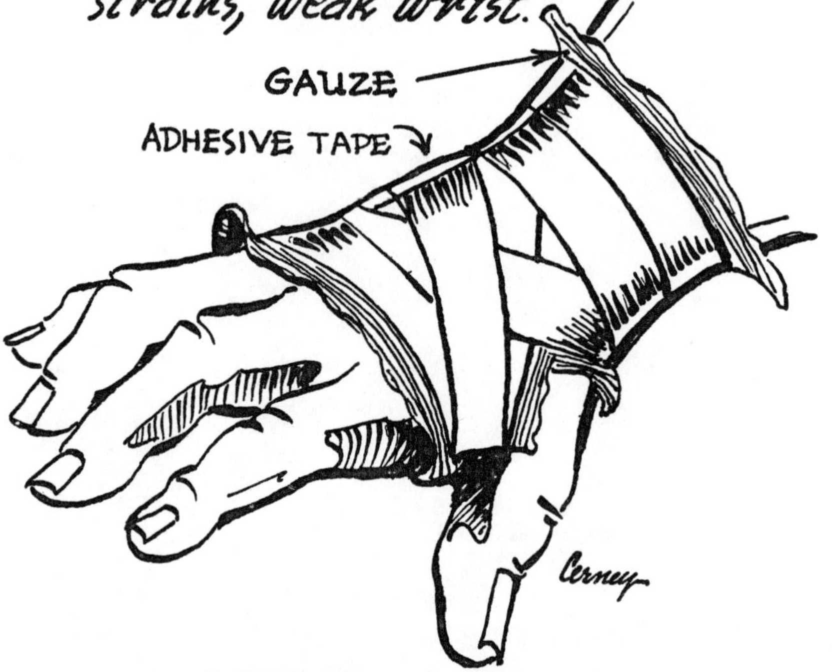

GAUZE

ADHESIVE TAPE

Cerney

METHOD of APPLICATION

1. With palms down athlete spreads fingers.
2. Wrap hand and wrist with gauze (2").
3. Swab gauze with rubber cement.
4. Apply 1" adhesive tape bisector straps.
   Crisscross over carpals and lock.

Figure 94

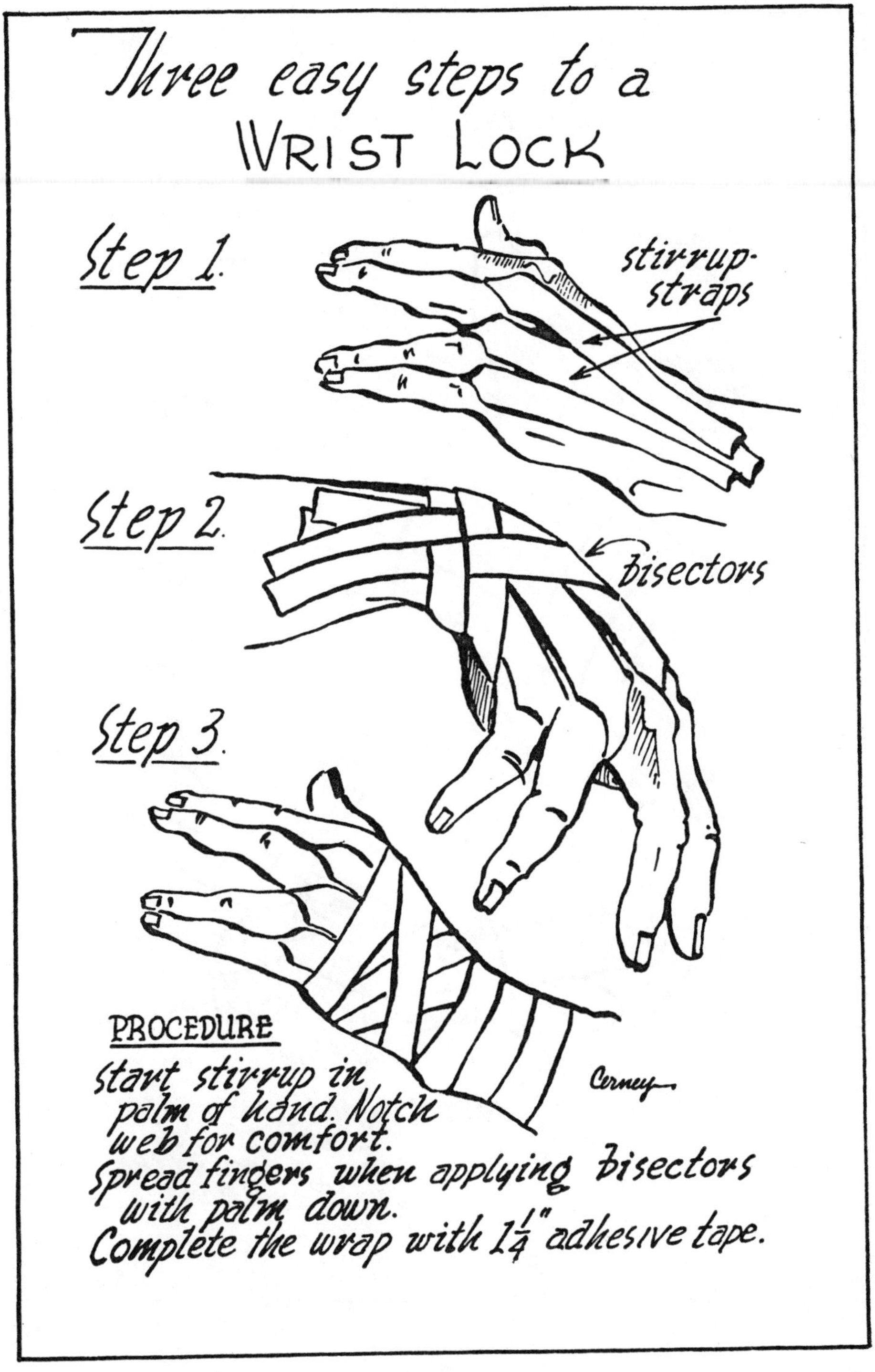

Three easy steps to a WRIST LOCK

Step 1.

stirrup-straps

Step 2.

bisectors

Step 3.

<u>PROCEDURE</u>
Start stirrup in palm of hand. Notch web for comfort.
Spread fingers when applying bisectors with palm down.
Complete the wrap with $1\frac{1}{4}$" adhesive tape.

Cerney.

Figure 95

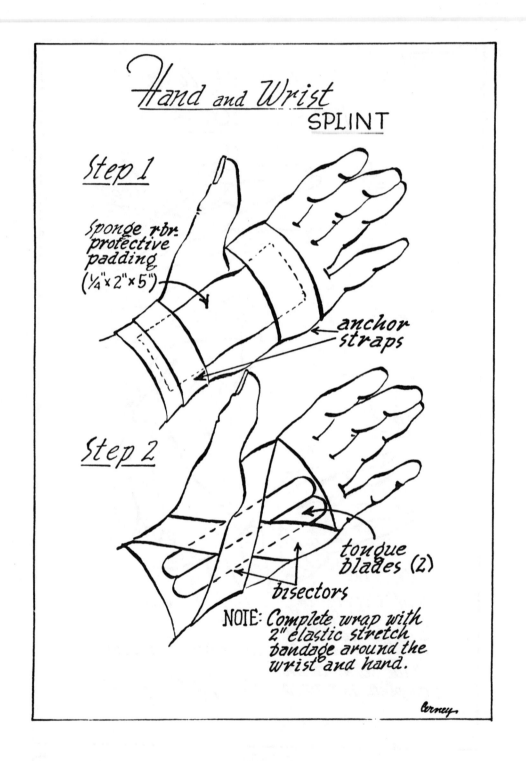

Figure 96

The FOREARM

<blockquote>
Suggested 1½"
Tape Width: 2"
</blockquote>

Purpose: Treat contusions, speed recuperation, prevent complications.
Position: Seated or standing.
Procedure: Same as for anterior thigh problems. Prep the skin after the earlier care of compression and cold compresses has been discontinued. To supplement any taping technique, elevate the arm by placing the elbow in a sling. The physician will check for complications and possible diagnostic X-ray filming. After 24 hours, start heat (moist or dry) on the arm. Provide protective padding and prescribe light activity.

(For taping techniques see "Thigh." The process is much the same.)

The ELBOW

Flexible Cast Techniques for:
> Elbow Limitation Strap
> Elbow Limitation (R. Bevan)
> Elbow Dislocation
> Tennis Elbow
> Elbow Sprain/Strain
> Displaced Radius

The ELBOW

> Suggested
> Tape Width: 1"

Purpose: Immobilize, control, protect.
Position: Elbow flexed.
Procedure: After skin-prep place *anchor* straps on upper and lower arm. Place restrainer straps immediately to prevent elbow extension. Pad the tender zones. Apply 1" adhesive tape as indicated in the drawings. If the team physician indicates additional support, supplement the flexible case with a 3" cotton elastic wrap and place elbow in a sling.

Trainer's Tips

Immediately after injury flex the elbow and apply elastic wrap and cold compresses to alleviate or control edema. Follow with diagnostic X-ray investigation. In 12 hours follow up with moist heat, electrotherapy or ultrasound, and an analgesic pack, but DO NOT MASSAGE THE ELBOW! Barring complications, return the athlete to competition wearing a protective elbow pad and/or an elastic brace or restrainer strap. Always pad the intercubital fossa before applying tape. Use a figure-8 final wrap over a basketweave. Design all straps to prevent extension of the joint.

Elbow Conditions Most
Amenable to Adhesive Tape

Athletic injuries to the elbow which are more responsive to adhesive tape control are: (a) *emergency care of elbow joint dislocation or dislocation of the head of the radius,* (b) *emergency care of a fractured supracondyle of the humerus,* (c) *fractured olecranon process emergency care,* (d) *emergency care of a ruptured obicular ligament,* (e) *periostitis,* (f) *bursitis,* (g) *epicondylitis,* (h) *tendonitis,* (i) *"tennis elbow."*

That "Tennis Elbow" or
"Tennis Arm" Problem

A common complication to *"Tennis Elbow"* is muscle spasm, myositis, periostitis and fibrositis. Too often these are end products of inadequate conditioning of the athlete, faulty nutrition, faulty delivery in throwing motions or a host of other personal problems. In any event *"Tennis Elbow" must be promptly immobilized and given rest.* Of special note in this injury is that IT POSITIVELY SHOULD NOT BE GIVEN COLD THERAPY! The elbow should be locked at right angles, a sling used, and the athlete instructed to follow an exercise program for the hand and arm. These exercises should be continued even though the part is bandaged.

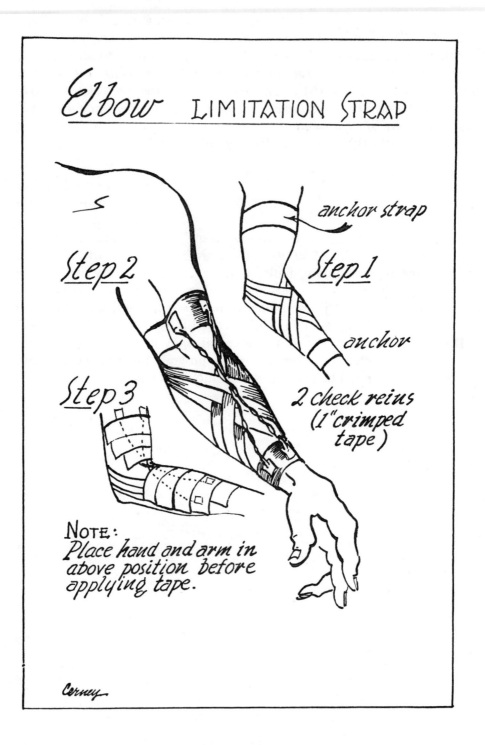

Figure 97

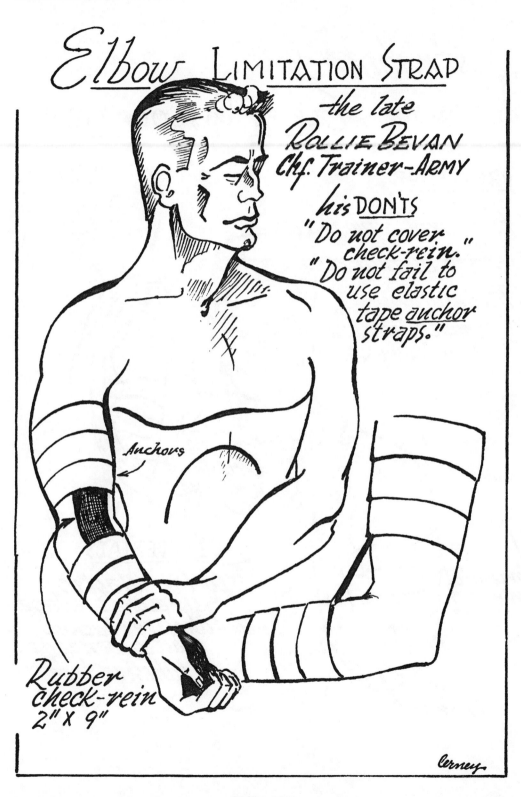

Figure 98

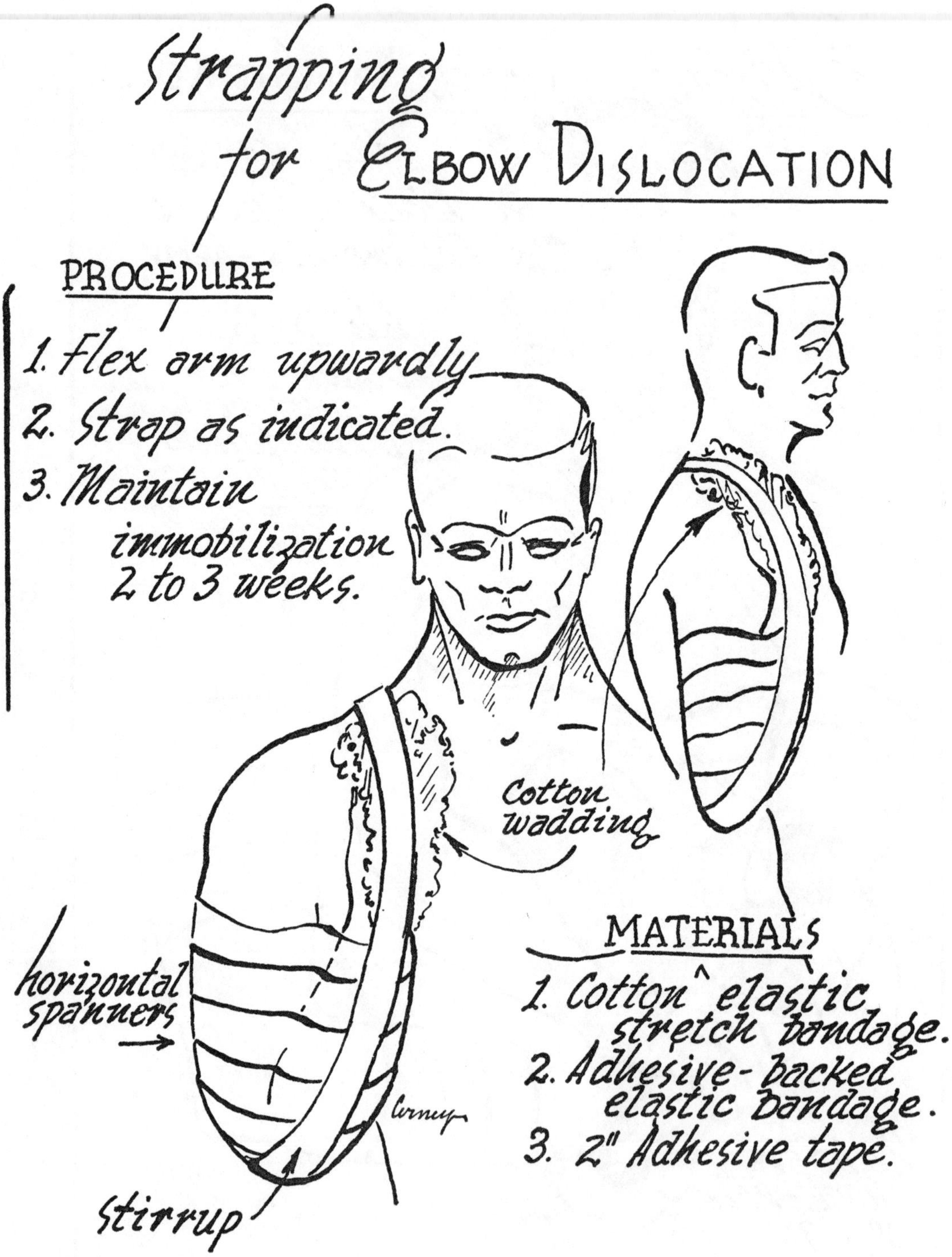

Strapping for Elbow Dislocation

PROCEDURE

1. Flex arm upwardly
2. Strap as indicated.
3. Maintain immobilization 2 to 3 weeks.

Cotton wadding

horizontal spanners →

stirrup

MATERIALS

1. Cotton elastic stretch bandage.
2. Adhesive-backed elastic bandage.
3. 2" Adhesive tape.

Figure 99

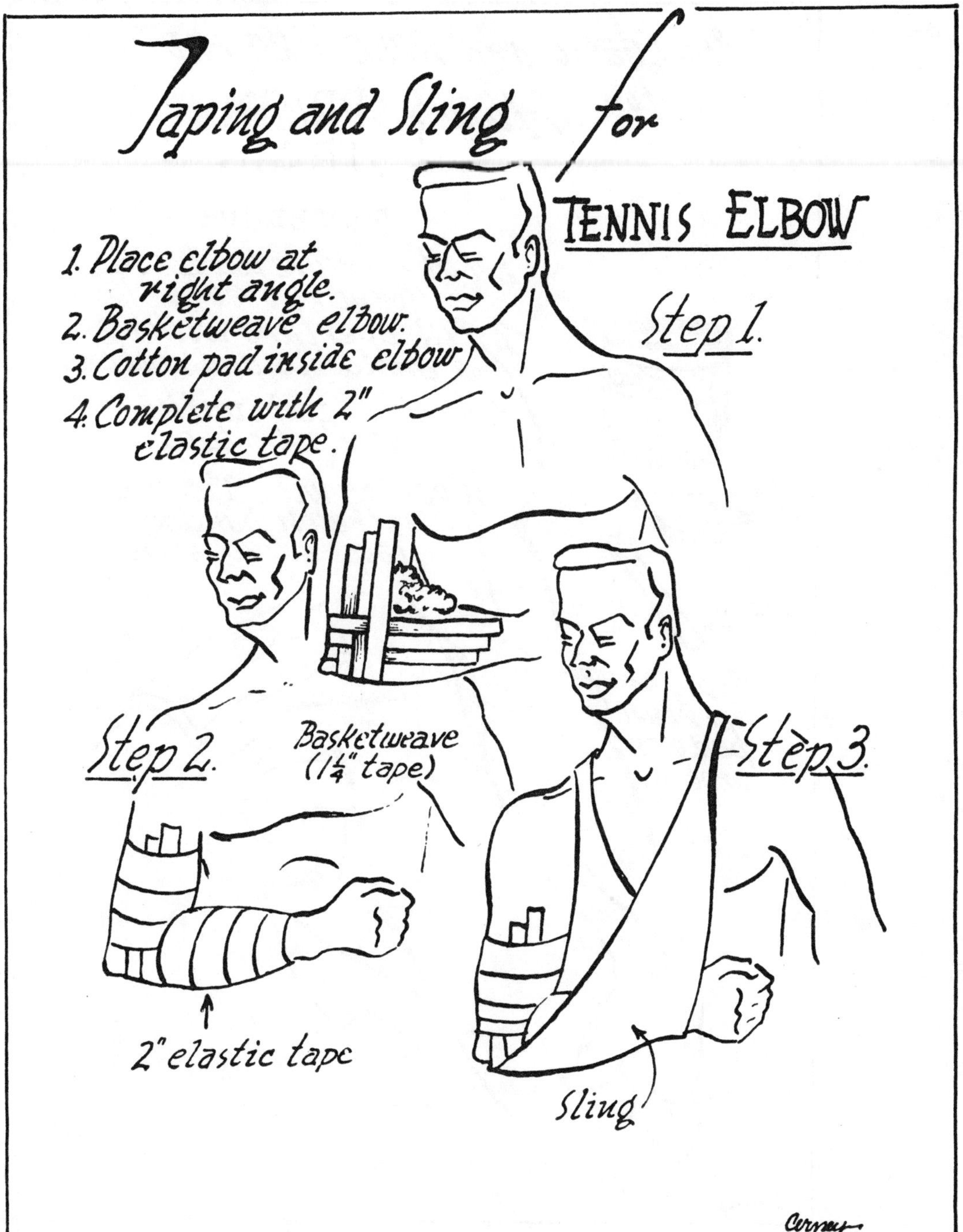
Taping and Sling for
TENNIS ELBOW
1. Place elbow at right angle.
2. Basketweave elbow.
3. Cotton pad inside elbow
4. Complete with 2" elastic tape.
Step 1.
Step 2.
Basketweave (1¼" tape)
2" elastic tape
Step 3.
Sling
Cerney

Figure 100

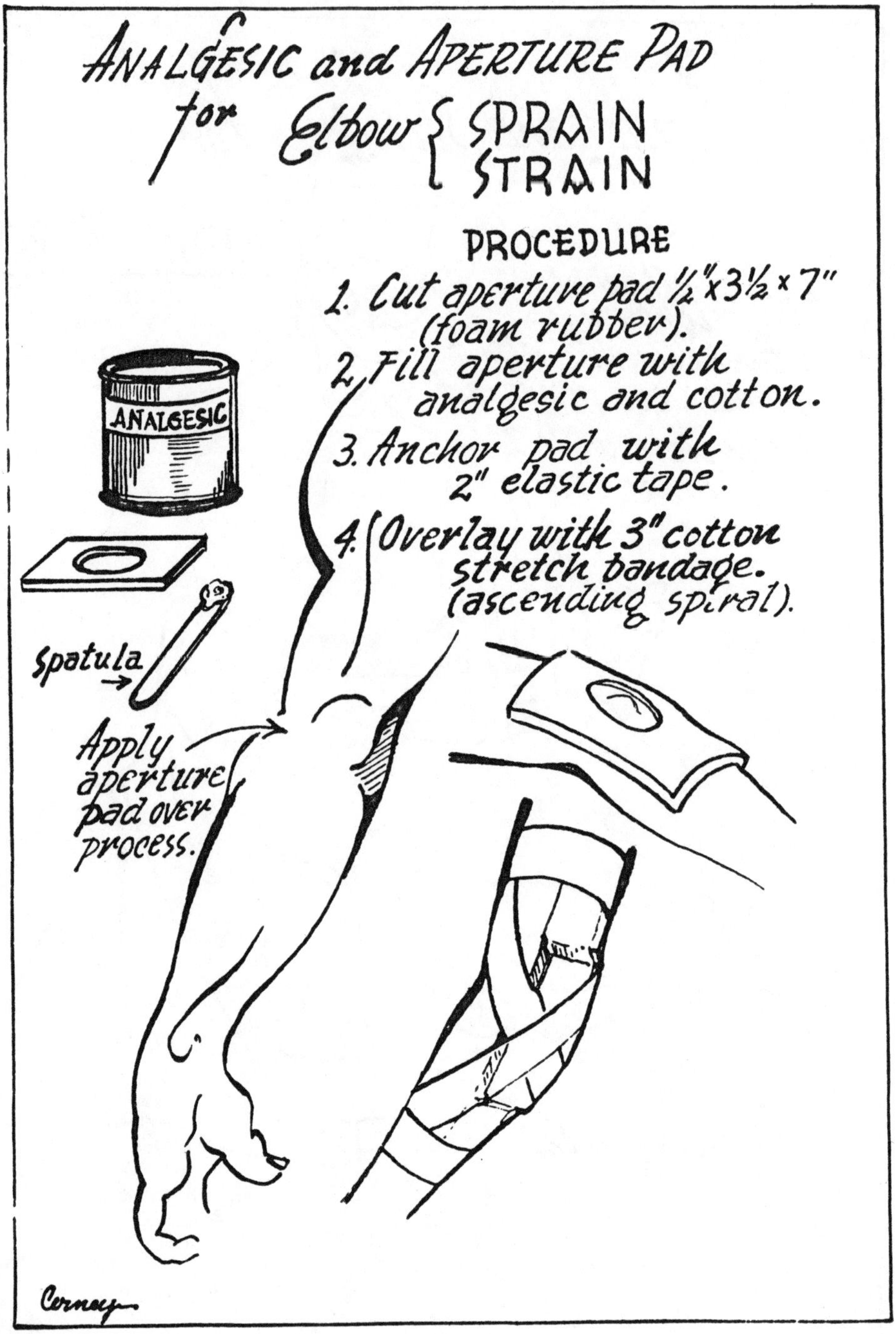

ANALGESIC and APERTURE PAD
for Elbow { SPRAIN
            STRAIN

PROCEDURE
1. Cut aperture pad ½" x 3½ x 7"
   (foam rubber).
2. Fill aperture with
   analgesic and cotton.
3. Anchor pad with
   2" elastic tape.
4. Overlay with 3" cotton
   stretch bandage.
   (ascending spiral).

ANALGESIC

Spatula →

Apply
aperture
pad over
process.

Cerney

Figure 101

Collar and Cuff

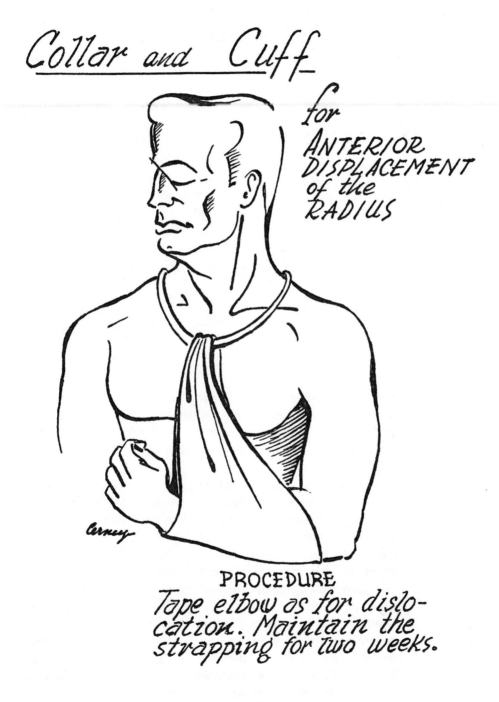

for ANTERIOR DISPLACEMENT of the RADIUS

PROCEDURE
Tape elbow as for dislocation. Maintain the strapping for two weeks.

Figure 102

The SHOULDER

Flexible Cast Techniques for:
"Glass Arm"
"Painful Shoulder"
"Football Shoulder"
"Weak Shoulders"
Deltoid Injury
Coraco-Brachialis Rupture
"Shoulder Separation"
Acromio-Clavicular Separation

The SHOULDER

Suggested   1½"
Tape Width: 2"

Purpose: Limit motion and relieve "arm drag" on the joint.

Position: Athlete seated, his elbow cocked at right angle, arm across abdomen and thumb hooked in trunks for support. Athlete is asked to raise his shoulder while flexible cast is being applied.

Procedure: Clip all hair, swab area with rubbing alcohol or other non-oily antiseptic. Apply your favorite adherent. Protect traumatized zones with sponge rubber slabs or "doughnuts" after the *anchor* straps have been established. Fix the sponge rubber to keep it from moving. Whether basketweave or other technique is used, the necessity is to approximate the acromio-clavicular joint or other problem. The joints must be "lined up" for correct positional healing. On the shoulder utilize strong tension or pull in applying from below upward. A shoulder cast should extend from sternum to shoulder to spinal column. The *biceps* and *pectoral* muscles should be partially immobilized. So should the scapula. Overlay all shoulder dressings with a 3" cotton elastic roller bandage. (A 6" stretch bandage is sometimes used for this purpose.)

Trainer's Tips:

(a) *Immobilize the offended joint immediately.* (b) *Place elbow in a sling.* (c) *Get shoulder X-rayed immediately for separation or fracture.* (d) *Lock analgesic pack in place with an elastic figure-8.* (e) *Prohibit arm-use till swelling and pain are gone.* (f) *Massage the triceps and uninvolved pectoral fibers as well as the cervical musculature and trapezius close to the spinal column.* (g) *DO NOT MASSAGE OVER OR AROUND THE EFFECTED JOINT.* (h) *When physical therapy is used DO NOT APPLY IT* (shortwave, ultrasonics) *THROUGH THE FLEXIBLE CAST.* (i) *Pad the axilla heavily.* (j) *"Locking" the clavicle in the "tape job" reduces pain even further.*

Shoulder Problems Amenable to Adhesive Tape Techniques

GLASS ARM isn't good medical terminology, but to athletes and trainers the title is self-explanatory. Muscles usually involved in *"Glass Arm"* are the *brachioradialis* and *biceps.* At the elbow the *supinator longus* may be similarly involved. The muscle inflammation *(myositis)* that occurs is almost instantly disabling, and the athlete should get at least a three-week lay-off.* Special TRAINER'S NOTES when using adhesive in this problem are: (a) *Lock the scapula down* with all "glass arm" strappings (almost dramatic relief is achieved). (b) *Relax all surrounding muscles* with massage but do not come near the shoulder "point."

DISLOCATION demands that a figure-8 type of wrap be used immediately after the joint has been "set." Utilize the elbow-to-shoulder lock strap for this purpose and supplement with an elbow sling.

BURSITIS is common in the shoulder and very painful for the athlete concerned. Throwing events accentuate inflammation of the bursae sacs. To ease the distension of these sacs, place a compression pad over the involved area and lock in position. DO NOT MAKE AN APERTURE IN SUCH A PAD. It is primarily a pressure pad, and to dispel any collected fluid its total milking compression action has to be sustained.

SYNOVITIS (Example: *bicipital tenosynovitis*) is an acute involvement of the tendon sheath. Usually it is near its insertion. It is quick to become chronic and effectively knocks an athlete out of sports if it's not given prompt and effective therapy. For effective control the shoulder has to be locked in such manner that it is permitted movement without pain and function is not restricted. A sling is a valuable adjunct.

SPRAIN/STRAIN problems should be promptly immobilized by a flexible cast. *Sprains should never be considered a minor injury in the shoulder.* Therefore, put the shoulder at rest. Limit the action of *biceps* and *supraspinatous* muscles.

SHOULDER FRACTURES demand immediate attention from the team doctor but *adhesive tape can be AN EMERGENCY MEASURE for temporary immobilization.* A broken humerus may be treated by traction using an adhesive tape technique but this is not within the domain of the trainer, coach, or student of physical education.

SUBSCAPULARIS INJURY occurs usually when there is sudden heavy lifting. Severe damage may necessitate surgery, but for lesser damage adhesive tape is an aid. The *subscapularis* extends from the lower lateral border of the scapula to the head of the humerus at the shoulder. When injured, all activity should stop. When weight-lifters first notice discomfort in this area, it is a sign to stop action. It is also a sign that it is already getting progressively worse. The Trainer will apply ice packs to the area for two hours with an elastic wrap. After 12 hours use deep heat, mild massage, area manipulation, and analgesic packs. Permit no weight-lifting until recovery is complete. This may take six months. In the interim maintain a conditioning schedule. Use no protective covering but *DO wear the arm in a sling when jogging.*

*For extensive details on "Glass Arm" see J.V. Cerney, *Care of Athletic Injuries* (Chas. Thomas Pub. Co., Springfield, Ill., 1963), pages 68 to 73.

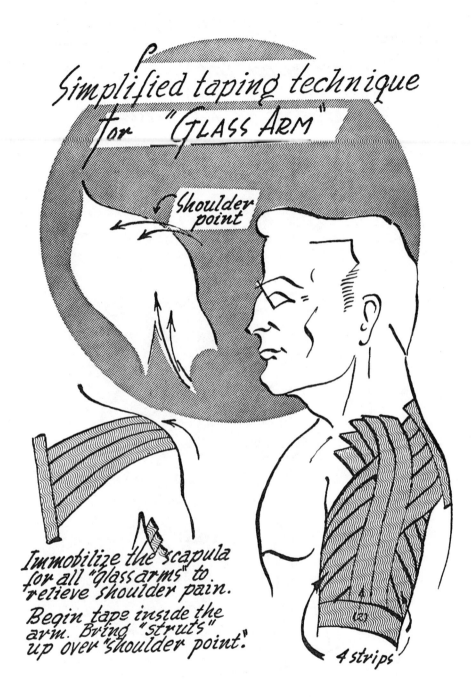

Simplified taping technique for "GLASS ARM"

Shoulder point

Immobilize the scapula for all "glass arms" to relieve shoulder pain.

Begin tape inside the arm. Bring "struts" up over "shoulder point."

4 strips

Cerney

(see following diagram for additional methods) →

Figure 103

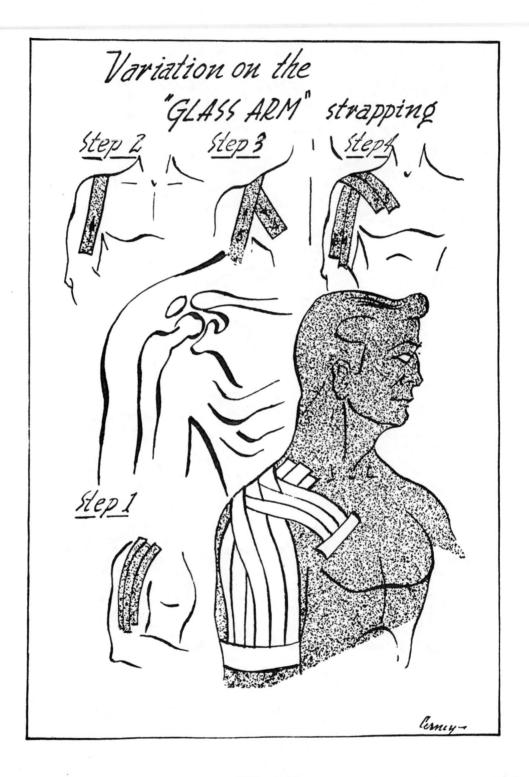

Figure 104

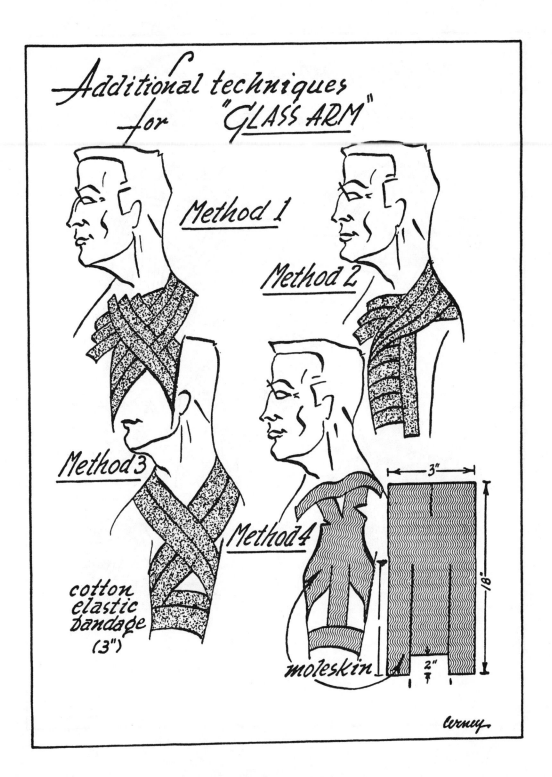

Figure 105

Figure 106

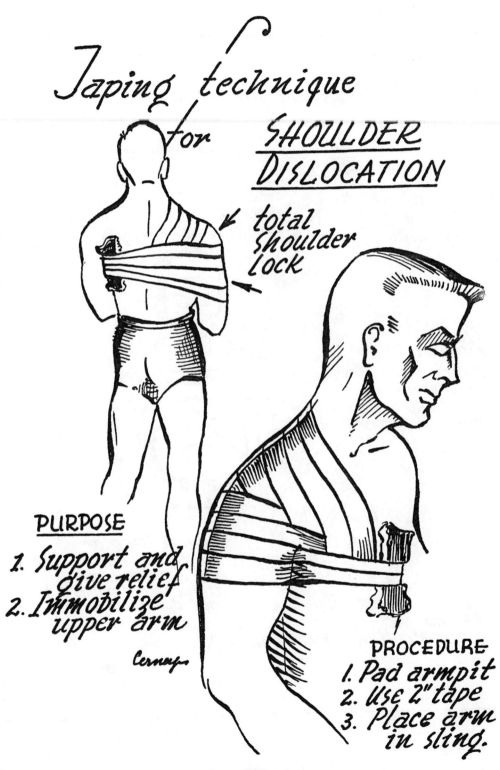

Taping technique for SHOULDER DISLOCATION

total shoulder lock

PURPOSE

1. Support and give relief
2. Immobilize upper arm

Cernay

PROCEDURE

1. Pad armpit
2. Use 2" tape
3. Place arm in sling.

Figure 107

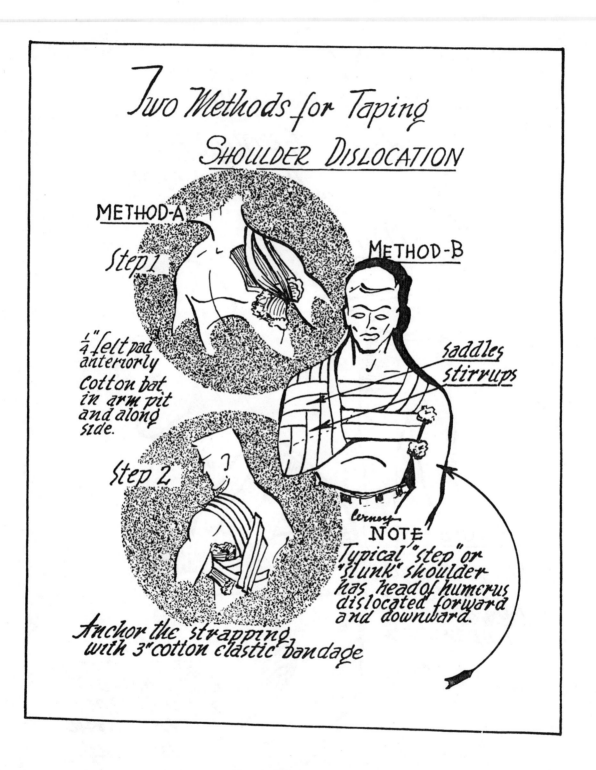

Figure 108

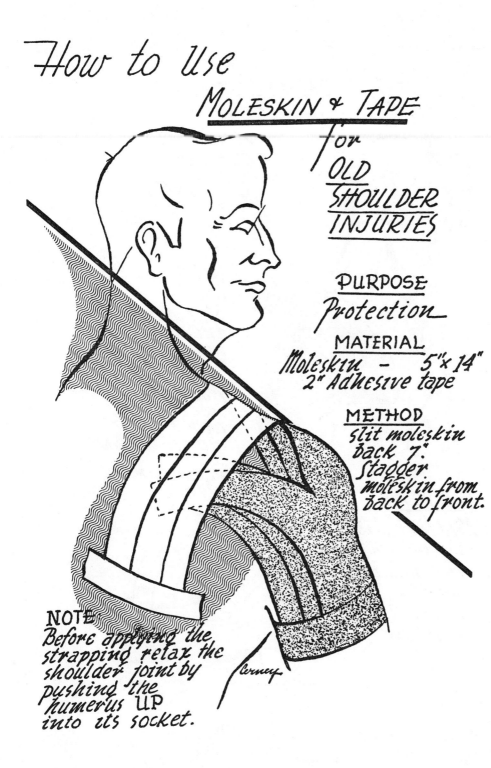

How to Use
MOLESKIN & TAPE
for OLD SHOULDER INJURIES

PURPOSE
Protection

MATERIAL
Moleskin — 5"x 14"
2" Adhesive tape

METHOD
Slit moleskin back 7".
Stagger moleskin from back to front.

NOTE
Before applying the strapping relax the shoulder joint by pushing the humerus UP into its socket.

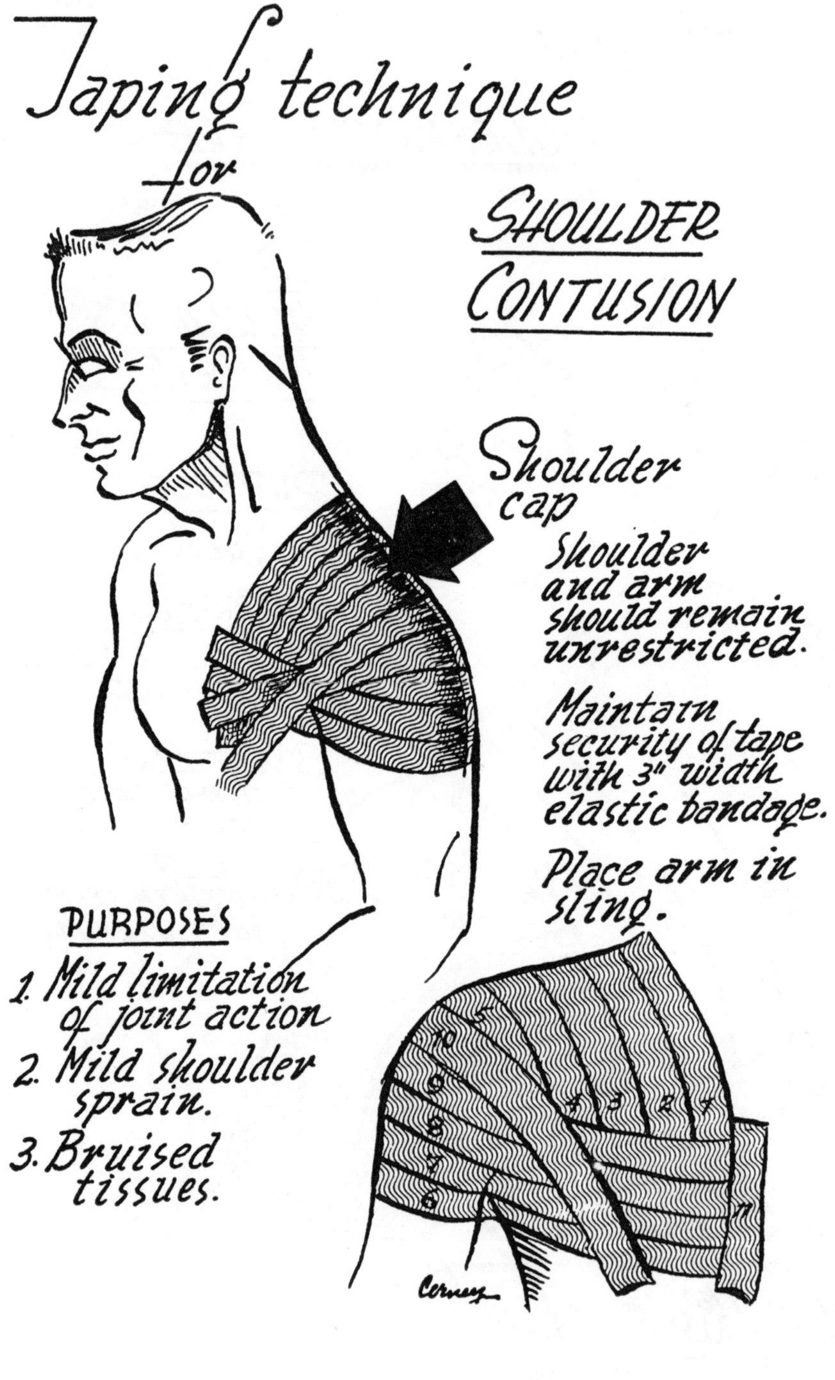
Taping technique for
SHOULDER CONTUSION
Shoulder cap
Shoulder and arm should remain unrestricted.
Maintain security of tape with 3" width elastic bandage.
Place arm in sling.
PURPOSES
1. Mild limitation of joint action
2. Mild shoulder sprain.
3. Bruised tissues.
Cerney

Figure 110

SHOULDER LOCK and SUPPORT

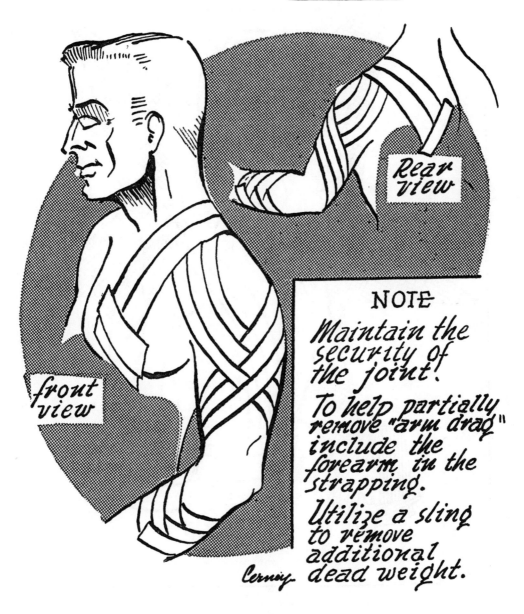

Rear view

front view

NOTE

Maintain the security of the joint!

To help partially remove "arm drag" include the forearm in the strapping.

Utilize a sling to remove additional dead weight.

Cerney.

Figure 111

Figure 112

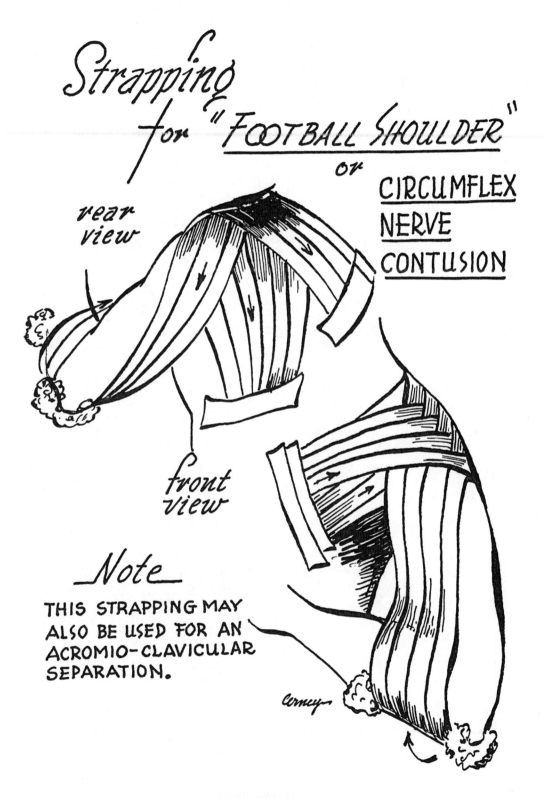

Figure 113

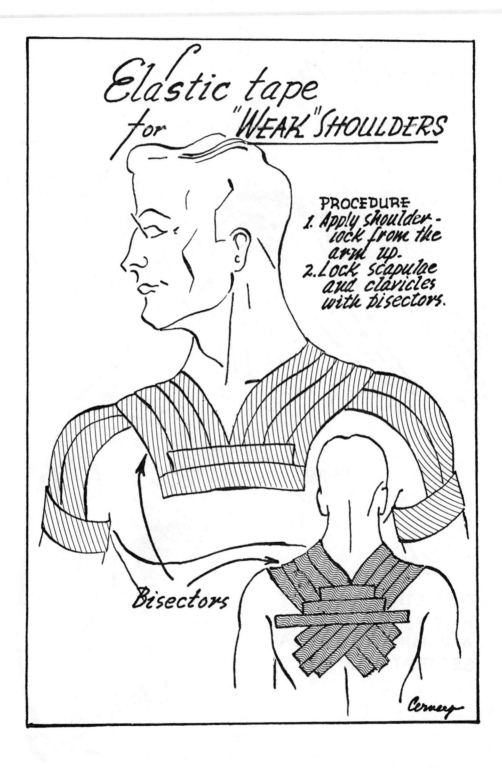

Figure 114

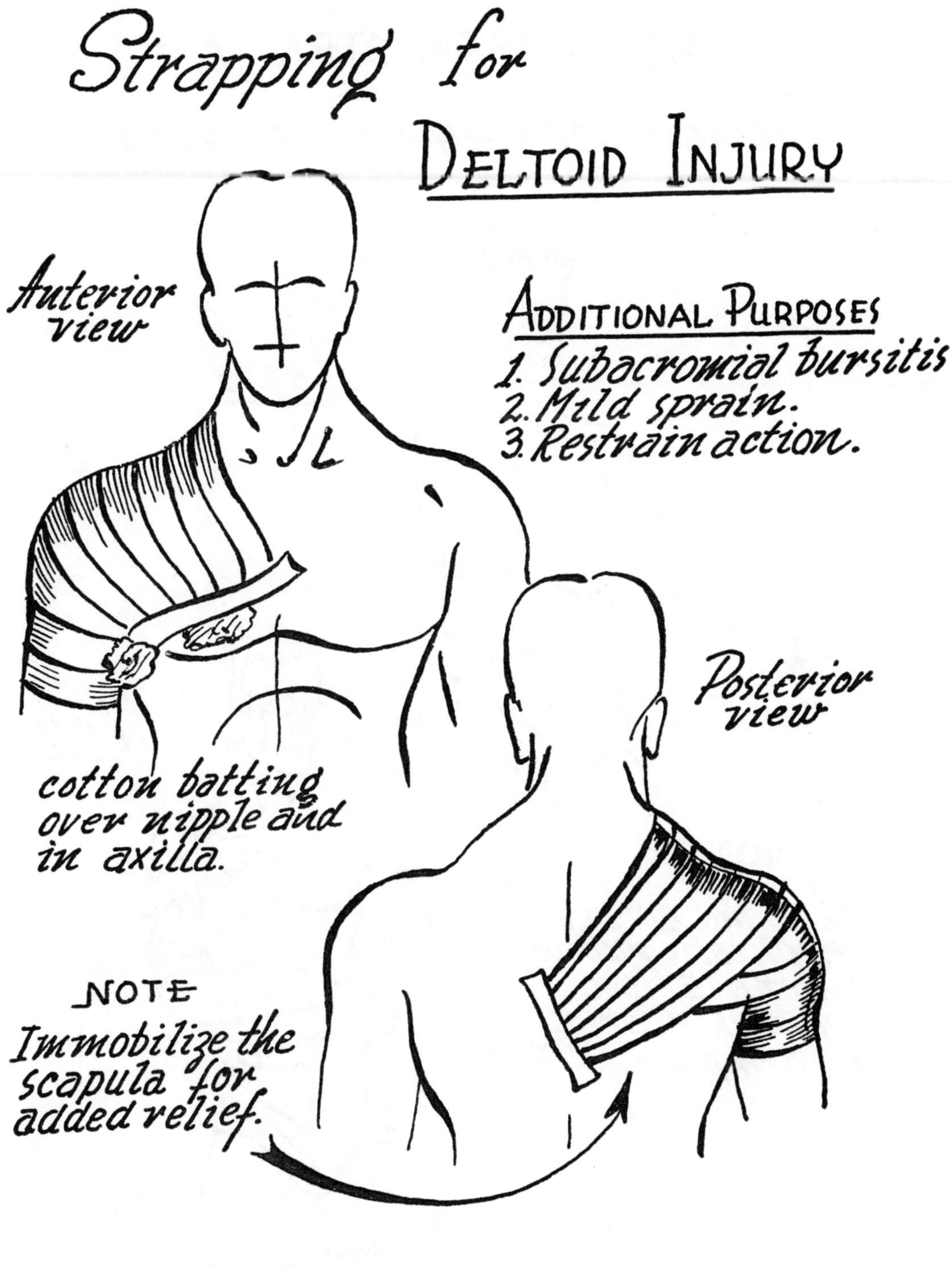

Strapping for Deltoid Injury

Anterior view

Additional Purposes
1. Subacromial bursitis
2. Mild sprain.
3. Restrain action.

cotton batting over nipple and in axilla.

Posterior view

NOTE
Immobilize the scapula for added relief.

Figure 115

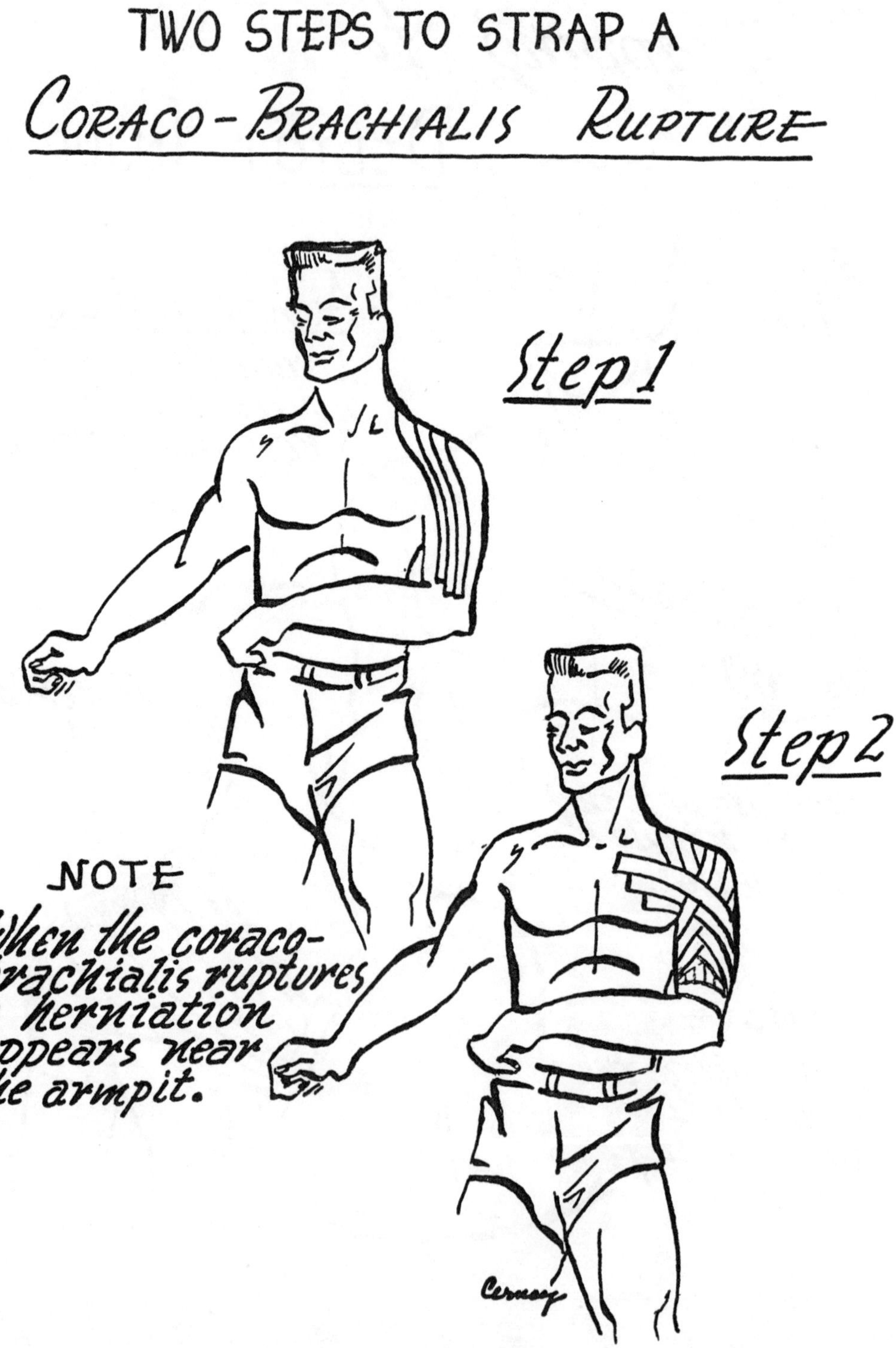

TWO STEPS TO STRAP A
Coraco-Brachialis Rupture

Step 1

Step 2

NOTE
When the coraco-brachialis ruptures, a herniation appears near the armpit.

Figure 116

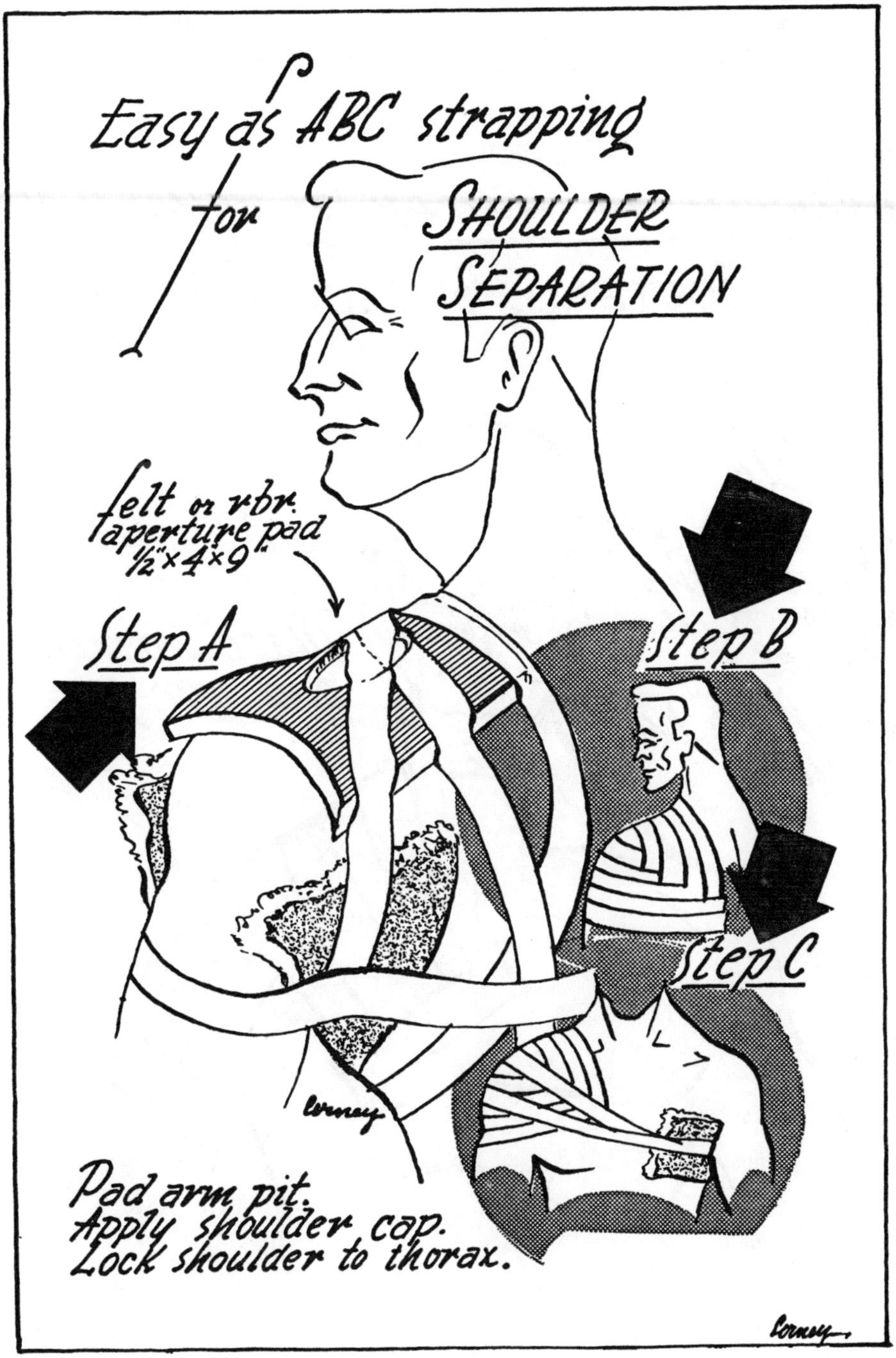
Easy as ABC strapping
for
SHOULDER
SEPARATION
felt or rbr.
aperture pad
½"×4×9"
Step A
Step B
Step C
Pad arm pit.
Apply shoulder cap.
Lock shoulder to thorax.

Figure 117

-Acromio-Clavicular Separation-

("Football Shoulder")

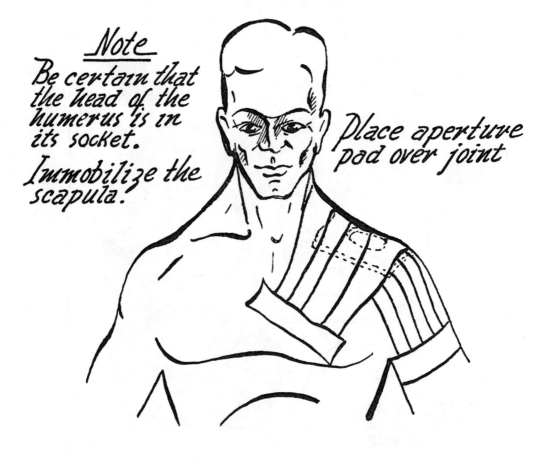

Note
Be certain that the head of the humerus is in its socket.

Immobilize the scapula.

Place aperture pad over joint

Figure 118

Section 3   The GROIN

Flexible Cast Techniques for:
>"Groin Pull" (Creghan)
>Groin Hernia and Inguinal Hernia
>Scrotal Injury Napkin Pouch
>Adhesive Tape Scrotal Bridge

The GROIN

> Suggested ½" 1"
> Tape Width: 1½"

Purpose: Relief and protection from groin strain or direct soft tissue trauma.

Position: Player standing for groin or inguinal flexible cast technique. The knee on the injured side is flexed anteriorly. Relax the buttocks and rotate the thigh mildly inward. Place the heel on a 3" high box. An adhesive tape container tube may serve the purpose.

Procedure: Groin involvements are best treated with non-adhesive bandage against the skin. For this purpose use a cotton elastic roller bandage. Start a 3" stretch bandage *below* the injury. Encircle the thigh for anchorage and then go up over the hip and around the waist in a *figure-8*. Overlay this bandage with adhesive tape in the same way. Start on the inside of the thigh. Spiral up. Add additional strips for added support. Where tape is to be applied directly to the skin, protect the genitals and pubic hair with one square foot of cotton or surgical wadding, gauze pack or flannel. The groin, inguinal area, and genitalia are normally warm moist areas. They are quickly irritated by tape. Since smegma glands in the area provide a typical odor unique to the male they have to be treated with diplomacy, so in prepping the skin for tape or elastic wraps: (a) *cleanse the skin thoroughly* with soap and water; (athlete does this in the shower), (b) *clip hair from thighs and abdomen;* (c) *apply a mild germicide or antiseptic* (BUT NOT ON THE SCROTUM!); (d) *cover with gauze or stockingette* before applying the flexible cast deemed necessary. *Bridge* straps and *locks* should be brought up over the hip, abdomen, or thigh for better anchorage.

How to Apply the Scrotal Injury Napkin Pouch

A blow to the testes is not only painful but is also immediately incapacitating. Rest and immobilization is the treatment of choice and a flexible cast for the sac and its contents is indicated. To achieve a soft suspension method, the following technique was devised: (See Figure 122):

Cut an aperture centrally in the upper one third of a female sanitary napkin (external type). *Insert the penis through the aperture. Bring the long end of the napkin down and the short end up. Tuck the long end back under the scrotum without pressure. This provides a soft nesting harness that promptly "feels good." Now lock the pad with adhesive tape and utilize narrow tape (½") for this purpose. It provides less pressure and less constriction on the contents.*

How to Apply a "Scrotal Bridge"

When the team physician orders the athlete to bed for a scrotal problem there will be a "pull" on the contents of the sac as the boy lies flat on his back. This can be prevented with an adhesive tape device. I call this device a "bridge," and it extends from thigh to thigh (See Figure 123). The bridge utilizes 3" tape, and soft padding is placed centrally to form a rest for the scrotum. NOTE: As a safeguard against having the hair (underlying the adhesive tape bridge) become enmeshed in the "tack" of the tape, place another piece of tape "tack-to-tack" on the middle four inches of the bridge. The balance will be on the thighs.

Psoas Magnus Injury—Often
Mislabeled "Groin Injury"

An injured *psoas* muscle is often given the wrong diagnosis. Mistaken as a "groin injury," it is handled as such. But *in psoas magnus injury, APPLY NO TAPE!* Constriction and pressure are wrong in this injury and the problem should be recognized for what it is. The psoas magnus muscle helps raise and externally rotate the thigh. Strain or direct trauma to this muscle causes local pain in the groin. Pain may be so great as to remove the athlete from competition. When such injury occurs, get the lad to the team physician immediately. The doctor will order diagnostic X-rays to rule out possible thigh, pelvic, or spinal fracture. If negative for fracture, the trainer may start deep heat and mild massage with mild rotation of the thigh. Cotton elastic bandage may be placed around thigh, hip, and waist. Rx: jogging.

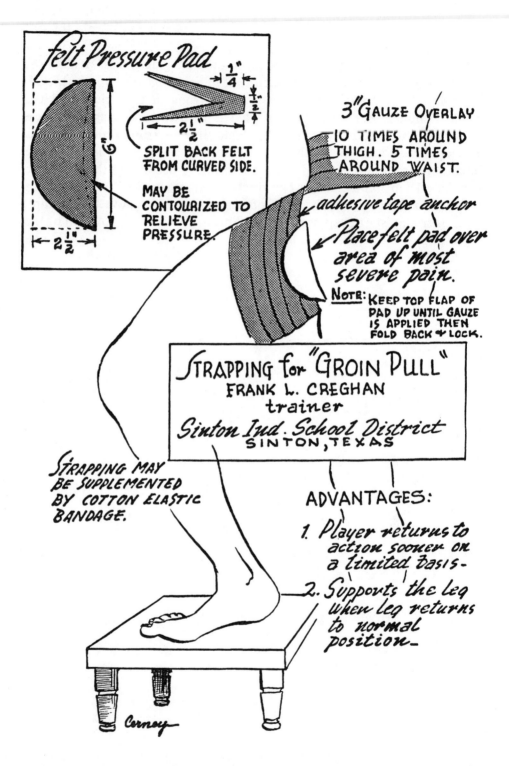

Figure 119

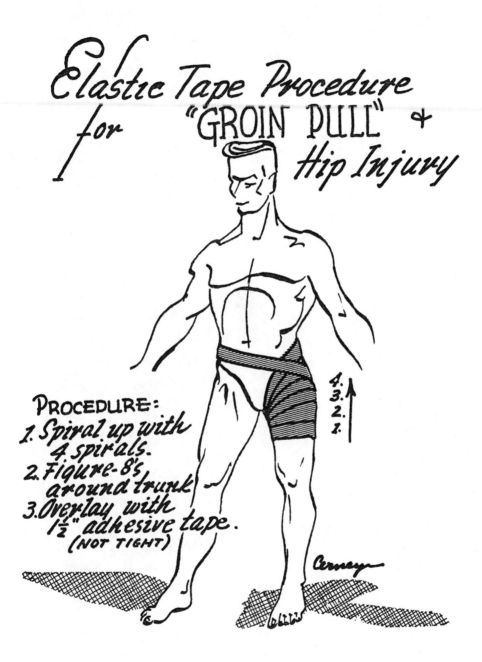

Elastic Tape Procedure
for "GROIN PULL" &
Hip Injury

PROCEDURE:
1. Spiral up with
   4 spirals.
2. Figure-8's
   around trunk
3. Overlay with
   1½" adhesive tape.
   (NOT TIGHT)

Figure 120

Three methods for strapping
INGUINAL and GROIN HERNIA

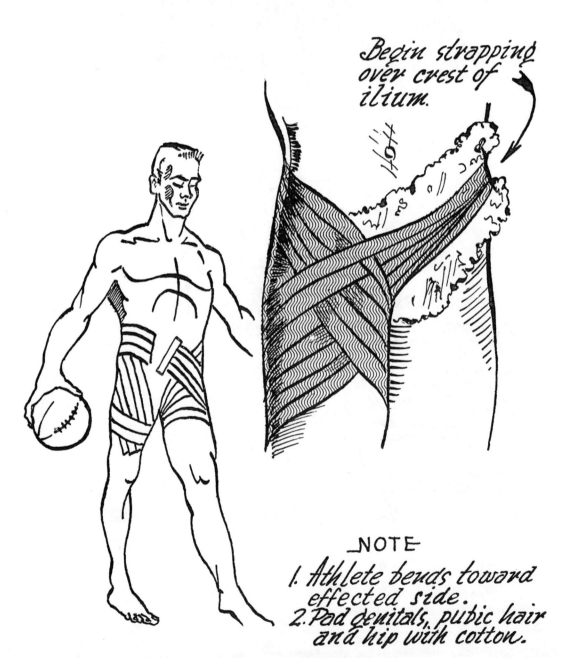

Begin strapping over crest of ilium.

NOTE

1. Athlete bends toward effected side.
2. Pad genitals, pubic hair and hip with cotton.

Figure 121

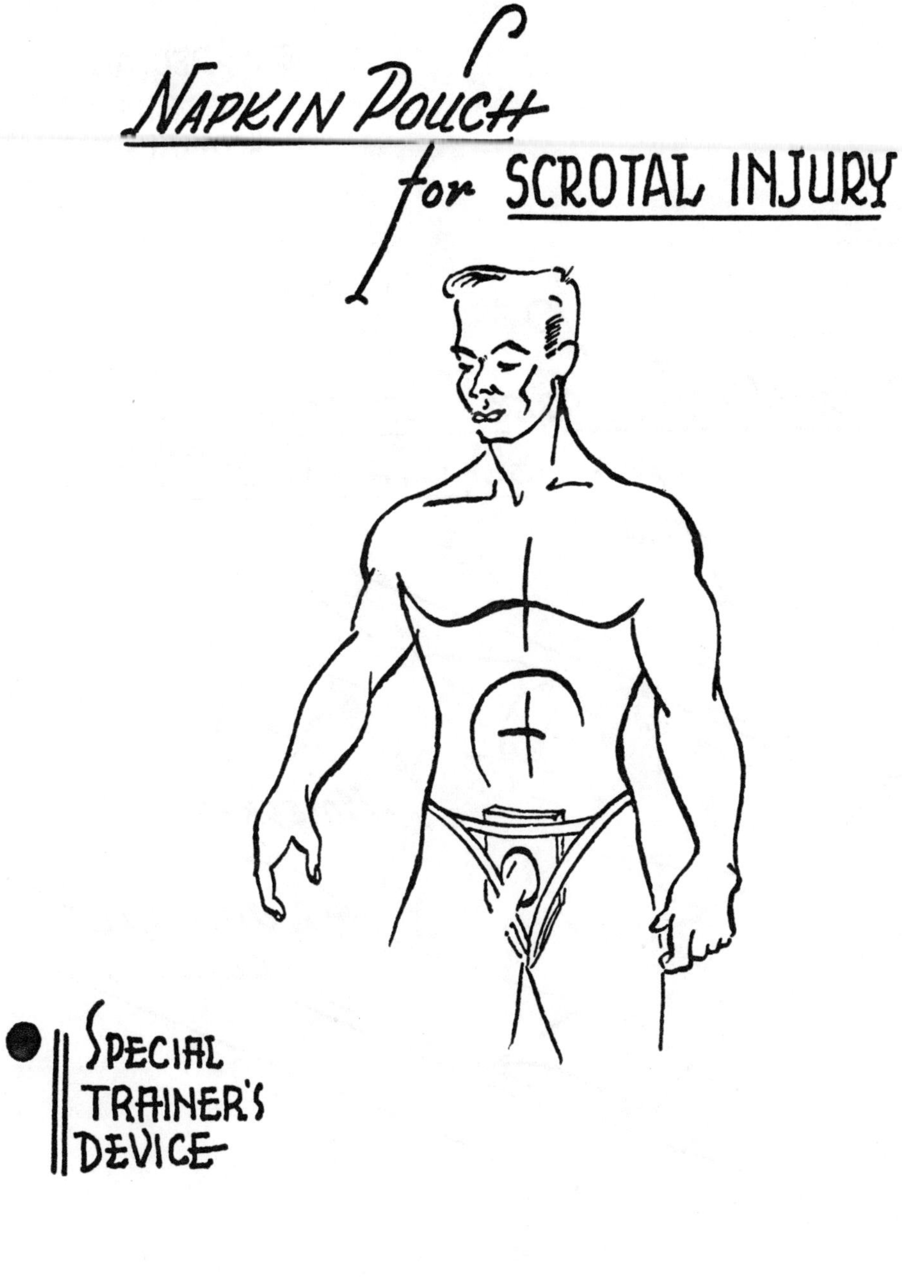

NAPKIN POUCH
for SCROTAL INJURY

SPECIAL TRAINER'S DEVICE

Figure 122

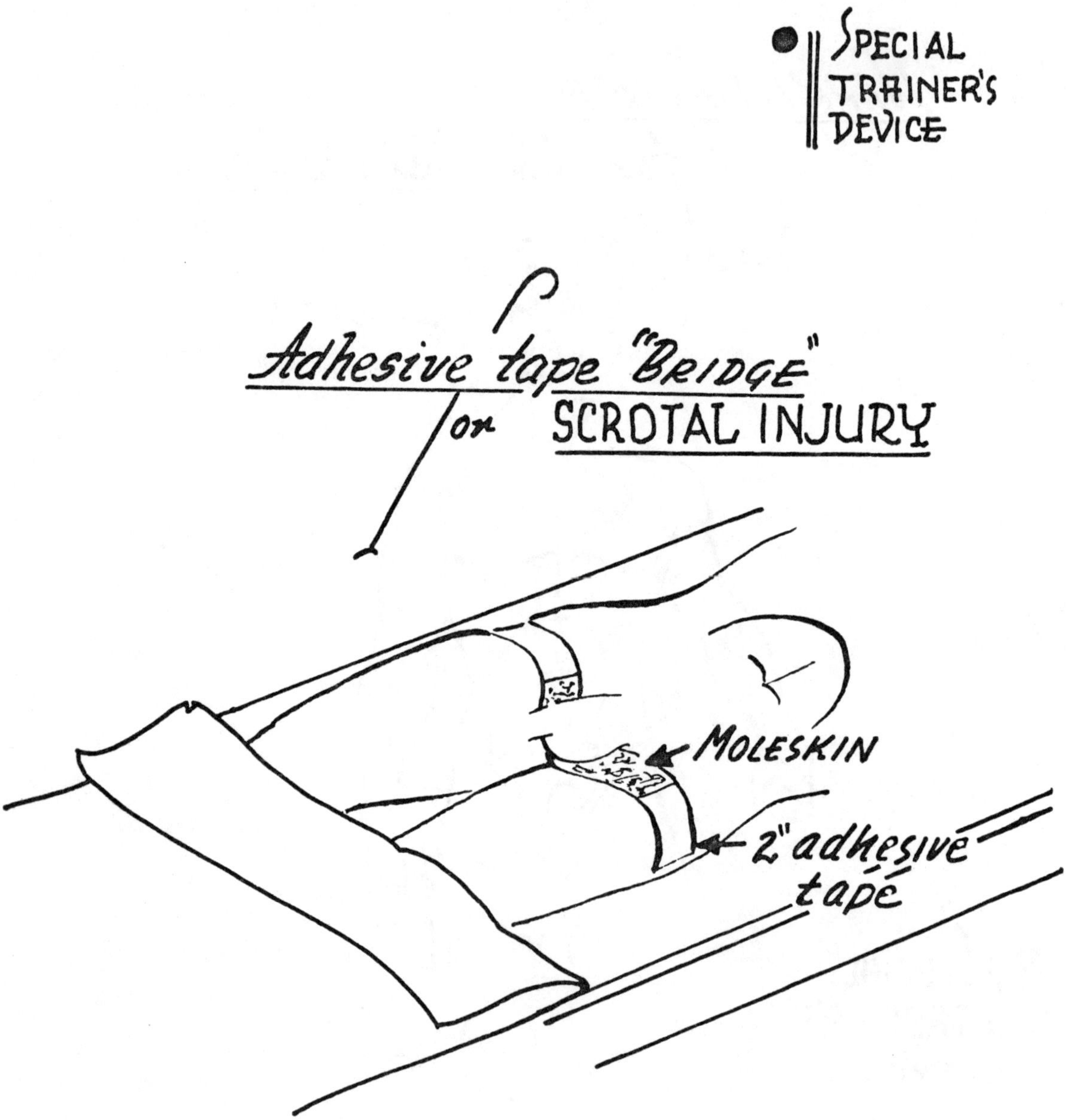

SPECIAL TRAINER'S DEVICE

Adhesive tape "BRIDGE"
or SCROTAL INJURY

MOLESKIN

2" adhesive tape

Figure 123

Section 4 The ABDOMEN

Flexible Cast Techniques for:
  Muscle Hernia
  Ruptured Abdominal Muscle

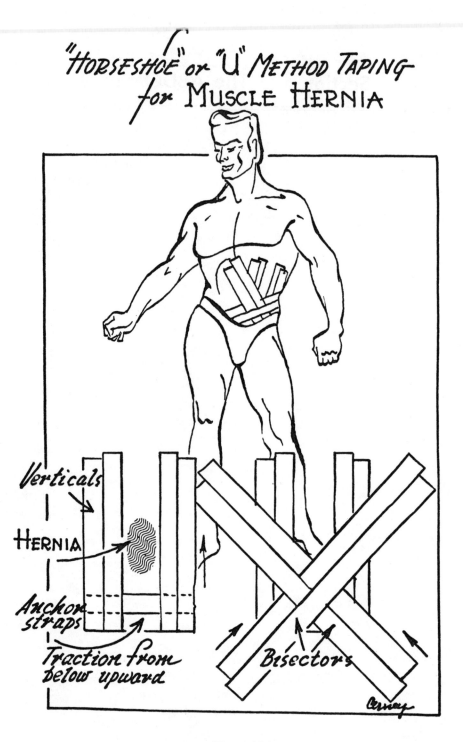

Figure 124

Elastic tape for RUPTURED OBLIQUIS ABDOMINUS
(Abdominal muscle strapping)

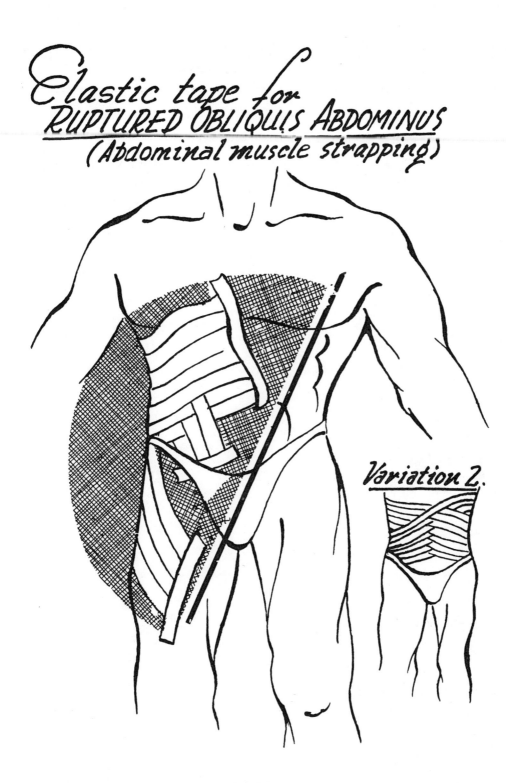

Variation 2.

Figure 125

Section 5   The FACE

Flexible Cast Techniques for:
 Facial Cuts
 Nose Splint (metal)
 Broken Nose (tape)
 Sweat Band (Hamel)

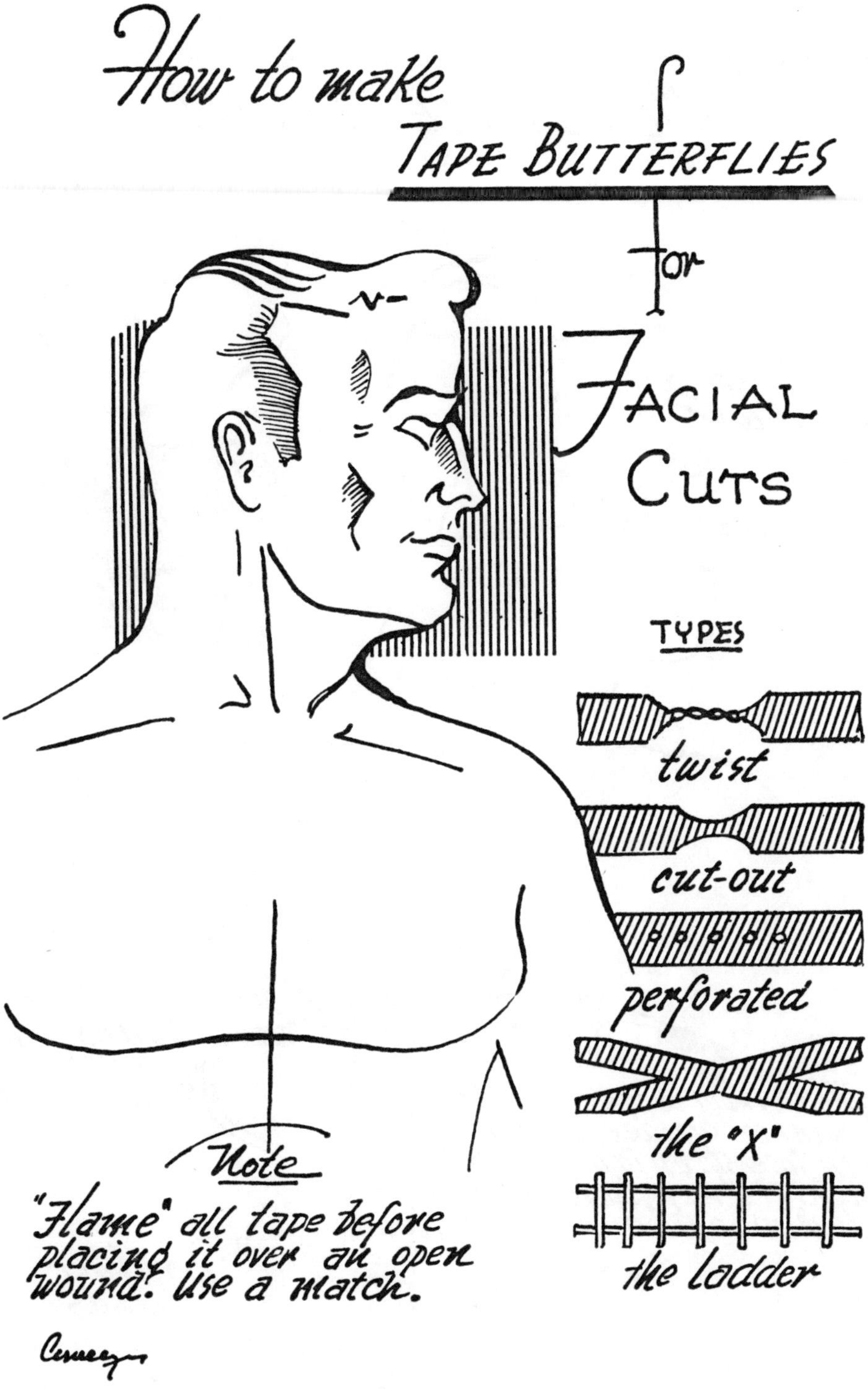

How to make TAPE BUTTERFLIES for FACIAL CUTS

TYPES

twist

cut-out

perforated

the "X"

the ladder

Note

"Flame" all tape before placing it over an open wound. Use a match.

Figure 126

Moldable METAL NOSE SPLINT

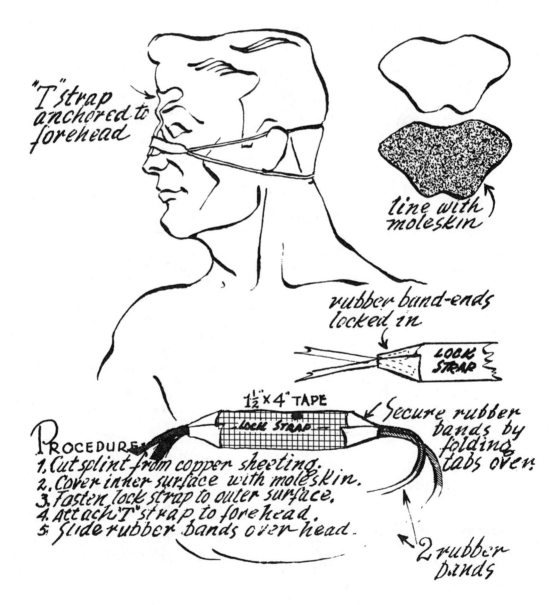

"T" strap anchored to forehead

line with moleskin

rubber band-ends locked in

LOCK STRAP

1½" × 4" TAPE

LOCK STRAP

Secure rubber bands by folding tabs over

2 rubber bands

PROCEDURE:
1. Cut splint from copper sheeting.
2. Cover inner surface with moleskin.
3. Fasten lock strap to outer surface.
4. Attach "T" strap to forehead.
5. Slide rubber bands over head.

Figure 127

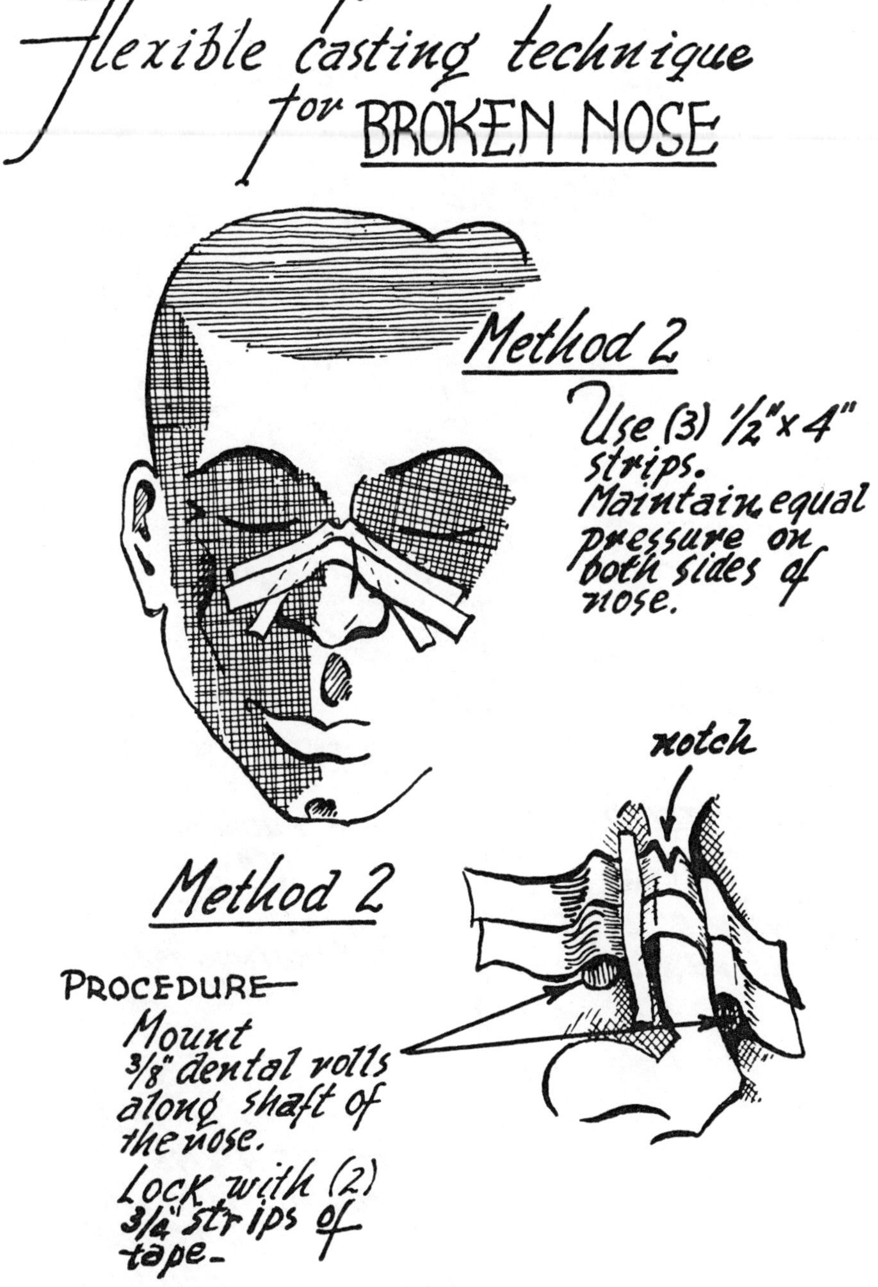

Flexible casting technique for BROKEN NOSE

Method 2

Use (3) ½"x 4" strips. Maintain equal pressure on both sides of nose.

notch

Method 2

PROCEDURE—

Mount 3/8" dental rolls along shaft of the nose.

Lock with (2) 3/4" strips of tape.

Figure 128

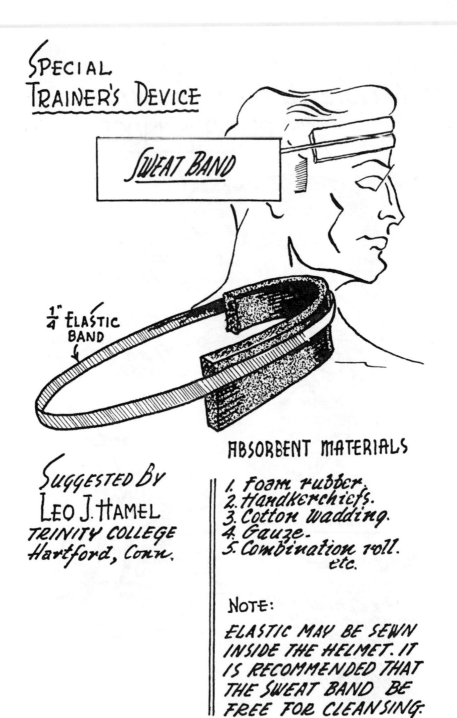

SPECIAL TRAINER'S DEVICE

SWEAT BAND

¼" ELASTIC BAND

Suggested By
LEO J. HAMEL
TRINITY COLLEGE
Hartford, Conn.

ABSORBENT MATERIALS

1. Foam rubber.
2. Handkerchiefs.
3. Cotton Wadding.
4. Gauze.
5. Combination roll.
                etc.

NOTE:

ELASTIC MAY BE SEWN INSIDE THE HELMET. IT IS RECOMMENDED THAT THE SWEAT BAND BE FREE FOR CLEANSING.

Figure 129

Section 6   The NECK

Flexible Cast Techniques for:
Torticolis ("wry neck")
Cervical Compression

The NECK

> Suggested
> Tape Width: 1½"

Purpose: Relieve neck muscle tension, provide support, control movement, protect against additional contusion or strain.

Position: Athlete seated or standing–head erect.

Procedure: In almost all neck involvements warranting adhesive tape, the
"torticolis" (wry neck) flexible cast can be used to advan-
tage. Most neck injuries in sports result from a pile-driving
block, tackle, or fall, causing muscle strain, twisting, contusion, and some hemorrhaging into the soft tissues. Before applying the flexible cast, do the following:

Trainer's Tips:

(a) *Apply ice immediately despite the fact that it may bring neck
stiffness on prematurely.* (b) *After 24 hours begin muscle relaxation
through heat and mild massage.* (c) *Player may be returned to the game or
practice after three to six days' rest, pending no complications.* (d) *Player
is to wear foam rubber cuff around neck during scrimmages or games if
playing football.* (e) *Be certain the team doctor has ruled out all possible
cervical vertebrae involvement.*

Other Neck Injuries
Amenable to Tape

STERNO-CLEIDO-MASTOID MUSCLE injury may occur from direct trauma. Using the "torticolis" flexible cast on the back of the neck will control the function of the sterno-cleido. *Apply no tape directly over this muscle.*

CERVICAL ARTHRITIS occurs when there is trauma to the neck, and leads to a host of problems. Arthritis in turn contributes to *cervical* and *brachial neuritis* (nerve inflammation) in which pain extends down the shoulder and arm. Because of this reflex extension of pain, the discomfort in the arm may be mis-diagnosed and certainly improperly treated.

CERVICAL MYOFASCIITIS is acquired in many ways in athletics. As the result of the head being whipped forward and back on the shoulders, like cracking a whip, it may occur in being *"clothesline tackled," "double tackled,"* or simply being thrown a block straight into the small of the back. Complications that follow are never "cured." The problem itself however is given relief through the use of the "torticolis" cast procedure.

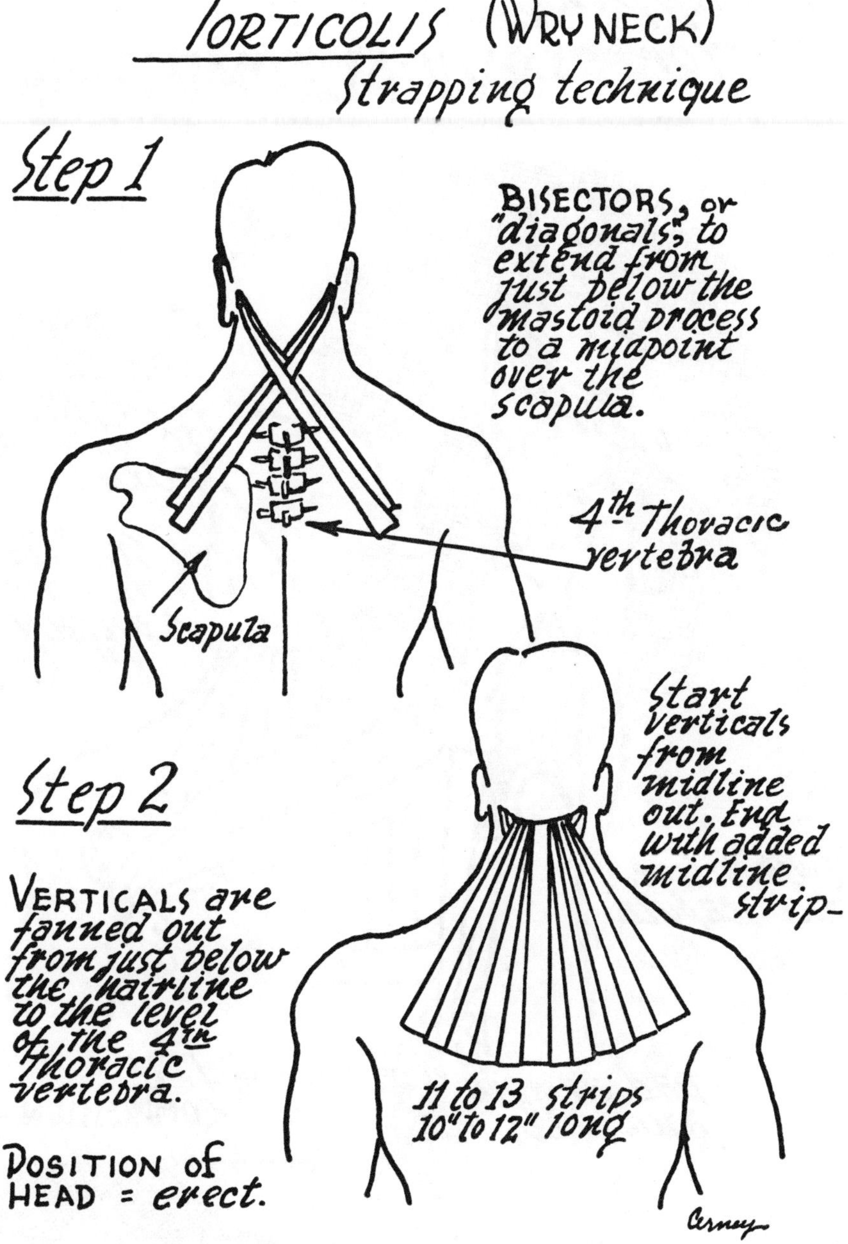

TORTICOLIS (WRY NECK)
Strapping technique

Step 1

BISECTORS, or "diagonals", to extend from just below the mastoid process to a midpoint over the scapula.

4th Thoracic vertebra

Scapula

Step 2

VERTICALS are fanned out from just below the hairline to the level of the 4th Thoracic vertebra.

POSITION of HEAD = erect.

Start verticals from midline out. End with added midline strip.

11 to 13 strips 10" to 12" long

Arney

Figure 130

Strapping for CERVICAL COMPRESSION

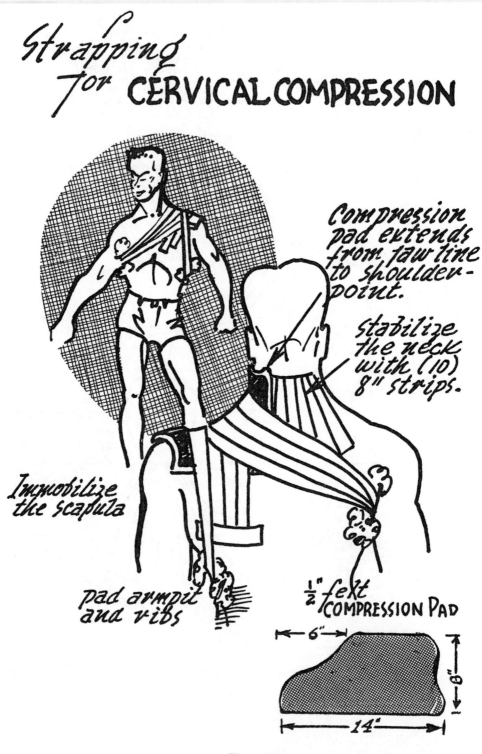

Compression pad extends from jaw line to shoulder-point.

stabilize the neck with (10) 8" strips.

Immobilize the scapula

pad armpit and ribs

½" felt COMPRESSION PAD

6"

8"

14"

Figure 131

Section 7   The BACK

Flexible Cast Techniques for:
Low Back Strap
Low Back Strain Basketweave
Low and Mid-Back Strap
Upper Back
Fractured Scapula

The BACK

| Suggested 1½" 2" |
| Tape Width: 3" |

Purpose: Support, compression, control.

Position: Depends on the part of the back involved.

       For example: Athlete seated, shoulders thrust back, in injury to the *trapezium.*

       Athlete standing in flexible casting injuries to the *lumborum* and *sacrospinalis.*

Procedure: Prep the skin; place *anchor* straps, *bridges,* or *bisectors.* Follow with *horizontals* and/or *spanners* from the hip level up. Apply firmly and complete the flexible cast by locking down the edges with *buttress* straps. Don't run tape into the crease between the buttocks. If *moles* or other skin lesions are present, cover them with gauze or surgical wadding.

The Methods Are Many

There are many causes for backache and many methods of applying a flexible cast to bring relief. In athletics the major problems result from one or more forms of strain/sprain or direct trauma. In all back injuries the diagnosis is the thing—but *it's the adhesive strapping that gives relief.* The relief from a *flexible cast* is dramatic.

Where both the upper and lower back are involved, there is usually some form of contracted musculature, inflammation, or tearing of soft tissue. Where bones and joints are involved there may be local arthritis or periostitis which may spread inflammation to surrounding soft tissues. For example, a subluxated lumbar vertebra may lead to *sciatica.* Stress on the sacroiliac joint may lead to intense low-back pain. Compression and support from adhesive tape in such cases is the treatment of choice until something better comes along.

Back Injuries Most Amenable
to Flexible Casting Techniques

LOW BACK INJURY usually has the *lumborum* and *sacrospinalis* involved. They go into spasm. As a result they "catch" when the athlete bends or raises. Usually it comes on when the athlete is cooled off. It is relieved when he's warmed up. It is brought on by twisting, overworking, direct trauma, nutritional deficiencies, and even fatigue. It subsides with care, and there are certain significant facts to remember in treating it.

Trainer's Tips
(Low Back Injuries):

(a) *Before the skin-prep, massage the muscles well to relieve their tension.* (b) *AVOID COLD PACK procedures* (use thermopacks or analgesic packs overnight). (c) *Set up a mild exercise program to stretch those low back muscles.* (d) *Render heat therapy twice daily* (rehabilitation may take a month). (e) In the application of a flexible cast for low back problems, have the athlete standing with his feet pointed out, duck-fashion. For security he rests with hands against the wall. In some cases you may want him prone to apply *spanner* straps and then have him erect for the *bisectors* or *obliques.* This gives added tightness.

UPPER BACK INJURY usually involves the *trapezius.* Muscles of the neck may get involved as well. To cope effectively with this problem with a *flexible cast,* seat the athlete and have him draw his shoulders up. Place *horizontal spanners* from below the scapula upward to the level of the third cervical vertebra. These spanners should run horizontally from shoulder point to shoulder point. Those skirting the neck should extend from the sterno-cleido-mastoid muscle on one side to that on the other. Diagonal *bisectors* should start at the clavicular space, descend obliquely across the scapula and the spinal column, and end at a point just below the opposite axillary area. Basketweave the *bisectors* or *obliques* and overlap each by half. Anchor all ends with *buttress* straps. The follow-through on this injury differs somewhat from low back care.

Trainer's Tips
(Upper Back Injuries):

(a) *Immediately on injury wrap the back with an elastic bandage and APPLY ICE PACKS.* (This not only renders relief but inhibits further hemorrage if present.) (b) *Have the team physician determine the extent of the damage.* (He may request an X-ray determination.) (c) *Apply deep heat and mild manipulation* if the X-ray film is negative for bone damage. (d) *Rotate the shoulders gently.* (e) *Apply overnight analgesic packs.* (f) *Advise athlete to work out regularly* with plenty of running. Forbid baseball pitchers, quarterbacks, javelin or discus throwers or shotputters to use their throwing arms. (Repair may take 2 to 4 weeks.) (g) *Apply protective padding and flexible casts for all practices and games.* Restriction from total activity may be necessary for some time.

LATISSIMUS DORSI DAMAGE results when the basketball player is slammed into the wall or a bleacher. It may come from getting tackled, from overwork, or from over-trying with the discus or shotput. It becomes exquisitely painful and necessitates a thorough examination. The team physician may also indicate broken ribs when he sees the X-ray film. In handling this back muscle problem, there are certain things to remember about tape.

Trainer's Tips
(Latissimus Dorsi Damage):

(a) *Apply cotton elastic (3") roller bandage* immediately after direct trauma *and follow with ice packs.* (b) Where diagnostic X-ray films are negative for fracture, *use heat and mild massage after 36 hours.* Maintain the elastic wrap. (c) *Keep athlete out of action for at least two weeks.* (d) *Keep athlete out of contact or throwing sports but DO* keep him active running. (If there is discomfort while running, put his arm in an elbow sling.) (e) REPEATED TIP: DO NOT USE A FLEXIBLE CAST on this problem. Tape causes too much constriction on this big muscle.

Significant Factors to
Watch for in Back Injuries

(a) *Where the flexible cast provides no relief,* look for the subluxation of a spinal vertebra or other joint involvement. Determine, through the team physician, whether the pain may not be referred from some abdominal organ. Check too to see if maybe the tape you are applying isn't at fault.

(b) *Where tape is to cover an area of hair* (pubic, inguinal, or abdominal), use stockingette before applying the tape.

(c) *Set a three day limitation* on all tape on the back. Preferably redress daily.

(d) *Where traction is being used,* LEAVE THE STRAPPING ON during treatment.

(e) *Where fracture is obvious, or even suspect,* DO NOT APPLY ADHESIVE TAPE on the back.

(f) *Shield the crest of the ilium,* or jutting spinous processes, with padding before applying adhesive tape.

(g) *Begin low-back straps with vertical* straps. Follow with *bisectors* and finish with the horizontals.

(h) *There are no anchor straps on the back.* All pieces of adhesive tape in the flexible cast are "lock" straps because of the mass of tissues to be covered and compressed.

(i) *Where back pain is severe,* and there is no fracture, strap the athlete lying face down. Place a firm pillow under his abdomen to reverse an accentuated anterior lumbar curvature. When it comes time to roll the boy on his feet there will be no torsion or twist in the corset-like *flexible cast.*

How to Handle That
Scapula Problem

Often involved in back injuries is the scapula. Direct trauma, without fracture, calls for a flexible cast in treatment of the injury. For best results place a sponge rubber pad over the lesion and anchor it in position. Overlay the padding with adhesive tape from chest to spinal column. Lock the shoulder point in. Protect nipples and axilla with cotton wadding.

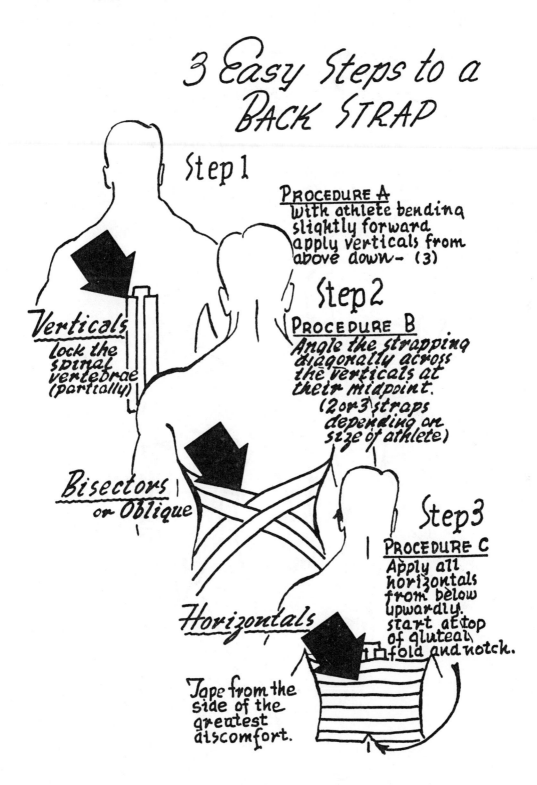

3 Easy Steps to a BACK STRAP

Step 1

PROCEDURE A
With athlete bending slightly forward apply verticals from above down~ (3)

Verticals
lock the spinal vertebrae (partially)

Step 2

PROCEDURE B
Angle the strapping diagonally across the verticals at their midpoint.
(2 or 3 straps depending on size of athlete)

Bisectors or **Oblique**

Step 3

PROCEDURE C
Apply all horizontals from below upwardly. start at top of gluteal fold and notch.

Horizontals

Tape from the side of the greatest discomfort.

Figure 132

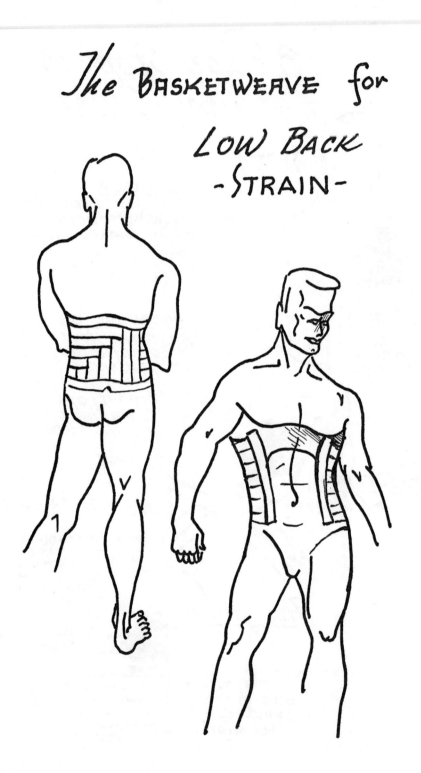

The BASKETWEAVE for LOW BACK -STRAIN-

Figure 133

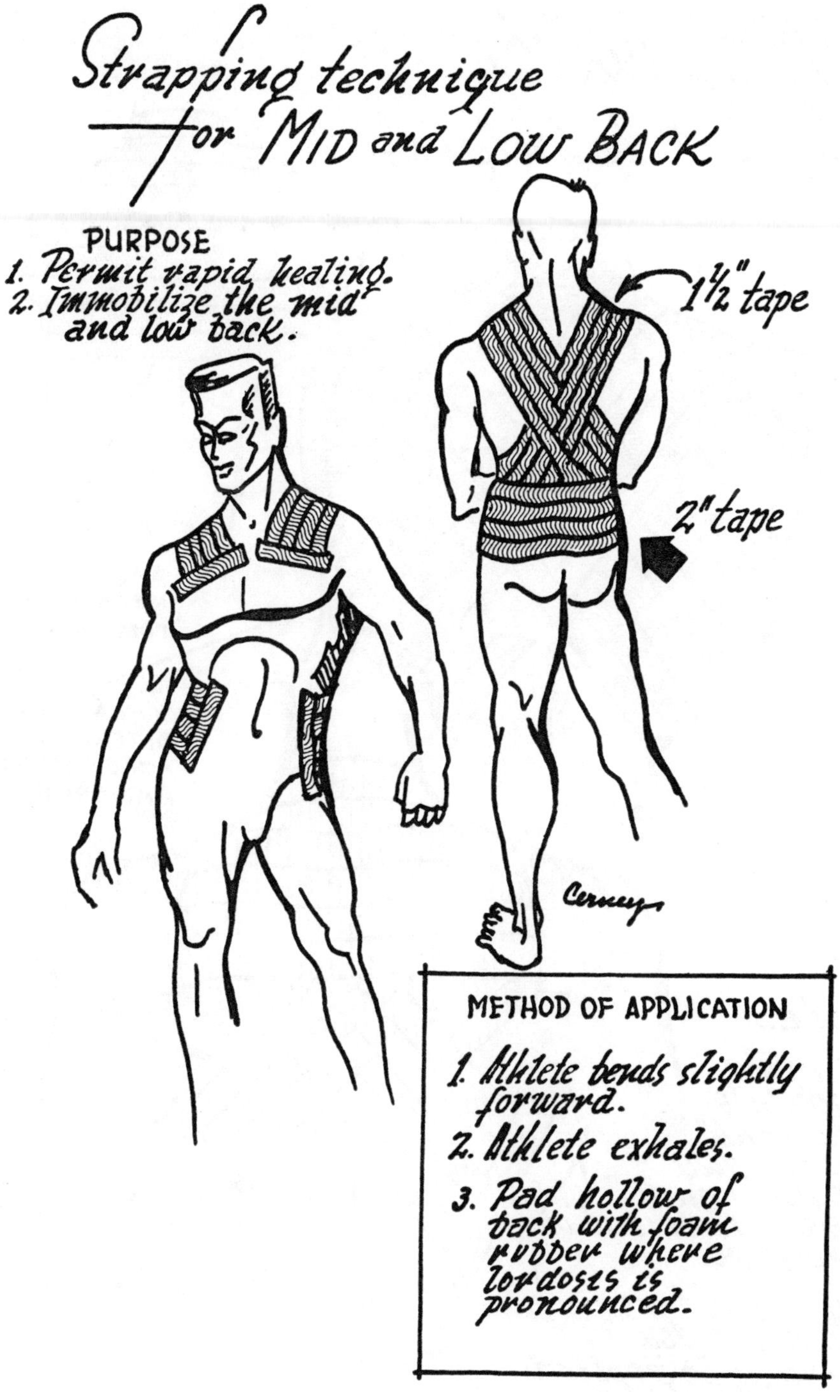

Strapping technique for MID and LOW BACK

PURPOSE
1. Permit rapid healing.
2. Immobilize the mid and low back.

1½" tape

2" tape

Cerney

METHOD OF APPLICATION

1. Athlete bends slightly forward.
2. Athlete exhales.
3. Pad hollow of back with foam rubber where lordosis is pronounced.

Figure 134

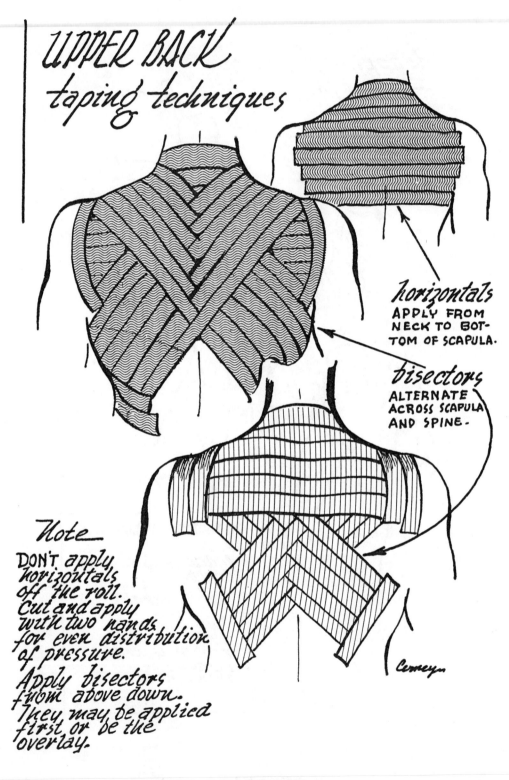

UPPER BACK
taping techniques

horizontals
APPLY FROM NECK TO BOTTOM OF SCAPULA.

bisectors
ALTERNATE ACROSS SCAPULA AND SPINE.

Note
DON'T apply horizontals off the roll. Cut and apply with two hands for even distribution of pressure.

Apply bisectors from above down. They may be applied first, or be the overlay.

Figure 135

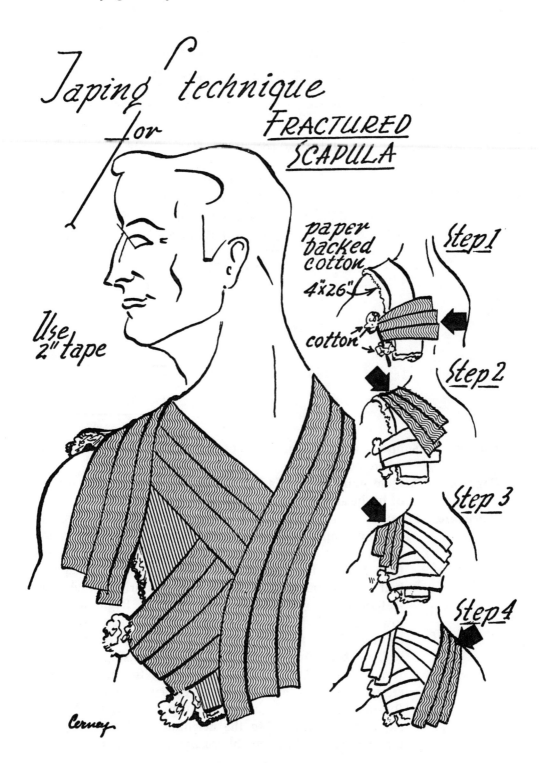

Taping technique for FRACTURED SCAPULA

Use 2" tape

paper backed cotton 4"x26"

cotton

Step 1

Step 2

Step 3

Step 4

Cerney

Figure 136

Section 8   The CHEST

Flexible Cast Techniques for:
Rib Fracture
Bruised Ribs
Over-riding Rib Fracture
Rib Contusion
Fractured Clavicle
Fractured Clavicle with Sternal Injury
Sterno-Clavicular Strain
Sterno-Clavicular Joint Lock

The CHEST

> Suggested 1½"
> Tape Width: 2"

Purpose: Support ribs and/or intercostal muscles, limit breathing where necessary.

Position: Athlete standing. He places hand, on the affected side, on top of his head. He leans slightly toward the side of injury.

Procedure: Prep the skin. Place *anchor* straps over sternum and spinal column. Apply bridge straps from back to front. Place tape and mould firmly along the line of the ribs. Cover no less than 2/3rds of the chest wall. Overlap all strips of tape by half and *buttress* the bare ends. Tape during exhalation. Deflate chest with each successive strap. Begin with the lowest and work upward. Tape must be applied with sufficient pressure to immobilize the excursion of the chest wall on breathing. Cover the nipples with surgical or cotton wadding. Use a strap that girdles the entire thorax ONLY where deemed vitally necessary to lock the chest. By overlapping each successive strip, the offended rib is successfully splinted to the neighboring rib. *Elastic tape* may be preferred for flexible casting of this area.

Thorax Injuries Amenable
to Flexible Casting Techniques

Certain conditions preclude placing the chest wall in an adhesive tape cast. Among these are rib fractures which involve the surrounding and/or underlying tissues.

CONTRAINDICATIONS for strapping fractured ribs are: (a) *where there is an over-riding and displacement of rib segments,* (b) *when the rib fracture occurs lateral to the attachment of the serratus anterior muscle* (strapping adhesive tape over this area creates additional pain and complications), (c) *where there is an under-riding edge projecting and possibly penetrating into the pleural sac,* (d) *where there is a definite penetration of the pleura and the alveoli are definitely punctured.*

INDICATIONS for chest involvements are: (a) *pleurisy,* (b) *strain or tearing of intercostal muscles,* (c) *separation of the costal-chondral junctions,* (d) *separation of the ribs at the spinal column or at the sternum,* (e) *neuritis* (non-infective), (f) *shingles,* (g) *rib fracture* (non-displaced). (Displaced rib segments may be flexible casted ONLY in emergency!)

Other Chest Wall Injury
for Athletic Consideration

SERRATUS MAGNUS INJURY is not uncommon in athletics and it has some remarkable characteristics that make it distinctive. The muscle itself covers the upper eight ribs just below the level of the armpit and is certainly easily available and unprotected when the arm is lifted. When it is injured by strain or tearing, the athlete finds it impossible to raise his arm higher than his shoulder. If he succeeds in doing so his scapula comes out uniquely like an angel wing—and this isn't always indicative of an angelic athlete. When the problem happens the trainer should: (a) *Compress the area immediately with an elastic wrap, and also lock the shoulder.* (b) *Place elbow in a sling.* (c) *Get physician to X-ray the part.* (d) *Place adhesive tape anchors after prepping the skin* (spinal column and sternum). (e) *Run ELASTIC TAPE from back to front following the rib line. Replace the bandage daily.* (f) *Use dry heat and mild massage and light manipulation of the arm* before each flexible cast is applied. (g) For scrimmages and games thereafter, follow with an *elastic chest supporter, rib guards,* and *longer and tougher football shoulder guards* lined with foam rubber.

CLAVICULAR INJURY appears consistently in the contact sports and two general types of *flexible casts* are used for involvement of the clavicle.

One type is the *figure-8* configuration or its variations. The other is the *"clavicular-cross."* Which one you use is determined by the parts involved.

For example: (a) when the clavicle is fractured, or the sternum is involved, the *figure-8* strapping is more efficient; (b) if there is deformity, or the clavicle is subluxated or otherwise mal-aligned, use the *clavicular-cross.* Where mis-alignment is present because of a fracture it may be necessary to supplement the strapping with a splint. In all shoulder and upper chest injuries there is an accompanying painful problem I call "arm drag," in which the arm's own weight pulls at the injured parts. You can alleviate this distress either with an adhesive tape loop from the shoulder to elbow or with an elbow sling. The first is more secure. Before applying the main body of the flexible cast, pad the traumatized area with a foam rubber compression pad. Anchor the flexible cast securely with a cotton elastic roller bandage (3" or 4") wrap.

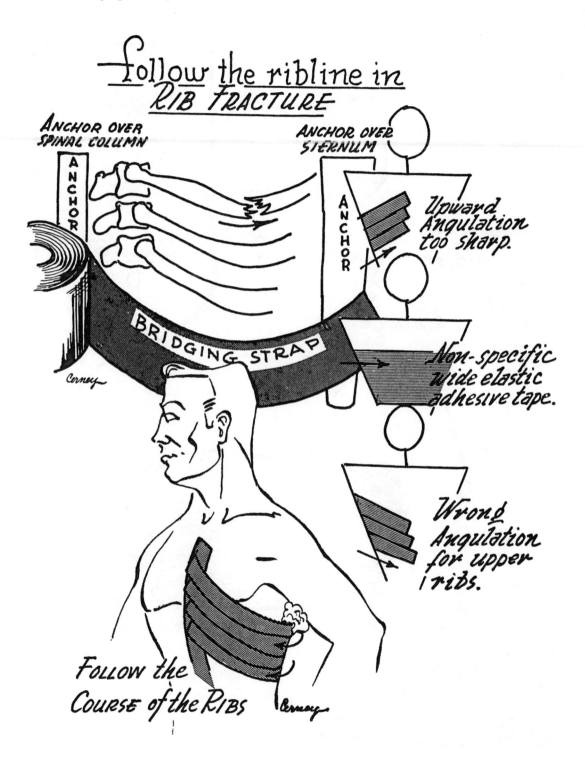

Figure 137

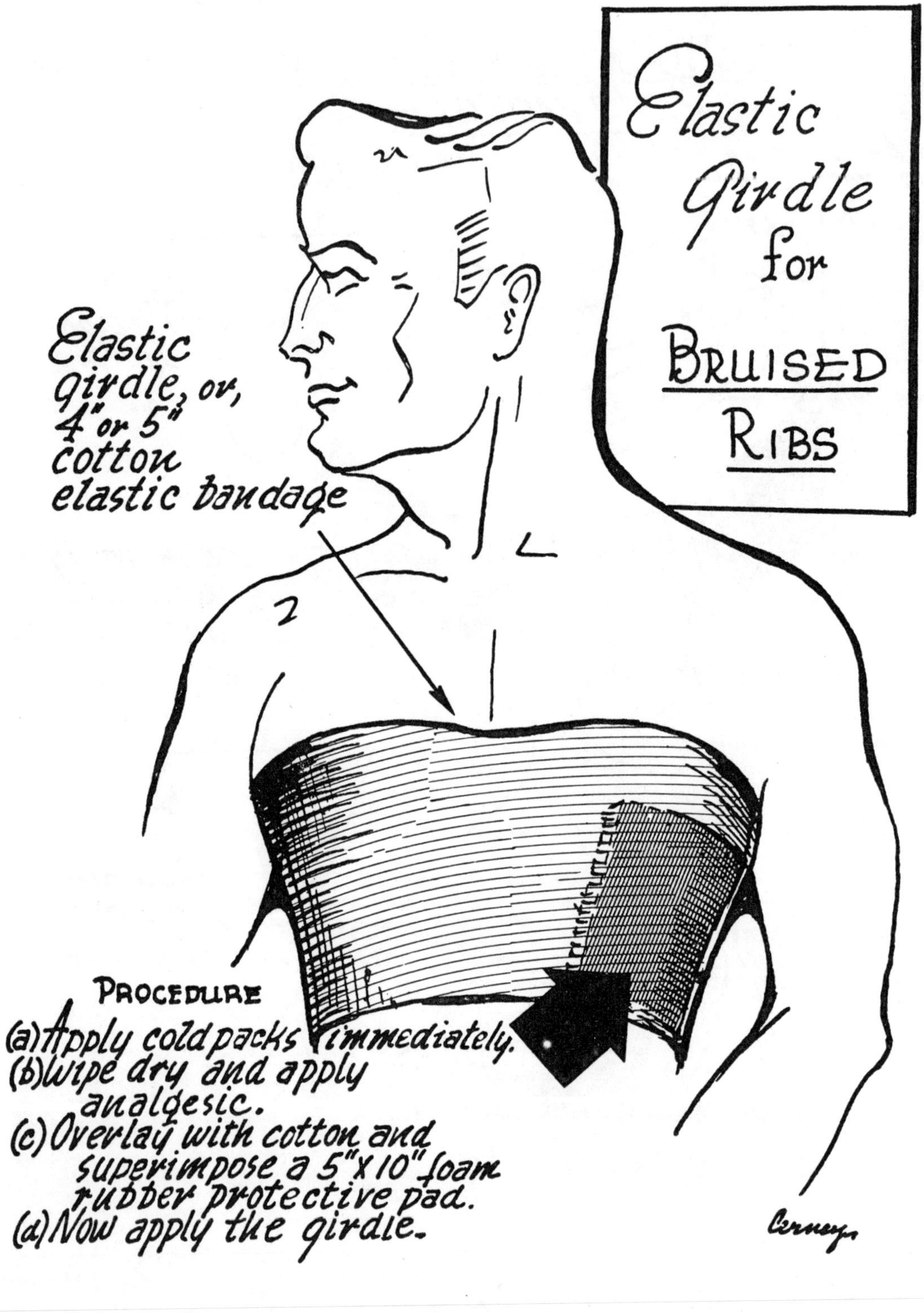

Elastic girdle, or, 4" or 5" cotton elastic bandage

Elastic Girdle for BRUISED RIBS

PROCEDURE

(a) Apply cold packs immediately.
(b) Wipe dry and apply analgesic.
(c) Overlay with cotton and superimpose a 5"x10" foam rubber protective pad.
(d) Now apply the girdle.

Cerney

Figure 138

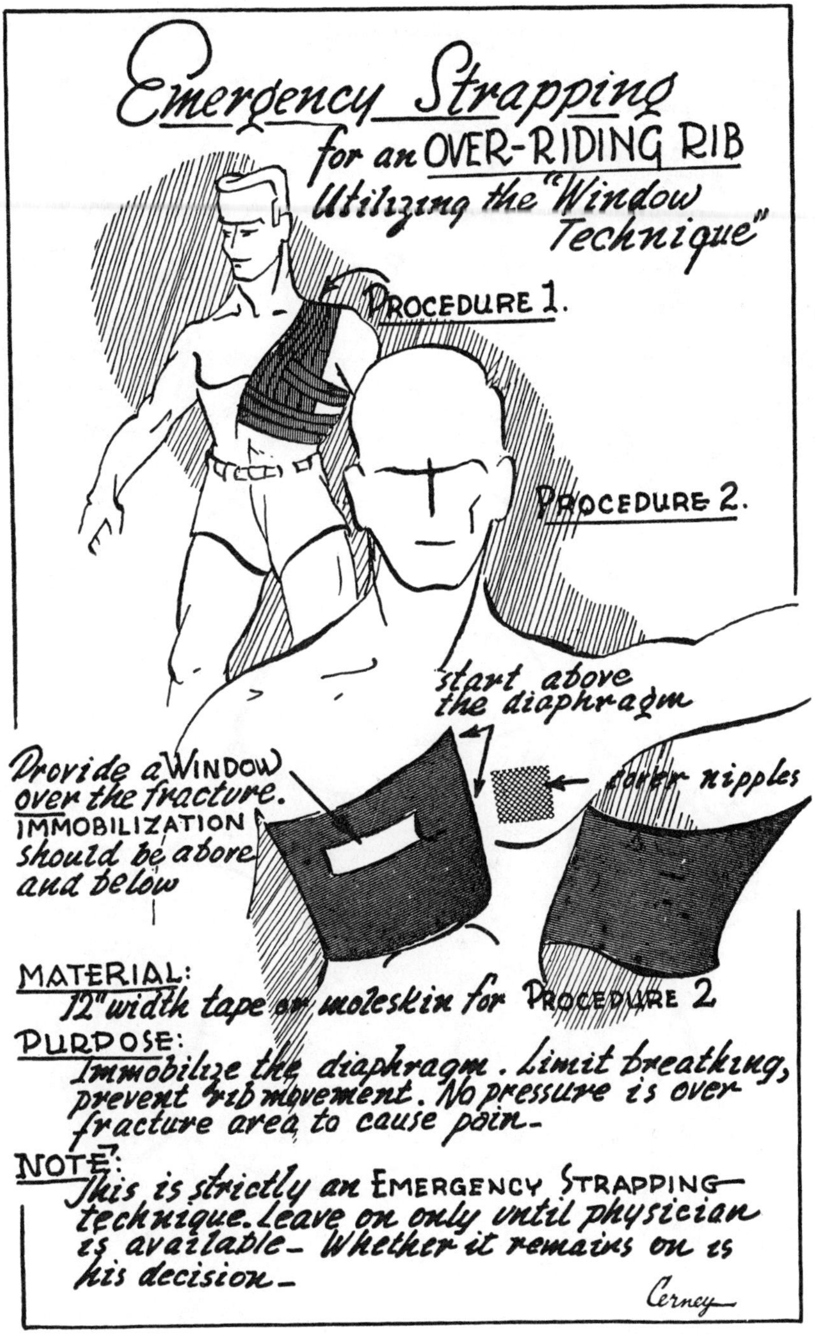

Emergency Strapping for an OVER-RIDING RIB
Utilizing the "Window Technique"

PROCEDURE 1.

PROCEDURE 2.

start above the diaphragm

Provide a WINDOW over the fracture. IMMOBILIZATION should be above and below

cover nipples

MATERIAL:
12" width tape or moleskin for PROCEDURE 2.

PURPOSE:
Immobilize the diaphragm. Limit breathing, prevent rib movement. No pressure is over fracture area to cause pain—

NOTE:
This is strictly an EMERGENCY STRAPPING technique. Leave on only until physician is available— Whether it remains on is his decision—

Cerney

Figure 139

Figure 140

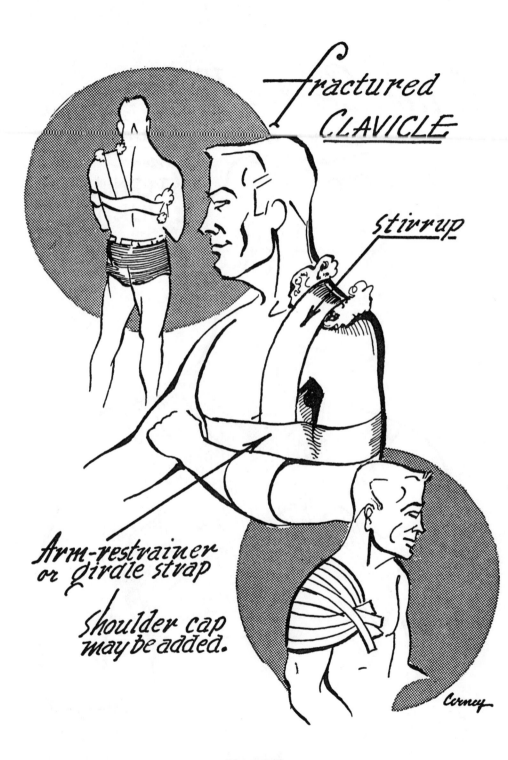

fractured CLAVICLE

stirrup

Arm-restrainer or girdle strap

Shoulder cap may be added.

Corney

Figure 141

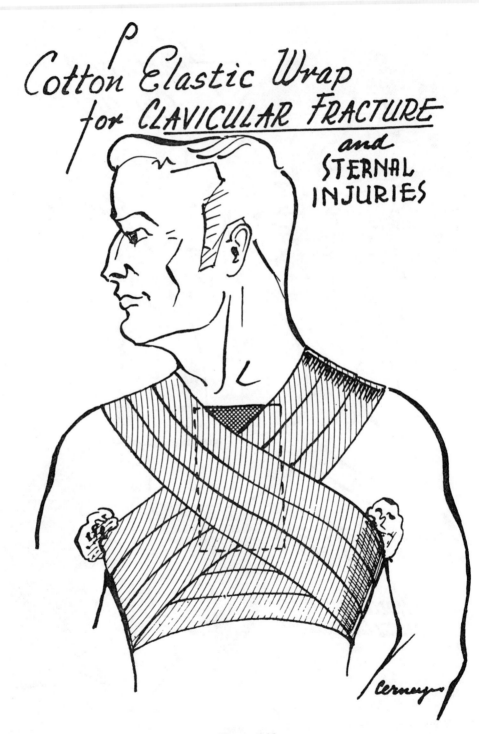

Cotton Elastic Wrap for CLAVICULAR FRACTURE and STERNAL INJURIES

Figure 142

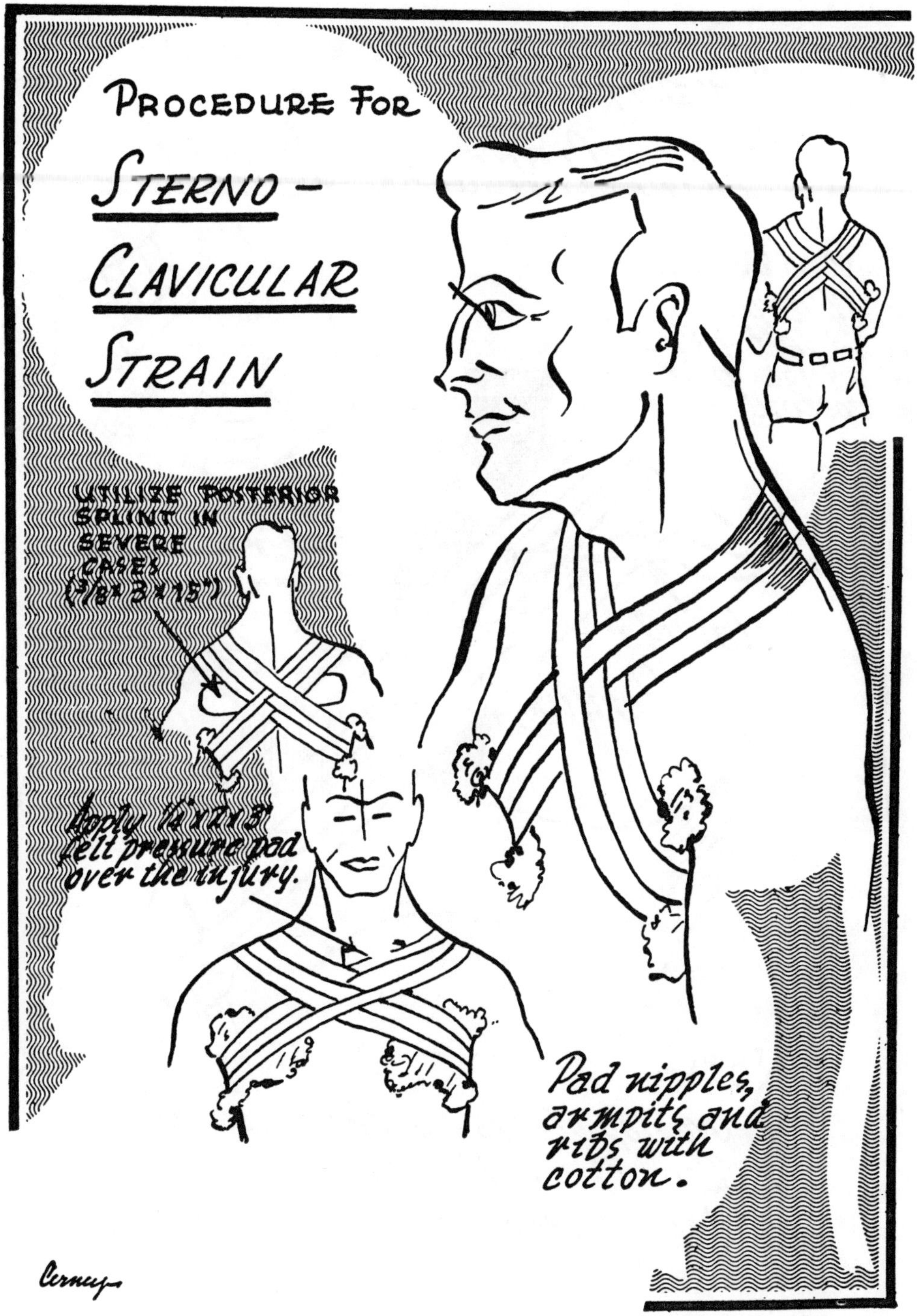
PROCEDURE FOR
STERNO-
CLAVICULAR
STRAIN
UTILIZE POSTERIOR SPLINT IN SEVERE CASES (3/8" x 3" x 15")
Apply 1/4" x 2" x 3" felt pressure pad over the injury.
Pad nipples, armpits and ribs with cotton.
Cerney

Figure 143

Simplified
Sterno-Clavicular Joint-Lock

MATERIAL
- 1½" tape
- ¼" felt (3"x4")
- gauze pad
- cotton

Back view

¼" Felt pad
or ⅜" firm foam rubber

Gauze pad

clavicle
Sternum

NOTE
1. Overlap straps by three fourths—
2. Use 3" elastic tape.
3. Anchor traction straps securely.

THE WRAP-UP

To anyone in sports medicine today, it should be self-evident that adhesive tape is an invaluable defensive offensive weapon in the care and prevention of athletic injuries—that there's an effective time and place for a *flexible cast* that creates compression/traction/tension—that even though it's no cure-all, adhesive tape can be converted by an efficient operator into a prime method for limiting function and supporting tissues without completely immobilizing the part—that *flexible casting* is an art and a science indeed, and from where I'm looking on now it's an effective treatment where athletic injuries are concerned.

The longer you use tape, and the more your capabilities grow, the more convinced of this you become. To those in the know it's the ideal choice . . . so *use* it! It's the best assistant trainer you ever had.

INDEX